BLACK PASSPORTS

BLACK PASSPORTS

Travel Memoirs as a Tool for Youth Empowerment

STEPHANIE Y. EVANS

Production by Jenn Bennett
Marketing by Anne M. Valentine

Library of Congress Cataloging-in-Publication Data
Evans, Stephanie Y.
  Black passports : travel memoirs as a tool for youth empowerment /
Stephanie Y. Evans.
    pages   cm
  Includes bibliographical references and index.
  ISBN 978-1-4384-5153-4 (hardcover : alk. paper) — ISBN 978-1-4384-
5154-1 (pbk. : alk. paper) 1. Self-control. 2. Performance. 3. Interna-
tional travel. 4. Blacks—Social conditions. I. Title.
  BF632.E93 2014
  305.896'073—dc23

                                                              2013025548

                    10 9 8 7 6 5 4 3 2 1

Dedication

To my husband, Curtis D. Byrd, a wise and kind man. Thank you for your passion and interminable will to live a full life. Thank you also for showing me the power of the one true force: LOVE. Sincerely yours, Yoda.

To my family, near and far. To grandmothers Mary Edmonds and Venella Byrd for your wit and vigor and especially to the young people in my family tree: this book is the most valuable gift I have to offer.

Credo

I believe
Wisdom illuminates paths to empowerment
Wisdom is a combination of guidance, self-control, and ethics

I define
Wisdom as
Heart
Brains
Courage

I write
To empower youth

The time of the psychological passing over from boyhood to manhood is a movable feast. The legal date fixed on the twenty-first birthday has little or no connection with it. There are men in their teens, and there are boys in their forties. This passing over is not really across a line, but across a zone.
—James Weldon Johnson, *Along This Way* (1933)

As black American women . . . we have been as invisible to the dominant culture as rain; we have been knowers, but we have not been known. . . . Aframerican autobiographical tradition encompasses survival, search for public voice, personal fulfillment, and self-creation.
—Joanne Braxton, *Black Women Writing Autobiography: A Tradition within a Tradition* (1989)

[While studying in Germany,] the unity beneath all life clutched me. I was not less fanatically a Negro, but "Negro" meant a greater, broader sense of humanity and world fellowship. I felt myself standing, not against the world, but simply against American narrowness of color prejudice, with the greater, finer world at my back.
—W. E. B. Du Bois, *Autobiography* (1968)

you show us
how to arrange our
worldly selves
—Sonia Sanchez, *Haiku (for Maya Angelou)* (2010)

CONTENTS

ILLUSTRATIONS

ACKNOWLEDGMENTS

This book was made possible by research funding provided by the University of Florida College of Liberal Arts and Sciences Colonel Allan and Margaret Crow Professor Award, 2010–11. Many thanks to Sharon Burney for her assistance in securing necessary sources in the early stages of this work. Parts of this research have been discussed at the following gatherings: Columbia University, Toward an Intellectual History of Black Women Conference (April 2011); Harvard University, Think Tank on Global Education (May 2011); Clark Atlanta University, Pearly Dove Lecture (March 2012); Clark Atlanta University, W. E. B. Du Bois Major Works Seminar on Autobiography (July 2012); the Association for the Study of African American Life and History (ASALH) Annual Convention in Pittsburgh, PA (September 2012); and Collegium for African American Research (CAAR) at Agnes Scott College in Atlanta, Georgia (March 2013).

Development of the *Swag Diplomacy* Viewshare online database was made possible by collaboration with the Emory University Digital Scholarship Commons (DiSC) Research Center and support from the Clark Atlanta University College of Education with technology support provided by the Clark Atlanta University Faculty Development Center. Thank you to Moya Bailey, Whitney Peoples, and Yvonne Nash for assistance in formatting and expanding the online resource. Thanks to Library of Congress staff for highlighting the Swag Diplomacy project in online publications to expand its usage. Special thanks to the African American Studies, Africana Women's Studies, and History (AWH) Department and the CAU community for encouragement and inspiration.

Many thanks to those who have offered substantive insight on working drafts, especially Dr. Natalie Graham, Dr. Charmayne Patterson, and Christy Garrison-Harrison. Thanks also to Augustus Wood, Esther Pervil, LaSella Hall, Tami Wheeler, Ondrea Rhymes, Tiana Thompson, and Faren Manuel for detailed comments, and Markiana Jackson, Michael Decuir, and Jaimi Carter for general feedback. Last, thanks to SUNY Press reviewers whose generous and detailed comments helped guide the editing process with care, compassion, and thoughtful critique. I am grateful to Beth Bouloukos at SUNY Press for her patience and support of this project, the SUNY editorial and production teams, and to editor Liz Pulcini for much-needed assistance in preparing this manuscript.

To my teachers, mentors, and role models: your guidance gave me a "window seat" to the world, and "I'm international because of you."

To my students: thank you for continuing to teach me about the joy and pain of lifelong learning.

To Dr. Erika Camacho: Mr. Escalante would be so proud of who you are, as a mathematician and a teacher. Thank you for challenging me to find the *ganas* to share my own story. Last, thanks to Saroya Corbett (mentee of Katherine Dunham) and Frank Moten (mentee of Dizzy Gillespie) for sharing their stories of how to continue legacies of creativity.

PROLOGUE

"Wisdom Is the Best of All Treasures":
Adolescent Development and the ABCs of Power

The Queen of Sheba's visit to King Solomon's court is recorded in numerous ancient texts, from the Bible to the Qur'ān. Makeda, as she is known in Ethiopia, traveled to Jerusalem to test Solomon's wisdom. One of the riddles she asked was how to distinguish girls from boys:

> Various boys and girls, all of a tender age, of the same height and dressed identically were placed before him, whereupon she said, "Distinguish the males from the females." At Solomon's command, nuts and roasted corns were distributed before them. The boys, without any sense of embarrassment, gathered them and placed them in their garments; the girls, who were more modest, placed them in their headdresses. Thus, Solomon was able to distinguish between them.[1]

Gender socialization and racial and national identity norms are all addressed in this book, but my main purpose, the heart of this text, is to provide resources that can help socialize youth—whether male or female—as wise global citizens. My definition of wisdom is simple: virtuous attitudes (heart-*altruism*), creative behaviors (brains-*balance*), and competent choices (courage-*character*) for success. It is the ongoing journey of guidance, self-control, and ethics. Wisdom is obtained through guidance (mentoring to understand history, potential, and voice), self-control (self-mastery and social/global competence), and ethics (the study of the tension between vices and virtues); wisdom is youth's passports to the world. Wisdom is a process.

James Weldon Johnson rightly observed that maturity has nothing to do with age. Similarly, wisdom is not automatically bestowed upon elders; wisdom is an ongoing process, hard won, and the most valuable asset that can be handed down from one generation to the next. In addition to political expediency, Makeda was compelled to visit Solomon because she valued wisdom and heard of his wise rule. *The Kebra Nagast* (*Glory of Kings*), a cornerstone of Ethiopian heritage, records Makeda's proclamation of wisdom's worth:

> I am smitten with the love of wisdom. Wisdom is far better than the treasure of silver and gold. It is sweeter than honey and finer than wine, brighter than the sun, and to be loved more than precious stones. What is stored within it is greater than oil, and it satisfies one's craving more than meat. It is joy to the heart, light to the eye, speed to the foot, and shield to the breast. *Wisdom is the best of all treasures.* He who stores gold has no profit without wisdom, and he who stores wisdom—no man can steal it away (italics added).[2]

In a quest for wisdom, Makeda was compelled to travel, but her case also demonstrates ethics is not as simple as striving for perfection; rather, ethics and morals involve learning to live well despite inevitable imperfection. In this research, I have identified two hundred Black autobiographies that contain international travel memoirs. Like the attractiveness of short stories, these narratives-within-texts can be used to impart wisdom to today's youth, providing a smorgasbord of worldly models to emulate—or avoid. This wisdom will be their passport to internal journeys of mind, body, and spirit as much as to geographical locations across continents.[3]

MESSAGE: GUIDANCE TO WISDOM

In this book, I identify life stories as tools with which youth can explore the mistakes and redemption of others in order to gain a semblance of self-control in their own lives. As evidenced by the Makeda and Solomon story, adolescent development and youth socialization are timeless topics, and the *bildungsroman* or coming of age story is of universal interest. Internationally, young people are searching for keys to reach their full potential, but with a lack of apparent mentors, many are left wondering where wisdom is found. The reality of the twenty-first century is that of a world moved by reverberations of racism, violent sexism, and a transnational hierarchy where Africans of any nation are slow to move from paralyzing hegemony and generations of exploitation, and adherence to gender roles can often be a matter of life or death. Thus, guidance must be considered in various international and national contexts as meanings shift with time and place.

Though we have "overcome" in many areas, Black youth still struggle to find positive and affirming answers to basic philosophical questions of ontology-being (Who am I?), epistemology-knowing (What do I know to be true?), and axiology-doing (What should I do?). Wisdom is a journey to balance being, knowing, and doing in a sustainable harmony between the self and the world. Race and gender, as anatomical phenomena, exist in an ambiguous, smoke-and-mirrors way. While there are noticeable physical variances, the meanings we give are purely historical and socially created. As much as ever, youth need philosophy—literally the love of wisdom—transmitted through moral examples and practical guidance of cautionary tales, and we must teach the broadest possible scope in which to understand the movable meaning of Black identity.

I offer this book as direction for teachers and mentors leading youth through the harrowing terrain of complex relations. In the introductory chapter and through an online resource companion to the book, called *Swag Diplomacy*, I use the acronym SWAG to stand for "start with a guide" and, specifically, guidance toward self-efficacy (organic power, control, and *mastery* over one's own attitude, behavior, and choices—ABCs). I define diplomacy as "youth empowerment," specifically where empowerment results in global competence, especially competence grounded in ethical action. Thus, *Black Passports* is a resource guide for youth empowerment to enhance self-control in all four levels of social location: micro (self), meso (community), macro (nation) and global (world).

In *Black Passports*, there are two key terms used to clarify dimensions of the concept "self-control": mastery and competence. Self-control is a central means to self-liberation. Beyond a deficient model usually invoked in social psychology texts that pathologize blackness (i.e., youth need constraint and discipline), I assume a strength-based model of self-control, which gives room for creative interpretation of how one exhibits control. Often it is not the youth who are out of control, but the adults around them. Mastery and competence are the two central concepts that Joyce West Stevens identifies as dual components of self-efficacy. In *Smart and Sassy: The Strengths of Inner-City Black*

Girls, Stevens defines self-efficacy as "the ability to exercise mastery and competence in one's social environment to achieve desirable social goals." She argues the concept of self-mastery is vital for adolescents who desire to establish healthy and purposeful identities. Given the oppressive environments that Black youth too often operate within, self-control and efficacy must allow for responses outside of the limitations of low-expectations.[8]

However, mastery and competence are only one part of the scale; social mores (ethics) determine how self-control is valued or measured in relation to others. Values vary greatly from culture to culture, and youth absorb the crass practices of greed, lust, wrath, and other normalized vices projected from the movie theater to the statehouse. Far from advocating a purist approach to morality, what most needs to be explored in the discussion of ethics is the tension between vice and virtue. Presenting questions for discussion may go farther than moralizing, given that children soon figure out that adults are not perfect; human perfection is an oxymoron. I present virtues and vices, not as an ultimate goal, but as a beginning of a process to move steadily toward goodness and, for those who desire a religious path, Godness.

Like opposite trays on a scale, the two main factors of self-control and ethics are a balance, and the scale is calibrated by guidance. Guidance, like mother or grandmother wit, can transform youth's view of themselves by lending a mirror that can reflect who they are. Guidance gives a sense of relation that helps us locate who and where we are. Guidance creates a grounding where one can more clearly spin a stable axis and identify an individual internal rhythm while creatively communicating with the outer world. I can attest to the fact that without guidance, the journey can be unsteady.

MEMOIRS: SHAPING A STABLE SELF
FROM A TRANSIENT CHILDHOOD

For Black youth who grow up in tough neighborhoods or who are raised without grounding in a positive family or close-knit community, the search for elders with sound advice or lives worthy of emulation can be daunting. As a daughter of a military family, I lived in six locations before I was eleven years old: Washington, D.C., New Mexico, California, Germany, Illinois, and Arizona. I was not grounded in any one community where mentors were readily available, so I turned to books. In the absence of consistent guidance in school or youth programs, I questioned texts for instruction and have ever since. But for young bookworms like me, availability of relevant books for instruction was as limited as culturally conscious teachers or consistent mentors.

I attended schools in places that had limited curricula and that ignored Black or female authors, which resulted in my very narrow understanding of the type of Black woman I could become. A quest for wisdom must necessarily include a quest for self-definition, and the widest possible notion of selfhood is necessary if Black children are to operate beyond stereotypes now rampant in media outlets like television, movies, music, social media, and the World Wide Web. As librarians and instructors of information literacy know all too well, more information does not mean better information. So, although today's youth have greater access to information and resources than I had in the 1970s, there are not necessarily clear pathways to the most diverse, culturally appropriate, or suitably complex resources. Youth need information literacy and critical thinking skills to interpret texts, as do those who mentor Black children globally.

But there are always gems on a journey, no matter how rough, so, although travel limited my interaction with a consistent group of peers, it also expanded my horizons. Benefiting from my adventures as a youth, I continue to travel widely as an adult, without modesty or embarrassment, in an insatiable search for answers hidden in crevices of the world. Today, I am at once drastically changed and strikingly identical to the person I was when my first global journeys began—in Hessisch Oldendorf, Germany—where my family and I lived on the air force base just outside of a town with titillating bakeries:

> *My First Trip Abroad* (1976)
> I became addicted to travel
> At age seven: running through torrential rain
> Searching for a German chocolate cake
> —Stephanie Y. Evans (2012)

Though I initially became enamored with travel through food, I now understand the sociopolitical aspects of exchange that are necessary to bring peaceful social relations and greater ecological sustainability. Now, gastronomic pleasure, cultural exchange, and justice are multiple interests in my explorations. As a result of my own adolescent ups and downs, youth empowerment through literary mentoring is my chosen form of improving the world. I hope this text winds through roots and branches of family trees, lingers through time, and traverses each continent.

My definition of wisdom is a result of me feeling out of place as a child. No matter where I landed, I was too Black, not Black enough, too womanish, not ladylike, or just too strange. Surely, as I have not always been a "modest" girl, I may have failed the gender test given in Solomon's court. I have often found myself disagreeing with limited social expectations for Black children and for women and I grew disillusioned as I uncovered political agendas behind so-called moral imperatives. Essentially, I discovered that many institutionalized declarations of right and wrong had nothing to do with social justice, but rather, emanated from those in power wanting to maintain all possible privileges. As Supreme Court cases continue to show, there are varying definitions of the seven sins (greed, gluttony, lust, envy, wrath, pride, and sloth). Similarly, my journey to self-creation, and constant re-creation, involved embracing the tension between virtues and vices and resting my spirituality on other-worldly intuitions that begin but don't end with organized religion. I am an informal student of world religions, an enthusiast but not an initiate of ancient belief systems, and I have found virtue (charity, temperance, chastity, kindness, patience, humility, diligence) as much outside of churches as in. The narratives show Black writers have taken many paths to peace and universal love, including Islam, Christianity, Judaism, Buddhism, Baha'i, Voodun, Rastafarianism, and environmentalism.

Ultimately, my internal /spiritual journeys have been as fascinating as my geographic ones, and they are motivation to provide youth with a variety of tools to track and map their own inner and outer movements. Literary mentoring—using books as tools for guidance—rests on people writing their ideas for others to consider. My own stories of life, school, work, and exchange are interwoven into this text to, in the words of Anna Julia Cooper, add my voice to the chorus.[5]

MODEL: LITERARY MENTORING AND TOOLS FOR GLOBAL COMPETENCE

Though personal empowerment is imperative, it is not enough to have individual "swag." Many of the narratives collected here demonstrate the value of outreach—diplomacy—connection to the world in an act of creative, peaceful exchange in resistance to existing narratives of violence, oppression, xenophobia, or hatred. Guidance gives us strength—strong bones—to carry us on our journey.

Not all Black travel has been pleasant, peaceful, or of good will. For example, problems of sex tourism and sex trafficking have been rampant since forced enslavement. The story of Saartjie Baartman, the so-called "Hottentot Venus" demonstrates the enduring oppression of Black women in every corner of the world. Baartman, a Khoi-San woman, was persuaded to travel to Europe in 1810 by William Dunlop, a British doctor. She left her South African home at approximately twenty years old, for promises of a better life for her and her family. She was exploited, and after her death (in 1815), "her genitalia and brain were preserved in a bottle and displayed at the Museum of Mankind in Paris until as recently as 1974." It was not until May 2002 that her body was returned to Hankey, the area of her birth near the Gamtoos River Valley in the Eastern Cape Province, and on South African Women's Day, August 9, 2002, afforded a proper burial.[6]

Baartman, like many authors examined in this book, possessed the nerve for international travel, a quest for adventure, and the ability to speak multiple languages, including Dutch, but that did not equate to her empowerment. In England and France, she was treated as a circus animal—caged, sold, and disgraced by those who had the power to exploit her. Despite her best efforts and any initial feelings of personal power she may have had at the beginning of her journey, her quest for "a better life" was thwarted by merchants of abuse and murder.

Today, there are scores of African American men who travel to Brazil or Colombia and other locations to prostitute women, and as Ramona Alston writes in her dissertation, "Race-crossings at the Crossroads of African American Travel in the Caribbean," African American women also travel to places like Jamaica to take advantage of Black men who are treated as exotic sexual commodities.[7]

Though university studies necessarily focus on adult learning, what is needed most in higher education is outreach to youth in an attempt to encourage loving attitudes at all levels and bridge the gap between self and world. In all nations, many homes, schools, and neighborhoods are violent places mirroring a violent world. This book is written for those most "at-risk" of being affected by debilitating conditions at home or abroad. These stories are presented in order to show them paths to improving the quality of life for themselves and their communities, despite harrowing challenges.

As all learning is self-learning, I do hope that youth will be compelled to access this guide directly and then read the primary texts themselves. Reading the actual autobiographies can help maximize self-guided development, mobility, and skill at navigating worlds of challenges. Reading also can help to access the worlds of opportunity. However, if wisdom is to shine through as the distinguishing factor of youth's character and behavior, it is up to adults to offer viable direction while continuing on their own pathways to growth. As such, my primary audiences for this work are high school teachers, university professors, agency directors, program staff, and mentors who provide service to youth in their development. In-depth biographies are not provided here; as a resource guide, the goal is to spotlight the wide assortment of biographies and suggest how, upon further investigation, life stories might enliven a school curriculum or mentoring program. In addition to the Viewshare online inter-active map that accompanies this book, university professors preparing auto-biography, study abroad, community-service-learning or community-based research courses will find online syllabi of special interest, including: (1) Mentoring At-Risk Youth; (2) Black Gender; (3) U.S. Women of Color; (4) Black Autobiography; and (5) African Americans in Paris. Secondary audiences are school reference and academic librarians, academic advisors and school counselors, or anyone interested in accessing or recording personal, familial, or organizational histories. This collection can be of use in teacher education and curriculum programs, adolescent development courses, and several courses from introduction to senior research courses in both Black studies and women's studies. As a member of the Association of Black Women Historians, the Association for the Study of African American Life and History (ASALH), and the Association of Personal Historians, I am invested in increasing the number of autobiographies that extend the historical record and expand understanding of the nuances of life stories, especially by Black authors.[8] As such, this collection will also make a significant contribution to the field of public history, moving the discussion beyond oral history to include self-written narratives.

Black Passports is a guide to wisdom for Black youth, and the narratives are maps to intellectual, geographical, and spiritual expeditions. The concept of lifelong learning is central to this text, so it is my hope that adults will gain much from these narratives for direction in their own life's journey. Through an exploration of our lives and sharing our stories, we can retain the best parts of ancient youth socialization while expanding opportunities relevant to today's global justice issues, regardless of race, gender, heritage, nationality, or other identity markers. Like Sheba learning from Solomon, I hope that adults will glean as much for themselves as for the youth they mentor when reading about the two hundred African American narratives presented here.

ONE

Introduction

SWAG DIPLOMACY
(Literary Mentoring for Self-Empowerment)

There are three things you need to be successful in life:
a backbone, a wishbone, and a jawbone.
Use your backbone for perseverance, your wishbone for goal setting,
and your jawbone for speaking out.

> —Paraphrased advice from Ohio State senator
> Nina Turner's grandmother, Inez Emerson[1]

From Linda Brent and Henry "Box" Brown in the mid-1800s to Maya Angelou and Malcolm X in the mid-1900s, African American autobiographers have offered relevant, interesting, and useful guides to personal and professional development for youth and young adults. This collection constructs a road map, beyond a "survival" or "how-to" guide; these narratives often are a guide of what *not* to do and how to learn from mistakes, grow a strong backbone, wishbone, and jawbone, and how to gain the courage to tell one's own life story.

By way of organizing an expansive bibliography, this book weaves a textured patchwork of Black lives. Each chapter is organized into three subthemes: *Message* (foundational scholarship and take away "main point" for the chapter), *Memoirs* (overview of relevant travel narratives and tribute to two authors), *Model* (example of program, resources, or ways message can be applied). This outline reflects the "What?," "So What?," "Now What?" model of applied learning that is often used in experiential education.[2]

MESSAGE: START WITH A GUIDE

This manuscript marks a decade of community service-learning classes and precollege youth summits, workshops, and lectures I have held at University of Massachusetts–Amherst, Brown University, University of Florida, Clark Atlanta University, and several high schools starting in 2001. Community partnerships were essential to the development of this curriculum for empowerment education as they are at the forefront of mentoring praxis. Much of the curriculum is based on those partnerships.

Manufacturing Empowerment and Black Diplomacy: Self, Communication, Tasks, and Innovation

Big Brothers Big Sisters (BBBS) is widely regarded as the premiere mentoring program in the nation. In "A Little Guidance," a promotional statement outlining their program's effectiveness, it claims, "83% of former Littles surveyed agreed that their Big instilled values and principles that have guided them through life."[3] As acknowledged by BBBS, in order to ensure cultural efficacy in these national programs in which African American youth are heavily enrolled, it is imperative that mentors rely on research in Black adolescent studies. These texts must include groundbreaking work such as Joyce Ladner *Tomorrow's Tomorrow: The Black Woman*, and Thomas Dortch (former president of the 100 Black Men organization), *The Miracles of Mentoring: The Joy of Investing in Our Future*. It is also crucial to employ survey research that privileges Black youth voices, places youth's self-analysis and worldview as the point of departure, and incorporates African diasporic youth perspectives as means of analysis for how to mentor Black youth regardless of location.

Charles Green's sociological research underscores connection of the term "mentoring" with the term "guidance" and shows that link exists regardless of national context. In *Manufacturing Powerlessness in the Black Diaspora: Inner-City Youth and the New Global Frontier* (2001), Green surveyed 686 youth ages 14 through 24 from New York, New Jersey, Washington, D.C., Richmond, Los Angeles, Trinidad-Tobago, Dominica, St. Thomas, Kenya, and Tanzania. In Green's study, U.S. youth identified lack of guidance (22 percent) as their highest concern. Guidance ranked as more important to address than drugs (19 percent) or lack of education (14 percent). Guidance weighs heavily on adolescents and young adults' abilities to envision a future beyond their present conditions. Green's approach of employing diasporic youth survey research is the only viable model for speaking intelligibly about Black youth in global contexts. In his findings, he argues that while there is an African diaspora in which youth operate, any attempt to alleviate burdens must be local in application because national and regional contexts prevent a "universal" approach to problem solving. Yet, as Africana scholars we must speak of the African diaspora in order to understand the larger context in which race has been formed in international contexts and racism and colonial waste has created recognizable patterns of cultural dismemberment for Black youth. International awareness must be an essential element of proposed solutions.[4]

Green argues that part of this lack of future vision stems from a cultural disconnection from the past: he writes that Blacks in the African diaspora are "without a clear understanding of their rich and diverse cultural history." Youth and "visionless leaders" are "distracted more and more from the important work of critical thinking and consciousness raising." This cultural disconnect can have a negative impact on youth's ability to gain expertise in basic functions needed to advance in the global workplace.

However, Black youth also need a working knowledge of global cultures, as they will be employed in a world of many nations. To that end, non-African-specific models of competence must also be consulted. Researcher Frederick Evers argues that competence in the work world is the ability to control or manage four specific areas: self, communication, tasks, and innovation/change. Evers, a researcher at McGill University in Canada, published *The Bases of Competence: Skills for Lifelong Learning and Employability*, in which he argues that teachers and university professors have a responsibility to more adequately prepare young workers for the dynamic challenges they will face in the "real world" after college life. He defines that preparation through concepts of "competence" and "lifelong learning."[5]

Evers and his research team surveyed three focus groups: graduates of a business school, employers that hired those graduates, and students currently enrolled in college. Results showed eighteen indicators as essential characteristics that students need to master in order to demonstrate "competence." These indicators fell into four categories of mastery that determined the relative success of young people joining the professional workforce: self, communication, tasks, and innovation.

"Self" is the foundation of knowledge skills needed for competence in employment; thus, *Black Passports* is grounded in a cultural necessity of African American youth to know dimensions of their rich history through historic examples of travel and global interaction in order to effectively advance in the twenty-first-century marketplace and fully participate in global democracy. Written and oral communication skills are a requirement for success and as job markets shift the ability to demonstrate flexibility to not only change but initiate and innovate change will determine a candidate's economic viability.

The legacy of Septima Clark, citizenship education, and the Freedom Schools are critical foundations of educational efficacy that show how empowerment education can change the world through local activism. Green argues that if powerlessness can be manufactured on a global scale, then so too can empowerment, especially through local action. Thus, this international memoir curriculum can assist Black youth in programs and schools both nationwide (locally) and abroad (globally).[6]

In *Black Diplomacy: African Americans and the State Department, 1945–1969*, Michael Krenn investigated the ways in which Black activists linked the civil rights movement to African independence, anti-apartheid, and anti-colonial struggles of the 1950s. However, he argues that, ultimately, the U.S. Department of State and Foreign Service "failed miserably" in efforts to provide necessary international space where Black voices could be heard.[7] Yet, diplomacy as a formal and informal exercise holds promise for the leadership needed to address many issues facing the world's Black youth. International outreach, connection, discussion, debate, concession, and—eventually—collaboration mirror the communicative process involved in mentoring work between agencies and individuals.

This curriculum goes beyond building self-esteem. In her self-empowerment theory model (SET), psychologist Carolyn Tucker argues that *self-control* is more important than self-esteem in the lives of Black youth. To this end, dimensions of self-control are explored in chapter 2, the first topical chapter of the book. Modeled after the Evers competencies of life, academics, employment, and growth through cultural exchange are the four core chapters that form the investigation of empowerment.

In my teaching, I have defined empowerment as having "strong bones," as suggested by Ohio State Senator Nina Turner's grandmother, Inez Emerson. Emerson identified three characteristics of success: backbone, wishbone, and jawbone, which are specifically explored in study abroad reflections where students recorded their interactions overseas.

In contemporary nomenclature the sense of self-love, strength, or power is often defined as having swagger or, in short, "swag." Yet, these guides offer ways to move beyond appearance of a cool "pose" to a grounded and real sense of internal peace and well-being despite inevitable social, political, cultural, and environmental hurricanes. In times of tumult, having real swag means using an internal compass and knowing which way to go when storms hit, when charlatans begin pedaling lies as truth, and when deciding what to believe when everyone else is confused. Real swag requires not only confidence, but also informed, historical, and studied conviction. Essentially, at its best, swag is the ability to exercise self-control regardless of environmental challenges.

Sass and Swag: Literacy for Life

In his assessment of Black historiography, Pero Dagbovie argues for a new approach to history that places student experiences and needs at the center of pedagogical approaches. He advocates a movement to "operationalize history." This builds on Columbia Teachers College Professor Carter V. Good's work on a "functional history of education." For those of us working with the millennial generation, this means incorporating the idea of swag in education or, more precisely, getting students to realize that swag is actually an aged and useful concept. For example, David Levering Lewis pointed out that people like W. E. B. Du Bois personified swag in the 1800s and 1900s: "Reduced to its essence, the legacy of W. E. B. Du Bois [includes] pioneering scholarship in the social sciences, investigative journalism and militant propaganda combined with organized protest, all of it distinguished by a courtly civil rights swagger through the corridors of academic, political, and economic power."[8] Part of what gave Du Bois his presence and wide sphere of influence was his international identity, gained by his fifteen trips to Europe, Asia, Russia, the Caribbean, and Africa throughout his ninety-five years.[9]

Parallel to the concept of swag, in *Smart and Sassy*, sociologist Joyce West Stevens identifies young Black girls' "sassy" behavior as a sign of resilience to an all-too-often hostile world. Youth need to find a stride to move past the many challenges they will face, and sass is a way of, as bell hooks advocates, "talking back" to those who would doubt or suppress youth's rise. Significantly, Stevens presents Black girls' agency via "sass" as a strength-based analysis rather than as a solely "at-risk" maladaptive behavior. Invoking "sassy" Sarah Vaughn, Stevens argues that resilience is a key factor of adolescent development in marginalized populations. Like "swag," sass becomes an adaptive behavior that, while sometimes turning into a reactionary and counterproductive response to stress or crisis, can in fact be nourished and shaped into a productive coping mechanism.

In the decade and a half of my college teaching experience, I have witnessed hundreds of students struggle to get a foothold on success and self-efficacy. Efficacy—the power to produce an effect—means focusing on both intention and outcome. This reinforces Tucker's assertion that "confidence" is not enough. Success means not just *feeling* successful, but also mastering the tools needed to overcome challenges. Essentially sassiness means being "bold, independent and courageous" in a way that propels one to *sustainable* success.[10]

An old adage warns, "You can lead a horse to water, but you can't make him drink." For youth to be successful, they have to be bold enough to thirst for guidance and humble enough to accept it when offered. Equally as important, they must demonstrate a focus on self without deteriorating into self-absorption. The concept of peer mentor is an imperative aspect of holistic youth development, and the concept of shared experiences is central to this discussion. Mentoring nurtures self-love and transforms that into self-determination.

Youth must start with a guide, but ultimately they must develop a unique persona and learn to trust their intuition to make their own decisions and find their own authoritative voice. Historically, Black Americans developed their strong sense of self-efficacy within a radically hostile environment. Both autobiography and travel writing exemplify precisely the types of intellectual and physical freedoms that the antiliteracy laws of the antebellum South, social strictures on women's voices, and efforts to stifle ethnic solidarity sought to prevent. As written in the "Act and Resolutions of the General Assembly of the State of South Carolina," penned in December 1800, denial of movement and literacy were essential to keeping African Americans subordinate: "Whereas, the law heretofore enacted for the government of the slaves, free Negroes, mulattoes, and mestizoes, have been found insufficient for keeping them in due subordination . . . be it therefore enacted . . . assembled or met together for the purpose of mental instruction . . . is hereby declared to be an unlawful meeting."[11] It took a strong will to provide a counter-narrative to the White supremacist images of lazy, ignorant, violent, or over-sexed stereotypes. Challenges to instruction that enable self-definition still linger, and twenty-first-century youth need self-mastery as much as ever. As Perry Hall acknowledges in his article, "Introduction to African American Studies," freedom and self-determination are the goals of literacy. In this case, I argue that real freedom moves beyond national boundaries and though literacy is no longer outlawed, wading through an ocean of misinformation requires a wishbone similar to those determined to travel the Underground Railroad.

Race and gender identities are not static, and exposure to international settings illuminates the kaleidoscope of ways individuals form identities that at once affirm and transcend race, ethnicity, gender, or national groupings. Autobiographical travelogues are sites of self-definition that show how identity expression and relationships play out in myriad complex ways that are usually rife with tension. With close investigation, identity expressions often lack the romanticism that accompanies what Benedict Anderson termed "imagined communities," and "we are the world" harmonies can easily fall apart when we interact with those *in* the world.

The narratives presented here blur lines of self/other and home/foreign. The voices provide readers with a wholly new opportunity for analysis of Black intellectual history, traditions of lifelong learning, and critical international studies. Above all, Black travel narratives demonstrate that writing, particularly self-writing in transnational contexts, in many ways reflects commitment to self-possession through evolving definitions and shifting perceptions of the world.

MEMOIRS: NARRATIVES OF EMPOWERMENT

By diverse pathways, well-known men and women such as Mahalia Jackson, Martin Luther King Jr., Althea Gibson, Ada "Bricktop" Smith, Bill Russell, Assata Shakur, Muhammad Ali, Tina Turner, Dorothy Height, and Malcolm X have penned their globetrotting stories. These travelers are joined by such lesser-known authors as cyclist Major Taylor, commercial pilot Janet Bragg, outrageous Black feminist lawyer and NOW (National Organization for Women) organizer Floryence Kennedy, and businessman activist Leon Sullivan. These narratives are filled with personal challenges, individual triumphs, community connectedness, national tragedies, and fascinating international encounters.

As technologies and economies draw nations closer together in the global web, children coming of age in the twenty-first century must increasingly understand their development in an international context. African American international memoir lends itself to a multidisciplinary lens—historical, sociological, geographical, and literary—and encourages insightful consideration of adolescent metamorphosis with the world as a textured setting. Resources abound.[12]

Methodology

I located two hundred *Black Passports* memoirs through three steps: First, I conducted a broad survey using search engines from the Library of Congress and academic journal databases such as JSTOR and PROQUEST to booksellers like amazon.com and bookfinder.com. Second, I scanned bibliographies by authors of groundbreaking publications about Black autobiography, particularly by V. P. Franklin, Margo Perkins, William Andrews, Roland Williams, and Joanne Braxton. Third, I combed tertiary sources in relevant bibliographies, encyclopedias, and list servs. The two most useful resources were Audrey Thompson's *African-American Histories, Biographies, and Fictionalized Biographies for Children and Young Adults: A Bibliography* (2001) and Henry Louis Gates Jr. and Evelyn Higginbotham's *African American Lives* (2004). Thompson's work identifies 494 names of biographies and autobiographies.[13] Gates and Higginbotham's *African American Lives* identified biographies and autobiographies of 611 African Americans including over 130 autobiographies. To narrow the data set to a manageable collection, only book-length publications were listed in this study.

A significant number of the names included are found in these two comprehensive texts, but there are many references here that are missing from one or both of the Thompson and Gates and Higginbotham sources, most notably activist Assata Shakur, actors Angela Bassett and Courtney Vance, pilot Janet Bragg, African or American students schooled in Africa such as Phillipe Wamba and Dympna Ugwu-Oju, surgeons Rose-Marie Toussaint and Claudia Lynn Thomas, educators Susie Mae Williams White and Jan Willis, and "Chef Jeff" Henderson. *Black Passports* increases focus on many narratives that are marginalized or largely unknown whether in academic or community circles. However, one major limitation of the data set is an outgrowth of the types of autobiographies available: most are stories by entertainers or athletes. Educators well understand that to be competitive in the national and local employment markets, youth must increasingly focus on science, technology, and medical professions. Scientists and health professionals must tell their stories to increase the diversity of perspectives, particularly those that might be provided by engineers, architects, nurses, veterinarians or others with technical careers. Further, sport narratives add context to health education.

There are approximately two hundred narratives included in *Black Passports* (see page 9).

Once introduced to a character and storyline, youth can access additional information online. In addition to encyclopedia references like *African*

Aaron, Hank
Ali, Laila
Ali, Muhammad
Ailey, Alvin
Anderson, Marian
Angelou, Maya
(Marguerite
Johnson)
Ashe, Arthur
Atkins, Cholly
Bailey, Pearl
Baldwin, James
Baker, Vernon
Baraka, Amiri
Basie, Count
Bassett, Angela and
Vance, Courtney
Bechet, Sidney
Beckwourth, James
Becton, Julius W., Jr.
Belafonte, Harry
Bragg, Janet
Bricktop (Ada
Smith)
Brooke, Edward
Brooks, Gwendolyn
Brown, Elaine
Brown, Henry "Box"
Brown, William
Wells
Broyard, Bliss
Bunche, Ralph
Bussey, Charles
Calloway, Cab
Campbell, Robert
Carlos, John
Carmichael, Stokely
Carson, Ben
Chamberlain, Wilt
Charles, Ray
Chuck D.
Clark, Septima
Poinsette
Cole, Natalie
Commings, Jeff
Cooper, Anna Julia
Coppin, Fanny
Jackson
Craft, William and
Ellen
Cruz, Celia
Davis, Angela
Yvonne
Davis, Belva
Davis, Miles
Davis, Ossie and
Ruby Dee

Davis, Sammy, Jr.
Dean, Harry Foster
Delany, Annie and
Sara
Denton, Sandy Pepa
Douglas, Gabrielle
Douglass, Frederick
Dryden, Charles
Du Bois, W. E. B.
Dunham, Katherine
Duster, Michelle
Dympna Ugwu-Oju
Early, Charity
Edelman, Marian
Wright
Elaw, Zilpha
Ellington, Duke
Estes, Simon
Fisher, Antwone
Foreman, George
Franklin, John Hope
Frazier, Joe
Gibbs, Mifflin Wistar
Gillespie, Dizzy
(John Birks)
Gordy, Berry
Gould, William
Benjamin
Gregory, Dick
Grier, Pam
Guillaume, Robert
Hampton, Lionel
Harris, Gail
Harrison, Juanita
Height, Dorothy
Henderson, Jeff
Henson, Josiah
Henson, Matthew
Heywood, Harry
Holiday, Billie
Hughes, Langston
Hunter-Gault,
Charlayne
Hurston, Zora Neale
Jackson, Janet
Jackson, Mahalia
Jacobs, Harriet
James, Etta
James, Rick
Jamison, Judith
Jefferson, Alexander
Jemison, Mae
Johnson, Jack
Johnson, James
Weldon
Johnson, John
Jones, Quincy

Jordan, June
Kelly, Samuel
Kennedy, Florynce
King, B. B.
King, Coretta Scott
King, Martin Luther,
Jr.
Kitt, Eartha
Lacy, Leslie
Alexander
Langston, John
Mercer
Latta, Rev. Morgan
Lee, Andrea
Leslie, Lisa
Lester, Julius
Lorde, Audre
Louis, Joe
Love, Nat
Lynch, James R
Malcolm X
Marrant, John
Marshall, Paule
Mays, Benjamin
Mays, Willie
McElroy, Colleen
McKay, Claude
Mingus, Charles
Montague, Magnifi-
cent Nathaniel
Morton, Lena
Morrow, Frederick
Moton, Robert
Murray, Pauli
Newton, Huey P
Obama, Barack
O'Ree, Willie
Oliver, Kitty
Owens, Jesse
Payne, Daniel
Pemberton, Gayle
Pickens, William
Poitier, Sidney
Powell, Adam
Powell, Colin
Prince, Nancy
Gardner
Pryor, Richard
Robin Quivers
Rangel, Charles
Reagon, Bernice
Johnson
Rice, Condoleezza
Ringgold, Faith
Robeson, Eslanda
Goode
Robeson, Paul

Robinson, Randall
Robinson, Sugar Ray
Ross, Diana
Rowan, Carl T
Rudolph, Wilma
RuPaul, Andre
Russell, Bill
Scarborough, Wil-
liam Sanders
Schuyler, George
Shakur, Assata
Simone, Nina
Smith, Amanda
Smith, Tommie
Steward, Austin
Steward, Theophilus
Gould
Sullivan, Leon
Taylor, Major
Terrell, Mary Church
Thomas, Claudia
Lynn
Thompson, Era Bell
Thurman, Howard
Toussaint,
Rose-Marie
Turner, Tina
Tyson, Mike
Vaughn, Donald
Verrett, Shirley
Vincent, Carter O
Walker, Alice
Walker, George
Walker, Rebecca
Wamba, Philippe
Ward, Samuel
Ringgold
Warwick, Dionne
Washington, Booker
T
Isaiah Washington
Waters, Ethel
Wattleton, Faye
Wells-Barnett, Ida
West, Cornel
White, Susie Mae
Williams
White, Walter
Wilkins, Roger
Williams, Patricia
Williams, Robert
Williams, Venus and
Serena
Willis, Jan
Wilson, Mary
Wright, Richard
Young, Andrew

American Lives, the best online companion resources for this collection are blackpast.org (University of Washington Professor Quintard Taylor's "Online African American History Reference Guide: Black Past . . . Remembered and Reclaimed"), aaregistry.org (the online education collective African American Registry), bio.com (The History Channel/Biography Channel's online resource), and wikipedia.com (the world-wide encyclopedia). The memoir collection benefits from existing resources that present the "facts" about these authors, but by focusing solely on autobiographies, *Black Passports* emphasizes self-definition in life writing. In this section, I offer possible paradigms for analyzing life writing; an increased collection of memoirs and autobiographies is sorely needed to enhance the primary source analysis of Black life and culture. Without rich, first-person primary sources, the reliability of research, efficacy of policy makers, and depth of insight offered by historians or social analysis will be limited.

Of course, as Marian Anderson's nephew duly notes in the introduction to *My Lord, What a Morning*, autobiography offers a unique perspective, but research-based definitive biographies, like that of Allan Keiler's *Marian Anderson: A Singer's Journey* "complete the story."[14] Readers are invited to begin with autobiographical sketches, but they are strongly encouraged to follow up with specifics offered by research-based biography. New work, such as Randal Jelks' *Benjamin Elijah Mays: Schoolmaster of the Movement* (2012), continues to enhance our understanding of important figures.

"Truth" in Autobiography: Promises and Limitations of the Genre

> Some names in this work have been changed and some of
> the characters and incidents are fictitious.
> —Charles Mingus, "Epigraph," *Beneath the Underdog*

In narratives by enslaved Blacks, authentication was essential. African American authors often had respected members of the White community attest that their narrative was true or real. Due to the propaganda of slaveholders, who portrayed Blacks as "happy slaves," narratives revealed the horrors of enslavement as recorded in the first person. There was an imperative for antebellum African American authors to assert the validity of their story, especially when the facts were "extraordinary," such as Linda Brent's hiding for seven years in a small space, Henry "Box" Brown's escape by shipping himself in a box through the United States Postal Service, or William and Ellen Craft's gender-bending escape from Georgia where light-skinned Ellen masqueraded as a sickly White man and William "escorted" his "master" to the North for treatment of a supposed illness.

This trend of authentication can most easily be seen in Nat Love's subtitle for his autobiography: *The Life and Adventures of Nat Love, Better Known in the Cattle Country as "Deadwood Dick" by Himself; a True History of Slavery Days, Life on the Great Cattle Ranges and on the Plains of the "Wild and Woolly" West, Based on Facts, and Personal Experiences of the Author* (1907). However, it would be a mistake for young readers to approach autobiography without any qualification of the notion of "truth" in self-writing.

As Charles Mingus writes plainly in the epigraph to *Beneath the Underdog*, autobiography is part fiction, either wittingly or unwittingly. For Mingus, the creative spirit that fueled his avant-garde jazz style on the bass also clearly influenced his autobiographical writing. Mingus wrote in the third person and took readers from the streets of Long Beach, California, to the halls of Bellevue mental institution. Discerning fact from fiction is a task for both author and reader. Autobiographical details are nuanced, and factual events are often incomplete with fabricated additions, as exemplified in Billie Holiday's autobiography, which was penned by William Duffy from piecemeal interviews. Facts, when investigated by scholars, are recorded differently by authors: for example, Muhammad Ali stated in his 1975 autobiography that he threw his 1960 Olympic gold medal in the Ohio River, which scholars such as Augustus Wood argue primary source documents do not substantiate.[15]

Clearly, there are challenges that autobiography presents to readers who desire historical accuracy. These challenges can readily be seen in the narrative of Jack Johnson, who misrepresented some of his fight record and was married several years after he stated, and also in Zora Neale Hurston's *Dust Tracks on a Road*, where she cited the wrong birth date and alluded to being born in Florida when she was actually born in Notasulga, Alabama. B. B. King openly admitted his memory clashed with scholarly record, but he wrote that he did not care because he was not telling a "cold-blooded history" but the tale of his life as his *heart* remembered.[16]

Even after accepting limitations when looking for "truth," in texts, autobiography as a genre is limited as a medium of study. Individual "great man or woman" narratives obscure millions of everyday people who have full lives and who impact their local or national landscapes by simply living regular, anonymous lives. Focus on individuals ignores how relationship to others, particularly in social movements, forms the foundation of impacting social or political norms. Further, international memoirs exclude important autobiographies or biographies like those of civil rights movement or activist workers

(especially by Ann Moody, Rosa Parks, Constance Baker Motley, Harriet Tubman, Fannie Lou Hamer, or Medgar Evers) and do not investigate relevant
cultural autobiographies or even memoirs like *Bourgeois Blues* by Jake Lamar,
who lives abroad but has not yet published a full-length book on the subject.

Also missing are incarceration memoirs (George Jackson in 1970), private
narratives like that of surgeon Dr. Vivien Thomas, businessman Earl Graves,
or as-yet unpublished memoirs like those of activist-journalist Charlotta Bass.
Last, nuanced race narratives or fictive autobiographies such as James Weldon
Johnson's *Autobiography of an Ex-Colored Man*, John Howard Griffin's *Black
Like Me*, or Ernest Gaines's *Autobiography of Miss Jane Pittman* might also
provide useful discussions of race and pursuit of personal and social identity
but are not presented here.

Autobiography is a valuable genre to explore in a quest to understand
meaning of human life in general and Black struggles for human and civil
rights in particular. In *Soliloquy*, his final autobiography, W. E. B. Du Bois
wrote:

> Autobiographies do not form indisputable authorities. They are always
> incomplete, and often unreliable. Eager as I am to put down the truth,
> there are difficulties; memory fails especially in small details, so that
> it becomes finally but a theory of my life, with much forgotten and
> misconceived, with valuable testimony but often less than absolutely
> true, despite my intention to be frank and fair.[17]

I argue that, despite admissions of omission, Dr. Du Bois's writing exemplifies
the narrative of a writer seeking truth while at the same time disseminating
a message of wisdom. Du Bois's series of three main autobiographies offers
a persuasive paradigm for the value of the genre. In essence, I support John
Blassingame's assessment, which situates Black people's writing in the first person as an indisputably important primary resource when interpreting Black
historical experience and when attempting to formulate political and cultural
possibilities for Black women and men.[18]

Self-definition is vital in a country where Black people are regularly portrayed as less than human. In the foreword to Jack Johnson's *My Life and Battles*, Geoffrey Ward goes so far as to call Johnson's autobiography "self-defense,"
revealing the level of persecution Johnson and others faced. Children labeled
"at-risk" often are in need of these strategies for self-defense provided by first-
person accounts.

In sum, this bibliography complements important work on Black travel like Farah Griffin and Cheryl Fish's groundbreaking anthology *A Stranger in the Village: Two Centuries of African American Travel Writing* (1998) and Elaine Lee's *Go Girl!: The Black Women's Book of Travel and Adventure* (1997). Whereas these texts focus on travel writing as a genre, this bibliography focuses on travel writing as memoir to situate travel within a larger life narrative. Exploratory exercises can be assigned by mapping one person's life: W. E. B. Du Bois, Dizzy Gillespie, Duke Ellington, Juanita Harrison, Katherine Dunham, and Coleen McElroy would be optimal examples because of their vast travel itineraries. The database can be fascinating from K–12 studies to advanced doctoral research and is a practical guide for addressing life's issues through memoirs. Of the hundreds of choices, I have selected a dozen authors as tantamount to virtuous models and as samples of possible instruction.[19]

The Guidance Council: Archetypes for Life Writing

Indeed, as will be discussed in the "Life" chapter, a "role model" is as complicated a notion as gender norms of "shameless" boys and "modest" girls in the tenth century BCE. Hero worship is a dangerous hobby because it obscures the necessity to celebrate icons without glossing over their faults. Even heroes have crises of character or, at the very least, actions that warrant "real talk" critique. Notably, though Makeda is hailed as a wise and honorable queen, also known as Bilqīs of Yemen, she actually beheaded her first husband because he was not ruling his inherited kingdom honorably. She allegedly got him drunk on wine, chopped off his head (which she displayed on the palace gate), and then retook her rightful power bestowed by her father. Yes, one must choose role models carefully, and even when hailing their virtues, we must pay close attention to the finer plot points of decision making, even with larger-than-life heroes.[20]

Despite the muddy terrain of defining role models, as a teacher, I cannot resist identifying those narratives that, according to my personal values of virtue, creativity, and competence, strike me as heroic and worthy of admiration. I call this list of twelve my "Guidance Council." These are life stories from the larger data set that I find inspiring. Mary McLeod Bethune wrote that the goals of higher education are to "investigate, interpret and inspire." Too often, researchers and teachers fail to divulge what inspires them. But many authors of autobiographies named their role models as sources of inspiration. Astronaut Mae Jemison admired performer Eartha Kitt, cut her hair short to model South African singer Miriam Makeba, and studied African dance, like Judith

Jamison. Most touchingly, when she earned her place in the NASA program, she was able to meet actress Nichelle Nichols, who played Lt. Uhura on the *Star Trek* TV show Jemison watched as a young science fiction enthusiast. Inspiration is in dire need in order to propel young imaginations to space and beyond and to adequately prepare youth for global political realities.

I have paired narratives with the parables afforded by close reading of memoir. Ida B. Wells and Frederick Douglass ("Introduction"), Katherine Dunham and Dizzy Gillespie ("Life"), Anna Julia Cooper and W. E. B. Du Bois ("School"), Mae Jemison and Jeff Henderson ("Work"), Jan Willis and Malcolm X ("Exchange") and Angela Davis and Barack Obama ("Conclusion").

There is ample opportunity for creative learning with this rich list. As a sample, I created a vocabulary list of thirteen hundred words from these twelve epic narratives from which geographic comprehension, historical analysis, academic confidence, and personal satisfaction can grow. This word list is introduced in chapter 4 and provided in full in appendix B.

Having reviewed this data set of two hundred narratives, I observed patterns in how Black travel narratives have been written. When considering a life narrative, readers must pay special attention to how the author shapes identity, knowledge, and power. As Margo Perkins argues in her comparative analysis of Angela Davis, Elaine Brown, and Assata Shakur, narratives reflect experience and also can help authors advocate for transformative action. Authors of autobiography continue to ask and answer these questions and, as Miriam Makeba sang, a luta continua: the struggle continues. Part of that struggle is self-definition. Yes, we need a "jawbone," but how are we supposed to sound and what shall we say?

After surveying the larger data set I propose a typography of eight narrative styles.[21]

Autobiographical Archetypes

> Activist—fights for something; generally uses institutionalized tools; advocate
> Survivor—recounts harrowing experiences of overcoming adversity
> Seeker—quests for knowledge, understanding, or adventure
> Relation—focuses on family, community, culture, or location
> Rebel—fights against something; generally operates outside of institutionalized norms

Icon—expresses selfhood; foregrounds ideas or image
Messenger—spreads gospel or heralds morality; brings word about
  life meaning
Professional—frames story through life work or occupation

Two most striking examples of this typology can be seen in two recent
publications: Theresa Runstedtler's *Jack Johnson, Rebel Sojourner: Boxing in
the Shadow of the Global Color Line* (2012) and Touré's *I Would Die 4 U: Why
Prince Became an Icon* (2013). The titles of the biographies explain the major
theme of the subject's life and, in Johnson's case, the tone of his narrative. The
categorical classification can also be seen in narratives like Ida B. Wells' title
Crusade for Justice, chosen by her daughter for the posthumously published
work.

In my assessment of the twelve Guidance Council narratives, there are
several ways we might characterize their voice:

Ida B. Wells, *Crusade for Justice* (1970): Survivor, Rebel
Frederick Douglass, *The Narrative of . . .* (1845): Survivor,
  Messenger
Katherine Dunham, *Island Possessed* (1969): Survivor, Icon,
  Professional
Dizzy Gillespie, *To Be or Not to . . . Bop!* (1979): Icon, Professional
Anna Julia Cooper, *The Third Step* (1945): Seeker, Messenger
W. E. B. Du Bois, *Darkwater* (1920): Messenger, Icon
Mae Jemison, *Find Where the Wind Goes* (2001): Seeker, Professional
Jeff Henderson, *Cooked: From the Streets to the Stove, from Cocaine to
  Foie Gras* (2007): Survivor, Professional
Jan Willis, *Dreaming Me* (2008): Seeker, Messenger
Malcolm X (Al-Hajj Malik El-Shabazz), *Autobiography of . . .* (1965):
  Rebel, Messenger
Angela Davis, *An Autobiography* (1974): Activist, Messenger
Barack Obama, *Dreams from My Father* (1995): Relation, Icon

The Guidance Council Reading List appears on the following page.

Students can access *Black Passport* narratives and the *Swag Diplomacy*
online resource to decipher ways these and other travelers have penned their
stories. They can use this paradigm to discover ways to tell of their own life
travels, past, present, and future.

Fig. 1.1. Ida B. Wells. 1897, Project Gutenberg.

Fig. 1.2. Frederick Douglass. circa 1879, National Archives and Records Administration.

Fig. 1.3. Anna J. Cooper. *A Voice from the South*, 1892. Book cover.

Fig. 1.4. W. E. B. Du Bois. 1918, Library of Congress, Cornelius Marion (C. M.) Battey, photographer.

Fig. 1.5. Katherine Dunham. 25 January 1956, Library of Congress.

Fig. 1.6. Dizzy Gillespie. Normandie, France 20 July 1991, Roland Godefroy, photographer.

Guidance Council Reading List. Pictures: public domain or used by permission.

Fig. 1.7. Jan Willis. Wesleyan.

Fig. 1.8. Malcolm X. Library of Congress, 12 March 1964.

Fig. 1.9. Angela Davis. 15 October 2006, Hunter Kahn photographer.

Fig. 1.10. President Barack Obama. 14 January 2009, Pete Souza, the Obama-Biden Transition Project

Fig. 1.11. Mae Jemison, 1992, Official NASA Photo, Endeavor.
Fig. 1.12. Jeff Henderson. 8 October 2008, foodnetwork.com.

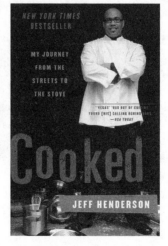

Literacy as Liberation: Frederick Douglass and Ida B. Wells

Many types of voices emerge from autobiography, sometimes within one text, so the genre is not a monolith, and certainly not all authors are heroes. However, African American life-writing, by virtue of the traditions of antiliteracy laws, slave narratives, and the audacity of "authoritative voices," epitomizes the heroic survival tradition of narratives, including Frederick Douglass ("*The Narrative Life...*") and Ida B. Wells (*Crusade for Justice*). In *The Black Scholar* (1973), John Blassingame identified Black autobiography as a foundational cornerstone of both literary and historical traditions. Citing Frederick Douglass as a primary example, he argued that autobiography is "one of the most important forums Blacks have used to state their positions, to leave a record of their resistance, to inspire future generations, and to promote their national development.... As a historical document, the autobiography was a counterweight to the White historian's caricature of Black life." Blassingame's essay identified the location of this genre at the intersection of two distinct disciplines and, in doing so, suggests a basis for an argument of autobiography's inherently interdisciplinary nature.[22] Regardless of the disciplinary approach, Douglass is widely recognized as the grandfather of Black narrative, as his powerful oratory and committed autobiographical efforts led the way for many others to tell their story. Though there were many powerful tales before him, including Olaudah Equiano more than fifty years prior to Douglass, his was the popularized account that came to personify the African American abolitionist imperative—the paradigm of freedom's voice.[23]

In a prefatory letter to Frederick Douglass's first autobiography, abolitionist Wendell Phillips wrote, "I am glad the time has come when the lions write history."[24] In his chapter on "narrative authority," Robert Stepto argues that Douglass's narrative has become the paradigm of voice and empowerment in the African American autobiographical tradition. Stepto lauds Douglass for his ability to offer compelling and creative prose that no other voice supersedes.[25] However, Douglass's fiercely independent voice is one that, at some point, benefited from nurturing or affirmation from those also engaged in the struggle, and in turn, he passed that affirmation to Ida B. Wells who passed the passion to those, like Michelle Duster her great-granddaughter, who are active today advocating for a long-overdue Ida B. Wells monument in Chicago. Many independent, proud, and creative people of power have themselves been nurtured into being by powerful mentors. We see this in the "young lions" like Soroya Corbett, Frank Moten, and Duster, whose lives are testimony to the benefits of mentoring.

Though he rightly acknowledged that not all autobiography is of exceptional literary quality, Blassingame situated Black people's writing in the first person or as the act of reflection as an indisputably important primary resource when interpreting Black historical experiences. As was standard for the times, he focused on the male contribution to literature by arguing that "the central theme which runs through these autobiographies is the demand for recognition of Black manhood." As women historical theorists and literary critics gained access to publication in the 1980s and 1990s, it became apparent that autobiographies were also about demands for recognition of Black womanhood.[26]

As outlined in chapter 5, Black women's narratives warrant special attention because their status as women meant they had to fight not only racial barriers to travel, but gendered barriers to mobility based on social expectations to conform to static existence circumscribed by the "Cult of True Womanhood." Piety, purity, domesticity, and submissiveness were also tied to stagnation and lack of voice. In *Black Women Writing Autobiography: A Tradition within a Tradition*, Joanne Braxton identified five types of subgenre in Black women's autobiography: slave narrative, travelogue, reminiscence, historical memoir, and modern autobiography. She then argued that the historical trajectory of Black women's autobiographical literature ranges from 'survival' narratives in the early stages to self-expression and self-identification, liberation via public voice, dealing with issues of acculturation, seeking personal fulfillment, and, ultimately, self-creation. Detailing representative stories of women, including Linda Brent, Ida B. Wells, Zora Neale Hurston, and Maya Angelou, Braxton traced the contributions of Black women's self-writing, much of which has provided guidance and fortification for this present study.[27]

In a more closely defined analysis that complements Braxton's comprehensive approach, Margo Perkins has compared three autobiographies of Black power movement participants. Perkins' *Autobiography as Activism: Three Black Women of the Sixties* provides a gendered alternative to well-known male narratives by figures like Malcolm X, George Jackson, and Eldridge Cleaver. Perkins argued that autobiographies by Angela Davis, Assata Shakur, and Elaine Brown "advocate and model transformative action" and allow women to "tell their own side of the story . . . to reinvent themselves . . . and contribute to the shaping of a people's collective consciousness." This idea of literary activism and constructing Black consciousness grounds ideas of self-efficacy, which is a foundation of global competence.[28]

Like Douglass, Ida B. Wells's autobiography is paradigmatic of a "strong bones" narrative because it traverses topics from her 1883 lawsuit against discriminatory treatment on the Chesapeake, Ohio, and Southwestern Railway and her research and reporting of the antilynching campaign. The train lawsuit helps inform civil rights movement discussions in the nineteenth century and enhances discussions of struggle long before the 1950s and 1960s.[29] The lynching of Wells' close friends in March of 1892 and the dissemination of her *Free Speech* newspaper in May of that year laid the groundwork for a lifetime of her *Crusade for Justice.*

Wells participated as a co-founder of the NAACP and marched for women's suffrage, seeing all causes for rights intertwined. In *Crusade,* she wrote, "Eternal vigilance is the price of liberty, and it does seem to me that, notwithstanding all these social agencies and activities there is not that vigilance which should be exercised in the preservation of our rights."[30] Despite a lifetime of struggle, Wells knew that as a country, we were not "there" yet; she understood the path to justice for all still lay ahead and required a collective diligence, not present even in the last days of her life in 1931. The killing of thousands, including Trayvon Martin in Florida, Kendrick Johnson in Georgia, and Phylicia Barnes in Maryland, shows we have a long way to go as a country to ensure the safety of Black youth.

Wells and Douglass are cornerstones of a civil rights curriculum because of the intersections of race, gender, and national politics, but also because they were both involved in bringing national issues to the attention of international communities. Wells' *Southern Horrors* and similar writings on lynching rightly place civil rights at the intersection of both governmental and public dimensions and identify the role that global advocacy plays in domestic issues. The crusade for justice continues in the form of discriminatory incarceration policies and what activists including Angela Davis have termed the "prison industrial complex." Michelle Alexander's book, *The New Jim Crow: Mass Incarceration in the Age of Colorblindness* (2010), outlines youth in marginalized populations and is a prime example of how youth must learn the history of activism, because much justice work remains to be done.

These stories directly connect self-education, desire for community building, and access to a passport, combined traits that social conservatives in the dominant culture have long understood make one particularly unsuitable for mental or physical enslavement. Frederick Douglass knew the value of learning: literacy and submission were incompatible. He also understood, as did Ida B. Wells after him, that calling international attention to oppression in the United States impacted domestic conditions. These two hundred diverse texts show that travelers' quests for identity, education, and empowerment were not uniform, and thus individually and collectively these narratives offer useful examples of suitably multidimensional Pan-African identities. The stories offer inexhaustible stimulation for young readers' malleable minds; Douglass and Wells offer foundational first steps to guidance in the right direction.

Frederick Douglass

Narrative of the Life of Frederick Douglass, An American Slave: Written by Himself (1845). England, Scotland, Ireland 1845.

> "Freedom's Ambassador"
> Wit sharper than Covey's whip
> Third-eye North Star clarity of purpose
> Firm as Haiti's limestone foundation

Ida Wells-Barnett

Crusade for Justice: The Autobiography of Ida B. Wells (1970). Europe 1893; Liverpool, Manchester, Bristol, London England 1894.

> "Vigilant Liberty. Run Tell That!"
> World's Fair, America's radical elocutionist
> Parading *Red Record* to Queen and Parliament
> Organizing protest campaigns; liberty's *Defender*.

MODEL: *BLACK PASSPORTS* OUTLINE, A PLAN FOR CREATIVE LITERACY

Oprah gained inspiration and insight from reading Maya Angelou's first autobiography, *I Know Why the Caged Bird Sings*, and Kareem Abdul Jabar recalls being profoundly impacted by *The Autobiography of Malcolm X*, after which he converted from Roman Catholicism to Islam.[31] Young men and women today can learn from books about how to create visible, mobile, and voluble lives. I define literary mentoring as readers gaining insight, perspective, inspiration, and guidance from a text in a similar way they would from a personal mentoring relationship.[32]

While literary mentoring can include a person using a book as a tool for mentoring, the focus here lies more on the person reading the actual text. This definition differs from the concept of literary mentoring presented by Irene Goldman-Price and Melissa McFarland Pennell in *American Literary Mentoring*, where they identify the term as authors of literature who mentor up-and-coming authors. For the purpose of mentoring youth, I invoke the term "literary mentoring" to mean youth reading memoirs as a path to self-empowerment, particularly empowerment that enables them to move more freely within global contexts.

At the 2011 Harvard University Think Tank on Global Education, the educational company World Savvy provided a helpful definition of global competency.[33] The organization exists to increase the quality and quantity of global interaction by schools and youth:

> At World Savvy, we've helped to develop more globally competent teachers and learners through integrated, interdisciplinary programs—youth engagement in arts, media and project based learning, and professional development which builds educators' capacity to embed global competency into teaching. This approach is focused on creating a global lens for all teaching and learning which illuminates the connections between issues, events and people, locally and globally, and promotes informed, positive action. . . .
>
> When our organization took on the task of defining global competence and developing an instrument to assess it among our students, we turned to our teachers, students and staff to understand the components of this dynamic concept, and settled on the following framework:

Knowledge:
Complexities and interdependency of world events and issues
Geography, conditions, issues and events
Historical forces that have shaped the current world system
One's own culture and history in relationship to others

Skills:
Research
Communication and collaboration
Coping and resiliency
Critical and comparative thinking
Creative thinking and problem solving

Values and Attitudes:
Openness to new opportunities, ideas and ways of thinking
Self-awareness about identity and culture, and sensitivity and respect for differences

Empathy and valuing multiple perspectives
Comfort with ambiguity and unfamiliar situations

Behaviors:
Seek out multiple opinions and perspectives
Form opinions based on exploration and evidence
Taking informed action on issues that matter to you
Sharing knowledge and encouraging discourse

At its core, this list reinforces my notion of ABCs (attitude, behavior, and choices) in adolescent development theory. I would add to this list the need to appreciate speaking multiple languages. Colleen McElroy, one of the ten study abroad cases presented in chapter 5, elegantly wrote about her acquisition of several languages: "My strange meanderings through foreign languages began with that first trip to Europe where I learned to breathe in the sounds of other languages, all the cacophonies and glides, the hums, clicks and hisses that unraveled into an abundance of new worlds holding lives so clearly unlike mine, yet somehow very familiar. . ."[34] It is imperative to take the time to learn to communicate effectively with others; though not all travelers will make the commitment to learn several languages fluently, the essence of communication—conveyed desire to talk and listen to others and the courtesy of learning at least elementary phases—is a must for global competence. Tools like omniglot.com, conversational humility, and what I call the "fab five" phrases (hello, goodbye, please, thank you, pardon me) can open doors across cultures, contributing to a sense of freedom.[35]

Historically as today, a passport and a notebook represent definitive types of freedom papers; however, reading books about others' freedom also can fan a fire in the bellies of those seeking to master their own destiny. This is especially important for youth put "at risk" by violent surroundings (whether personal, intellectual, or structural).

Global literacy as an approach for Black youth is strengthened by Dr. Greg Carr's notion of the need to "rescue, reconstruct and restore" Black global networks through "literacy and scribal good speech." In 2012 Carr, head of African American studies at Howard University, lectured about the role of Black studies at Black institutions. In his spiritually pragmatic excavation of Black continuities in "maroon" spaces, or places of African cultural retentions, Carr presented an intellectual legacy of African humanities before and after the Maafa or "Middle Passage" of enslavement. His talk offered a reconnection to forms and functions of cultural ways of knowing ready-made for international communication. In this he presented a path away from "dialectics" (an African

European binary) to "globalectics" (a scholarly recentering of African diasporic thought) grounded in Ngugi wa Thiong'o's book *Globalectics: Theory and the Politics of Knowing*. For Black youth, literary mentoring for global competency must identify roots in ancient African knowledge systems. With roots in African thought and a culturally competent curriculum, Black youth will be best equipped for their journey to global competency.[36]

A Decade of Mentoring through Higher Education

While an undergraduate at California State University–Long Beach (CSULB), I was introduced to community service-learning through the Kellogg Fellowship program housed in the School of Social Work at the same time I began to explore Black studies and women's studies. The result congealed identity education with applied learning for social justice. After working in the CSULB Office of Community Service-Learning, I earned a summer research internship with Nadinne Cruz at the Haas Center for Public Service at Stanford University, where I explored how cultural identity impacted definitions of service. Later, as a graduate student in Massachusetts, I investigated Black women's definition of community in their educational philosophy and practice. From early in my undergraduate studies, central themes in my work revolved around identity, knowledge construction, education, and community service.

Beginning in 2001, I co-taught a Mentoring Youth of Color class in the Honors College of the University of Massachusetts–Amherst. The class was an answer to demands by Black students for more substantive diversity in course offerings, but it was also designed to meet the community's call for a greater diversity of college volunteers in local after school programs. After co-teaching the class for two semesters, I took on the class as my own and expanded the partners to include Amherst Regional Middle School's Savuka program (a 21st-Century Learning Center program), the Men's Resource Center, and a young women's club begun by Shellian Smith, one of the students in the original class. At Brown University, while completing my UMass dissertation, I worked as the assistant director of Youth Education Programs at the Swearer Center for Public Service, where I supervised students who coordinated after school programs in Providence, Rhode Island.[37] The cycle of community engagement was completed when I began as a junior faculty member at the University of Florida, where I re-established the mentoring class and developed long-standing partnerships with Big Brothers Big Sisters, the Boys and Girls Clubs, Eastside High School, Lincoln Middle School, the Reichert House for boys, and the Practical Academic Cultural Education (PACE) program for girls and developing partnerships with various organizations in Atlanta, Georgia.

For the past decade, I have also conducted workshops that incorporate creative writing and college preparation. The 2003 summit I held at Brown included participants of Def Poetry Jam, and by the time I developed the program in Florida, I incorporated technology, creating a "NIA Statement" assignment where college students crafted an educational autobiography, spoken word, and Haiku to create a YouTube video for use as a mentoring tool. The take-away message from the partnerships is that these service-learning courses and summits provided empowering education, especially when located in critical disciplinary sites like Black studies or women's studies. When applied, identity studies amplified by creative expression provide an opportunity for youth to enhance their understanding of self by connecting with college students who "look like them" and who personify educational opportunity that may not exist within marginalized communities.

Moreover, college students who have entered a class wanting to "help" or "do good service" have learned how difficult it is to work with children, parents, grandparents, court-appointed caretakers, agency supervisors, law enforcement officers, state and federal policy makers, teachers, principals, guidance counselors, health care or social workers, doctors, and others involved in children's lives. In chapter 3, I provide excerpts from the 2010 course syllabus that outline the framework for creating this learning environment.

BOOK OUTLINE

There are four objectives for *Black Passports* and the corresponding online *Swag Diplomacy* resources. I have created these resources to enhance student knowledge of:

1. self in sociological contexts ("Life")
2. family, peer, and community and school relations ("School")
3. Black identity development within career and professional spaces ("Work")
4. diasporic interactions ("Exchange")

Exploration of these texts should strengthen all four levels of what Gwen Kirk and Margo Okazowa-Rey call "social location": micro (personal), meso (community), macro (nation), global (international). Students reading these texts will be better positioned to understand the concept of ecology, or interrelatedness of life and culture, and can seek to more effectively interact with—and change—their social, political, and natural environments.[38]

In chapter 1, I have outlined the need for youth guidance, defined self-mastery, and global competence as components of empowerment, introduced developments that inspired this research, previewed the collective portrait of the academic memoirs, and explored the complexities of defining role models in literary texts useful in mentoring.

The core four chapters of the book provide substantive exploration of the 200 narratives. Chapter 2 explores many challenging issues that youth face (identity issues including sexuality, religion, political ideologies) and highlights memoirs that raise those issues. Also included in chapter 2 are reflections by Saroya Corbett and Frank Motten, (mentees of Katherine Dunham and Dizzy Gillespie) about how mentoring and performing arts positively impacted the ability to shape their lives. In chapter 3, I identify narratives that can be used in conjunction with national and State of Georgia high school social studies and language arts standards in the subjects of history, geography, vocabulary, and writing. This chapter includes the full list of authors and the geographical guide to their travels, as a basic curriculum ripe for assignments based on travel location. As a southern state with the internationally significant urban city center of Atlanta, Georgia offers one significant point of entry that, if effective, would hold curricular implications and great promise for teaching and mentoring models nationwide.

Students of all ages need guidance through a variety of environmental and behavioral risk factors and frank discussions about work expectations in order to comprehend themselves as positive participants in the global citizenry. These central chapters offer curricular tools that address basic needs of secondary school-aged youth, but they are also very relevant for college-aged adults in an ever-increasingly challenging global job market (chapter 4). I also share my own professional memoir as a sample of how one can view a career (as opposed to just a job) as an extension of personal passions. Chapter 5 demonstrates how ten historic study abroad narratives reflect empowerment characteristics (backbone, wishbone, and jawbone). This is an imperative counternarrative to fight the cultural ignorance of mandated limitations like the 2010 Eurocentric Arizona HB 2281 "antiethnic studies" bill. These ten traveling Black bodies demonstrate the shifting meaning of blackness in tricky international contexts. I focus on the meaning of Black women's "immodest" travel, given that Black men autobiographers have traveled at a rate of at least twice as much as women, and this data set allows an unprecedented scope in which to interrogate the contours of the phenomenon of women moving through a world that seeks to circumscribe their bodies and sequester their minds.

In the closing chapter, we revisit the ABC basics through reflections of my own upbringing, and reflections on study abroad courses through which I have taken forty students to Paris. Chapter 6 ends with advice for the next generation of "young lions."

The appendices offer an alphabetical listing of authors (appendix A), Passport Geography: Data Set for Viewshare Online Project (appendix B), the full Guidance Council vocabulary list of thirteen hundred words (appendix C), and tributary "epic" poetry to some *Black Passports* authors as samples of creative homework that might be assigned in classes that use this curriculum (appendix D). Also provided are syllabi for five courses available online at www.professorevans.net/teaching.

By exploring the experiences of African Americans on several continents, we get a keen glimpse into how human development of race identity is fascinating and infinitely useful to youth in the process of forming their own self-concept. Each chapter offers an entry point into an aspect of Black life at home and abroad to expand youths' horizons.

—

TWO

LIFE

Developing an Authoritative Self (Micro)

No matter where you travel,
You still be Black,
You carry all your history
On your own damn back.
Your momma raised you proper
Your daddy caused you pain
You understand Beethoven,
But you still love Trane.

—Houston Baker Jr., "No Matter Where
You Travel, You Still Be Black" (1979)

MESSAGE: EXPLORING SELF, HEROES, AND ROLE MODELS

There are numerous possible questions students might ask when approaching this body of narratives. These questions are not only about how authors lived, but how life was translated. Questions include: What is the overall tone of the narrative and portrayal of self (in terms of personal values)? Where were authors from? What challenges have they faced, and what attitude did they have when facing them? What countries did they visit and at what age? Why did they travel? What were the major life choices they faced? At what age did they pen their memoirs? Was there a stated purpose in choosing to write their story? What models of resilience do the narratives offer? How did their

observations of countries differ from other travelogues? What events demonstrate the author's primary struggle with vice or virtue?

Discussion questions can be derived from mission statements and agendas
of organizations such as the Boys and Girls Club or Big Brothers Big Sisters.
Many of these questions are about how to approach or interpret the hardships
of life. For example, by engaging memoirs about survival of rape or moles-
tation (Katherine Dunham, Maya Angelou, Pam Grier, Antwone Fisher) or
recovery from drugs (Billie Holiday, Rick James, Richard Pryor), students and
mentors can discuss themes of risk, growth, decision making, and choices with
an eye toward surviving and moving beyond devastating circumstances. This is
especially important in urban areas like Chicago and Detroit, where youth are
raised around normalized violence. Exploration into the lives of others who
grew and thrived in urban centers offers poignant inspiration.

Exposing students to a broad data set can encourage them to find a topic
that interests them and research it in a way that fulfills both personal curiosity
and academic requirements. For example, student researchers might compare
authors' spiritual quests. Students may investigate missionary Amanda Smith,
who, in 1893, published an extensive account of her work in England, Ireland,
Scotland, India, and Africa and compare that with the personal journeys of
Al-Hajj Malik El-Shabazz (Malcolm X) on the Hajj to Mecca in 1964 and Professor Jan Willis's trips to Tibet in the 1970s. This would encourage exploration
of different world religions (in this case, Christianity, Islam, and Buddhism). A
topical approach to comparing memoirs offers many areas of potential interest
that clearly reflect agency and classroom plans:

- *City histories:* Chicago (Sidney Bechet, Janet Bragg, Bricktop,
  Gwendolyn Brooks, Cab Calloway, Katherine Dunham, James Fore-
  man, John Hope Franklin, Dick Gregory, Lionel Hampton, Mahalia
  Jackson, Etta James, Mae Jemison, John H. Johnson, Quincy Jones,
  B. B. King, Malcolm X, Benjamin Mays, Barack Obama, Gayle Pem-
  berton, George Schuyler, Major Taylor, Era Bell Thompson, Ida B.
  Wells, Richard Wright); Detroit (Vincent O. Carter, Berry Gordy,
  Diana Ross, Rick James, Ben Carson, Joe Louis, Robert Williams,
  Mayor Coleman Young, Donald Vaughn)
- *State histories:* South Carolina (James Lynch, Daniel Payne, Ben-
  jamin Mays, William Pickens, Eartha Kitt, Althea Gibson, Dizzy
  Gillespie, Septima Clark, Marian Wright Edelman, Joe Frazier)
- *Caribbean life and culture:* Trinidad (C. L. R. James); Jamaica
  (Harry Belafonte, Sandy "Pepa" Denton); Bahamas (Sidney Poitier);

Barbados (Paule Marshall); Haiti (Rose-Marie Toussaint, Edwidge Danticat)

- *Significant events:* Marian Anderson's 1939 concert at the Lincoln Memorial (Walter White, Marian Anderson); Ghana's 1957 independence celebration (Martin Luther King Jr., Coretta Scott King, Adam Clayton Powell); 1968 Olympics in Mexico (Tommy Smith, John Carlos); "Rumble in the Jungle" 1974 boxing match in Zaire (Muhammad Ali, George Foreman, Etta James, Celia Cruz); Nelson Mandela's 1994 inauguration (Maya Angelou, Quincy Jones, Charles Rangel, Colin Powell)
- *Family, personal, or professional relationships:* adoring friends (Duke Ellington, Mahalia Jackson); interplaying musicians (Duke Ellington, Cab Calloway, Dizzy Gillespie, Miles Davis, Quincy Jones); parents (Berry Gordy, Diana Ross); lovers (Pam Grier, Richard Pryor); siblings (Barack Obama, Auma Obama); mother/daughter (Alice Walker, Rebecca Walker); mentor/mentee (Alvin Ailey, Judith Jamison); sports rivals (Wilt Chamberlain, Bill Russell)
- *Passages on historic vessels: Queen Mary* (Benjamin Mays, Janet Bragg, Cholly Atkins, Lisa Leslie); *Queen Elizabeth* (Lena Morton); *Ill de France* (Ethel Waters, Cab Calloway); *America* (Bricktop), *Bremen* (Adam Clayton Powell)
- *Activist causes:* Caribbean activism (Frederick Douglass, James Weldon Johnson, Katherine Dunham); antilynching (Ida B. Wells, Walter White, James Weldon Johnson, W. E. B. Du Bois); suffrage (Ida B. Wells and Mary Church Terrell); South Africa/antiapartheid (Ralphe Bunche, Lionel Hampton, Arthur Ashe, Leon Sullivan)
- *Interesting jobs:* Congressional representatives of Harlem (Adam Clayton Powell, Charles Rangel); performers in *Porgy and Bess* (Pearl Bailey, Sammy Davis Jr., Eartha Kitt, Cab Calloway, Simon Estes, and Maya Angelou)
- *Military combat:* Civil War (William Gould); WWII (Berry Gordy, "Red Tail" pilots Alexander Jefferson and Charles Drydon); Vietnam War (Colin Powell)
- *Music types:* jazz (musician Dizzy Gillespie, dancer Katherine Dunham); classical music/opera (W. E. B. Du Bois and Marianne Anderson's love for Schubert; concerts by Dionne Warwick, Natalie Cole, Sherley Verrett, Simon Estes)
- *Sports:* tennis (Arthur Ashe, Althea Gibson); swimming (Jeff

Commings); hockey (Willie O'Ree); baseball (Hank Aaron, Willie Mays); soccer (Pelé); cricket (C. L. R. James); boxing (Jack Johnson, Sugar Ray Robinson, George Foreman, Muhammad Ali, Joe Frazier); basketball (Lisa Leslie); gymnastics (Gabrielle Douglass)

- *Writing styles and voice:* travelogue (Amanda Smith, Juanita Harrison, Ralphe Bunche, Eslanda Goode Robeson, Era Bell Thompson, Susie Mae Williams-White); analysis/advocacy (Fanny Jackson Coppin, Walter White, Charlayne Hunter-Gault); vignette (Gwendolyn Brooks, Kitty Oliver, Colleen McElroy); third person (Charles Mingus, Katherine Dunham)
- *Conflicting philosophies:* nonviolence (Martin Luther King Jr. vs. Robert Williams); rap music (Dionne Warwick vs. Salt-n-Pepa); the word "nigga" (Chuck D, Richard Pryor, and Kitty Oliver vs. B. B. King and Rick James)
- *Exchange experiences:* critiquing America (William Wells Brown, Bejnamin Gould, Rose Butler Brown, Mary Church Terrell, Dorothy Height, Huey P. Newton, Gayle Pemberton); critiquing visiting country (James Baldwin, Billie Holiday)
- *Motivations for world travel:* adventure (Nat Love, Matthew Henson, Juanita Harrison, Sarah and Bessie Delany, RuPaul); career military (Colin Powell, Henry O. Flipper, Gail Harris); military as escape (Antwone Fisher, Magnificent Montague, Langston Hughes); career politics (Condoleezza Rice, John Mercer Langston); sharing culture (Faith Ringgold, Duke Ellington, Count Basie, Lionel Hampton, Celia Cruz).

Herein lies limitless opportunity to discuss men's and women's socialization, environment, language use, and cultural norms, media, and other relevant topics to adolescent development that arise in community agencies and in the high school or college classroom.

As a final example, those interested in the idea of mentoring as a topic can compare the motivations and impact in two narratives by authors who dedicated a significant part of their lives to mentoring: George Foreman (who came out of retirement to save his community center in Houston, Texas) and Marian Wright Edelman (advocate of the Children's Legal Defense Fund . . . originator of the Leave No Child Behind program, before the language was co-opted). Regardless of the subject, narratives provide many levels of compelling guidance relevant to youth development and increased global awareness.

ABCs of Self-Empowerment and the Search
for Epic Heroes in the Literary Tradition

Carolyn Tucker's research is reflected in her local findings in Gainesville, Flor-ida, and while some aspects are generalizable, the value of her practical work emerged from connecting with specific aspects of the community in which she worked for over a decade. In her thirteen years of working with youth in Florida, Dr. Tucker, a psychologist, concluded that youth desired control more than esteem. Tucker's work focuses on attitude, behavior, and choices, form-ing what I call the "ABCs" of adolescent development. Her work emphasizes how children often must learn their ABCs while navigating within challenging home, school, work, and socioglobal environments. Tucker's "Self-Empow-erment Theory" (SET) involves three strategies: (1) teaching youth the asso-ciations between thoughts (e.g., self-talk), feelings, and behaviors [*attitude*]; (2) emphasizing that youth and not others are in control of their behaviors [*behavior*]; and (3) teaching them that they can change behaviors [*choices*]. Essentially, these ABC strategies are at the core of local and national programs intended to impart life skills to youth at risk of being overtaken by cycles of poverty, violence, and limited opportunity. In order for them to be exposed to the ABCs, they must have mentors.[1]

Mentors are often portrayed as heroes because they share their life expe-riences with protégées who follow in their footsteps. Many heroic tales can be found in the epic narratives of autobiography. Content analysis I used to approach *Black Passports* narratives is based on the African "epic hero" tradi-tion found in Modibo Caulibaly's dissertation, "The Characteristics of the Afri-can Epic Hero as a Reflection of the Kemetic Tradition." He defined ancient Mali poems as hero tales that include the *Epic of Sundiata* and *Mansa Musa*. This paradigm roughly follows a three-tiered trajectory, tracing the hero's background, battles, and life lessons:

1. Background: family background, birth, and growth. Exile, educa-tion/training, return.
2. Battles: social battles, fights/struggle, and victory. Character flaws to overcome.
3. Life Lessons: leadership. Building of a harmonious community and society.

Equally significant to the idea of Black voice in epic literature, theorist Evie Shockley distinguishes Black poetry as a tradition of the "renegade" and characterizes the Black experience as inherently indicative of the struggle for justice. In *Renegade Poetics: Black Aesthetics and Formal Innovation in African American Poetry*, Shockley exposes the new language constructions of Black "rebel" narratives. With these two traditions of hero and renegade in mind, we account for the validity of community folk heroes and collective heroes outside of the "great man, individualist" interpretation of "hero." The recognition of the wide range of authors (particularly through poetic tributes in appendix D) embodies praise song traditions. The two hundred life stories broadens the classification of those who are recognized as worthy of praise. Recognition does not ignore pervasive imperfections in all authors, but it does show that all stories are worth investigation in order to form a greater historical understanding of the tellers.

"I am Not a Role Model"

Though I love stories of rebels and heroes it is necessary to interpret terms such as "empowerment," "role model," and "guidance" in complicated ways that beg broader questions: How do we define worthiness in a role model? and How important are texts that demonstrate what youth should not emulate? For example, the artist Faith Ringgold revealed a whirlwind overnight love affair in Paris with a man she had just met, and the gay transvestite entertainer RuPaul also details his tantalizing, round-the-way, drive-by (literally) sexual "encounters" while he was a correspondent for a British television show. And then there are Rick James, a self-professed "super freak," and Charles Mingus, a would-be pimp. In 1993, when professional basketball player Charles Barkley insisted in a Nike Air tennis shoe commercial, "I am not a role model. I am not paid to be a role model. I am paid to wreak havoc on the basketball court," he was speaking the truth. Black celebrities in the public eye cannot be counted on—just because they are celebrities—to act with common sense or responsibility for youth any more than non-Black celebrities.

In the most glaring contemporary example, Jay Z and Kanye West not only insisted in naming themselves "Niggas in Paris," but sang the song *twelve times in a row* in a June 2012 concert in an attempt to break the world record for number of times one song was played at a single concert. Of all possible songs, this choice confirms they are anything but global role models.[2] But their memoirs, if ever produced, would certainly warrant examination to find out what, in their own words, would compel them to repeat that particular song in the international arena. Even "Mr. International" himself, Talib Quali demonstrates that progressive or positive figures may not always pass the role model test either. His public discussions exploded with Crunk Feminist Collective and Lupe Fiasco over Rick Ross's 2013 "U.O.E.N.O." song lyrics where he raps about slipping a "molly" into a woman's drink and having sex with her when "she didn't know"–essentially rapping about date rape. The thoughtful point and counterpoint Twitter-based interaction shows "Black conscious" entertainers also have a tough time upholding static expectations of the public ideal.[3]

Though many listed in *Black Passports* are arguably not "role models" in a positive sense, surely there is much to learn from their adventures and life reflections. In addition, we must complicate those who are more commonly portrayed as role models. Notably, though some may cite Condoleezza Rice as a poster child for Black women's highest achievement, many disagree. Ula Taylor, professor of African American studies at Berkeley, presented a rousing paper at the 2012 conference Beautiful Struggle: Transformative Black Studies in Shifting Political Landscapes, at Northwestern University. The paper, "Rice over Rivers," equated Rice's actions in perpetuating myths of "weapons of mass destruction" that resulted in unnecessary deaths to the same type of treacherous behavior of nurse Eunice Rivers, the Black woman who assisted in causing death and disease in the Black men who were used as subjects in the Tuskegee, Alabama, syphilis case of medical abuse from 1932 to 1972. Taylor argued that both women willingly participated in betraying the interests of Black men in trade for apparent power from White hegemonic institutions. In essence, Taylor, like Carter G. Woodson, pointed to the miseducation of would-be Black leaders. Taylor's argument built on an earlier presentation by Evelyn Higginbotham at the 2005 Association of Black Women Historians' keynote luncheon address titled, An Open Letter to Condoleezza Rice, where Rice was weighed and measured in terms of the same type of social justice efforts that created opportunities for her success. Her work in that area was, ultimately, found wanting.

Professor Higginbotham's "politics of respectability" also remains a central concept to consider, because the assumptions of upper-middle-class desirability remain problematic; "outreach" and "uplift" are patronizing notions at best, deadly at worst.[4] In a classic article entitled, "Why Service Learning Is Bad," John Eby identified the pitfalls of altruistic intent, namely the band-aid approach to enduring structural problems not addressed by soup kitchens and after school programs no matter how abundant or well intended. Equally problematic, there are not always clearly "right" or "wrong" positions in Black thought, as the expanding field of graduate research in Black studies demonstrates.

Nonviolence is a perfect case in point. Stokely Carmichael is credited with extending the civil rights movement into the Black power movement and demonstrates the perceived shortcomings of operating within nonviolent paradigms. Largely as a result of the 1968 assassination of Martin Luther King Jr., many activists saw armed struggle as the only viable way to justice, and their willingness to commit to nonviolence waned in an era filled with state-sanctioned violence. Before Dr. King, activists like Ida B. Wells were frustrated by an inability to get an antilynching bill passed in the early twentieth century, and after King, Carmichael, Huey P. Newton, Assata Shakur, and others railed against a system of violent Whites in their mid-twentieth century demand for equal rights. Whereas Black veterans who returned from World War II participated in the "Double V" campaign—indicating victory in democracy both abroad and at home—those like James Foreman (*Making of a Black Revolutionary*) and Robert F. Williams (*Negroes with Guns*) returned from Korea and Vietnam also determined to claim freedoms at home as due compensation for the sacrifice serving the country. Scholar-activist Akinyele Umoja's recent work *We Will Shoot Back: Armed Resistance in the Mississippi Freedom Movement* brings to the fore the depth of disagreement about non-violence as a viable strategy in the Black struggle for justice. Scholars and activists who lived during the 1960s still vehemently disagree about the right course of action for empowerment, so it is important not to take the introduction of this wide range of Black players as an oversimplification of motives or outcomes.

It is likewise important to not overstate the claims of empowerment of African American freedom or voices. Though many claimed power by having their story told, that telling did not always equate to obtaining sustainable power. For instance, Billie Holiday's autobiography was published right before her death when she was at her most vulnerable, still struggling with addiction and fighting for license or stage to perform in the United States. In fact, she did not even write her autobiography—it was ghostwritten like quite a few others on the list, which requires readers to again qualify voices when co-authors are involved or stories are presented "as told to . . ."

Of further issue is the need for interpretation of dense texts provided by writers such as Fanny Jackson Coppin and George Schuyler, who penned seemingly derogatory portrayals of Africans or African Americans as primitive or backward. Young readers must interpret authors within their own times and not give in to anachronistic assessments of historical figures. This data simply offers a wide range of choices as a starting point, so youth understand the rich palette of options they have to use in creating their own portrait. And there are many creative portraits from which to choose.

MEMOIRS: NARRATIVES OF LIFE

Readers interested in racial identity will be intrigued by longtime NAACP activist Walter White's discussion of his blue eyes and white skin because it will open the door to asking the question I often challenge my students to answer: "What makes a Black person Black?" Walter White subtitled his text *The Life Story of a Man Who Crossed the Color Line to Fight for Civil Rights,* getting to the very heart of the phenomenon so eloquently captured by Du Bois: the color line. White's racial development from his home in Atlanta placed him in the heart of America's race struggle, but he was also often mistaken for being Caucasian, even by Blacks in Harlem. Resolving to live as Black even though he looked White, he used his appearance as a cloak to infiltrate spaces dominated by Jim Crow racist organizations such as the Ku Klux Klan. Working for the National Association for the Advancement of Colored People (NAACP), he witnessed atrocities like the 1906 Atlanta Race Riot in Georgia, which added to his resolve to fight for justice. White's light skin and blue eyes allowed him to "pass" in Estill Springs, Tennessee, where he went to investigate a lynching. He also traveled to Europe during World War II as an advocate for equal rights for Black troops. He made a life out of investigating attitudes about the physiological construction of race, which can definitely fuel discussions about the tenuous nature, perceptions, and experiences of racial life inside and outside of America. Professor Yaba Blay's *(1)ne Drop* analysis expands discussion.

Decades after White's coming to terms with his racial identity, scores of authors (Kitty Oliver, Charles Mingus, and Jesse Owens) pored over their racial and cultural makeup in an effort to discern what is "authentically" Black. President Barack Obama's account of his racial identity development provides a similarly fascinating journey. President Obama's stories of home (White American mother and African father), school (White, Pacific Islander, or Asian contexts), and social development (interracial dating and elite educational institutions) are gripping, elaborate, and evolving narratives. President Obama's two autobiographies mainly encompass his identity development through race and nation. The focus on his mixed-race heritage demonstrates that, despite talks of a "postracial" society, the question of race remains an immovable cornerstone of American politics. During both of his presidential elections, the birth certificate challenges to Obama's right to hold office by the so-called "birther movement" exemplify the 1960s feminist adage that the personal is political and that politics is literally embedded in the physical body. Throughout Obama's text, he traces his innermost personal thoughts between Hawaii, Kansas, Indonesia, Kenya, Chicago, and Washington, D.C., and unmasks much of how his experiences have impacted the formation of his political agenda. Surely, his rotating environments contributed to his eventual success at Harvard and in national politics.

Similarly, Charles Mingus, who grew up in California, embraced his Japanese friend who taught him judo and subsequently rejected static notions of blackness. Kitty Oliver, one of the first students to integrate the University of Florida in the 1960s, admitted liking Santana or Peter, Paul, and Mary as much as Sly and the Family Stone or Otis Redding. Each author presents an image of racial self and explores cultural amalgamations that defy homogenous portrayals of blackness.

These authors offer entryways to discussion about what is authentic or "acting Black" in today's context. This identity "crisis" also touches the "white" community as explored in Bliss Broyard's book *One Drop: My Father's Hidden Life Story of Race and Family Secrets*, where well-respected *New York Times* critic Anatole Broyard called his children to his deathbed and confessed that he was born in New Orleans and born Black, but spent his entire life passing as White. Their reactions and the daughter's subsequent book offer much intriguing fodder for critical race studies, as her exposure so drastically differs (perhaps due to changing times) from the rejection of blackness chosen by her father.

In contrast, Mae Jemison's embrace of the short afro hairstyle, African dance, and her decision to major in African American studies also points to choices youth make in determining their racial direction and, as they grow older can embrace Blackness to a greater extent, reconciling their professional lives with their cultural selves without difficulty. Claudia Lynn Thomas's detailed recollection of the student protests for Black studies at Vassar College offers a glimpse into the centrality of racial identity beyond the middle and high school years. How this development exists in varying adult contexts and evolves over time in shifting historical epochs is a constant point of negotiation. Sidney Poitier pointedly addresses changing times in his chapter, "Why Do White Folks Love Sidney Poitier So?" in *The Measure of a Man: A Spiritual Autobiography*. Because of his success in gaining starring roles in Hollywood, he was labeled as "Uncle Tom" in the late 1960s by young radical activists. As writer Langston Hughes and educator Pauli Murray also described in their public lives, Poitier moved from being viewed as a radical cultural warrior in his youth to out of step with Black identity progressives in his adulthood.

Like Poitier, many African Americans operate within shifting planes of nationality. Black narratives of U.S. immigration abound and complicate notions of American blackness. Authors of immigrant narratives include Celia

Cruz, Harry Belafonte, Claude McKay, June Jordon, Edwidge Dandicat, Phillipe Wamba, Paule Marshall, Ugwu-Oju, and Sandy Denton. Authors express varying degrees of connection to their Caribbean or African homelands, from Cruz's painful separation from Cuba or Dandicat's torn family in Haiti to a wistful revisiting by Marshall to the Bahamas or Wamba to Tanzania. In a poignant reaffirmation of her Caribbean roots while on a return visit to Haiti after graduating from medical school, Rose-Marie Toussaint recalls that the local *oungan* (a priest and community elder) foretold of her destiny in healing arts when she was a young child. Though the sports and entertainment industry often operate as if Black America is the center of the Black universe, close observation of African American constructs of cultural blackness are often firmly built upon pillars of other nations in the diaspora.

Spiritual and religious aspects of Black autobiography expose change over time within individual lives. Some stories chronicle personal journeys to faith and belief systems: examples include the spiritual awakening of Jan Willis to Buddhism; proclamations of Muslim faith by Muhammad Ali, Kareem Abdul Jabar and Malcolm X; Andrew Young and Sidney Poitier's memoir of Christianity; and Sammy Davis Jr. and Julius Lester, who inherited Jewish traditions as their religious choice. Many texts not only follow authors through their own conversion or commitment, but also extend to their missionary work and testimonies, such as those by Christian messengers Amanda Smith, Zilpha Elaw, Benjamin Mays, Pauli Murray, George Foreman, and Cornel West. Some authors allude to their religion or faith without making it the centerpiece of their total narrative: Dr. Ben Carson is affiliated with the Seventh Day Adventist Church, and Dizzy Gillespie embraced the Baha'i faith.

Throughout history, authors moved by faith have grounded their lives in religion, whether through Reverend Morgan Latta, Fanny Jackson Coppin, and other educators building schools and missionary curriculum on the rock of the church, through the comparative religion of Howard Thurman, through the gospel music of Mahalia Jackson, or through Septima Clark's civil rights community activism as an ongoing act of faith.

Issues discussing family will be infinitely helpful for youth, especially those experiencing loss or strained relations. Several authors (Ida B. Wells, Marian Anderson, Katherine Dunham, B. B. King, Zora Neale Hurston, Arthur Ashe, Pauli Murray, Bill Russell) lost a parent while young; Ray Charles recalls the enduring pain of his brother's drowning as a youth; and Natalie Cole recounts the painful loss of both her brother and sister as an adult. Sharing the sense of loss is surely an important point of connection to those who are currently going through such trials.

Other narratives of family challenges can be instructive. The tension expressed between mother and daughter Alice and Rebecca Walker is palpably painful, as both seek to express their perspectives in a difficult—and public—relationship. Similar parent-child problems are exposed by parents (Faith Ringgold) or children (Langston Hughes, Janet Jackson). Others have struggled with parenthood in the inability to conceive (Mary Church Terrell and Angela Bassett) or with the experience of having an abortion (Beneditta de Silva), and the openness of the stories invoke empathy and might be a salve for effected readers.

These heart-wrenching stories are balanced by encouraging tales of strong family ties found in works by married couples, such as Martin Luther King Jr. and Coretta Scott King; Ozzy Davis and Ruby Dee; Angela Basset and Courtney Vance; William and Ellen Craft, or works co-authored by siblings Sarah and Annie Delany. Also present are tomes of parental adoration by Gayle Pemberton, June Jordan, Condoleezza Rice, Paule Murray, Nina Simone, Diana Ross, Martin Luther King Jr., Adam Clayton Powell Jr., Mary Church Terrell, Marian Wright Edelman, and Maya Angelou. Michelle Duster, the great-granddaughter of Ida B. Wells, traced her ancestor's trip to England, and Duster's drive to continue social justice work through writing uplifts Wells's legacy in a touching and important way that links "ancestor" to "family."

Many narratives tackle the topic of health, whether mental or physical. Audre Lorde's journal of her losing battle with breast cancer is a stark contrast to Natalie Cole's tale of surviving kidney failure and the relationship that developed with her donor's sister, even as she lost her own sister to cancer during her hospitalization. Claudia Thomas, after graduating from Vassar, became a medical doctor and gained a greater appreciation for the profession when she eventually found herself a patient after a grand mal seizure. Interestingly, Sammy Davis Jr.'s account of the car accident that resulted in his losing an eye is a harrowing tale of determination to live a full life despite a partial disability. Physical and psychological health and relationship to one's body can be read between the lines of almost all *Black Passports* memoirs.

Like health, sexual identity is a site of discussion of much interest to youth and mentors alike. Ripe examples of robust sexuality like B. B. King's self-professed love of women, which led to his fifteen children, beg extended rap sessions. King even flirted with nurses when he was in the hospital for a painful adult circumcision at forty years old, which complicates notions of defining healthy sexual behavior. Questions of sexual health can be addressed through Faith Ringgold's explicit fling with an African beau in Paris, to the (literally) countless escapades of Wilt Chamberlain. Gay and lesbian writers like Audre Lorde, RuPaul, and swimmer Jeff Commings also provide models of overt self-acceptance and self-love, despite the rejection of an often-cruel world. The portrayal of Eartha Kitt as a "sex kitten" but also as a loving mother helps transform a sensationalized topic of Black women's sexual identity to a human one.

Several authors mark their survival despite other barriers such as violence and drugs. Survivors of sexual violence offer significant points of inspiration in autobiography. Oprah has often cited that reading Maya Angelou's account of surviving rape became an impetus for shedding her own shame around abuse. In turn, her desire to help others overcome shame was the cause for making the topic a staple in her long-standing television show. In the same vein, reading Pam Grier's details of being gang raped by cousins at six years old and then raped by a date while at a house party offers young women who may have experienced the same difficulties a pathway to finding voice and healing. That Grier in the same life story triumphantly faced cancer and still portrays a strength of spirit and quest for balance prepares young women for the many types of physical challenges that may come their way and demonstrates the will it takes to persevere and keep coming back. Other women—Linda Brent during her enslavement in North Carolina, Katherine Dunham in her father's home in Chicago after her mother's death, and Billie Holiday, raped by a neighbor on Christmas Eve when she was eleven years old—reveal their trials with sexual abuse that add to Angelou's well-known testimony and get the topic to the level of attention it deserves.

Antwone Fisher, a male survivor of adolescent rape, provides an important addition to this chorus of voices. His shame at being raped by an older woman as a teenager gives significant opportunity to discuss gender expectations of masculinity in society and the myriad ways boys are hurt and are largely encouraged to ignore, mask, or disregard their pain. With the 2012 conviction of Pennsylvania State University coach Jerry Sandusky, the public had an unprecedented opportunity to discuss how vulnerable boys are, particularly those boys in "at-risk" programs. Fisher's narrative broached the topic of abuse, foster care, and caretaking of Black boys in a difficult but creative style that compels readers to consider the vital service of mental health professionals. The gender dynamics in Fisher's case were palpable because the socialization of boys assumes that it is impossible to be "raped" by an older woman. The open national discussion about all violence against youth offers much-needed points of entry to counseling discussions that must take place if healthy adult relationships are to develop.

Domestic violence is another topic covered by authors. Clearly, Tina Turner's account is the most prominent example, but other important examples are Nina Simone and Sandy Denton (Pepa), textbook cases for young women to consider. Pepa's revelation of terror in several episodes in which she was driven to the woods in the middle of the night with a threat of murder gives readers a look at the difficult process of extracting oneself from a situation of domestic violence. Given the saturation of sensationalist media around the Rihanna/Chris Brown saga, and the popularity of the topic with teens, deeper reading is necessary.

Male perspectives of relationship violence are also very much present, with Miles Davis, Richard Pryor, and Bill Russell bringing the topic to the fore, though in drastically different ways. On the one hand, Davis shared truncated contours of his physical abuse of Cicely Tyson, while Richard Pryor gave details of his drug use and domestic violence toward his wife (including shooting at her). On the other hand, Bill Russell insisted that violence can occur both ways. In Russell's relationship with a woman named Iodine, her violent episodes occurred in the home and also in a potentially deadly car chase through the streets of Boston.

Deterioration of health through drug abuse is also widely discussed in life stories, especially in narratives of entertainers like Miles Davis, Ray Charles, Richard Pryor, Rick James, and Etta James. Mary Wilson's account of how alcohol slowly took the life of Florence Ballard, her childhood friend and also a member of the Supremes, shows how disease impacts loved ones as well as the addicted. Jeff Henderson provides a particularly relevant memoir involving dark shadows of substance abuse: that of a big-time drug dealer. Henderson became a crack dealer in San Diego who did a decade of jail time after getting busted with drugs at the Mexican border, and his prison sentence eventually provided the path to his redemption: cooking. Having worked for a decade as a cook while he served his time, when released, Henderson worked his way up to become the head chef at Caesar's Palace. He authored *Cooked: From the Streets to the Stove, from Cocaine to Foie Gras* (2007), and now he hosts his own cooking show on Food Network television, which he calls the "culinary and life skills boot camp." His online biography gives the details:

Jeff Henderson grew up on the tough streets of South Central L.A. and San Diego. At 19 he was running a $35,000-a-week cocaine operation. At 24, Jeff was arrested and sent to prison, where he spent the next ten years. While incarcerated, Jeff discovered a passion for cooking and the drive to turn his life around. Jeff became Executive Chef at Café Bellagio in Las Vegas, wrote a best-selling book, and now he is focusing on giving back. In *The Chef Jeff Project*, he takes six at-risk young adults and commits to turning their lives around by putting them to work in his catering company, Posh Urban Cuisine. He arms them with the knowledge, the skills and, ultimately, the opportunity for a new life with a culinary career.[5]

"Chef Jeff" now grounds his work in mentoring programs and challenges youth to value their own future inside the kitchen and beyond.

The path to health, especially mental health through counseling, is also a point of interest in youth development. Richard Pryor's candid reflection of his sessions highlights the importance of mental health counseling, as it was his counselor who suggested he take a trip to Africa, "the Motherland," to get his mind right, which, in turn, helped curb his self-destructive habits. However, Charles Mingus's trip through Bellevue shows a drastically different view of counseling: both the patient and his account of institutional treatment are nothing short of disturbing. His use of third person throughout the text reflects a dissonance ripe for interpretation by those interested in Black psychology. But even there, one reading the Mingus text cannot escape the mastery of his writing and a sense that the life of a written Mingus is infinitely healthier than the life of one unrecorded. Here, we see a clear tie between self-writing (relatively) healthy living, and outer limits of creative genius.

Human Will, Cultural Production, and Political Identity

Goal setting and the quest for freedom—wishbone—are central themes raised by some authors. Olympian Althea Gibson's autobiography title, *I Always Wanted to Be Somebody,* demonstrates a personal perseverance that gave her a verve for life through sports, whether tennis or golf. Professional prowess, impeccable reputation, and quest for excellence are also found in the work of choreographer Cholly Atkins. His impact on all major Motown acts, including the Temptations, the Supremes, and Gladys Knight and the Pips, is legendary and recognized as a key ingredient of success for major entertainers of that golden era. Of course, polished perfection permeates the life story of Mr. Entertainment himself: Sammy Davis Jr., especially in his account of bringing the house down when performing for the Queen of England. Davis's performances are multifaceted, and his religious identity (Jewish) is further complicated by his political identity (a supporter of Richard Nixon). The multifarious Black human spirit shines through with a will to find excellence on the path to self-realization.

Of all identity-development and life skills narratives, Richard Pryor's story of how he developed healthy approaches to attitude, behavior, and choices by embracing a historical and cultural lens is most instructive. Not only does it encompass many of the struggles mentioned above (drugs, domestic violence, mental health), but it also involves a central connection of international travel to identity development: travel to Africa.

When answering poet Countee Cullen's question, "What is Africa to me?," more than sixty African American authors have presented vastly different autobiographical interpretations of visits "home." A partial list of people who have made the trek to the Motherland include Katherine Dunham, Pauli Murray, Celia Cruz, Fanny Jackson Coppin, Eslanda Goode Robeson, Charlayne Hunter-Gault, Shirley Verrett, Amanda Smith, Etta James, Janet Bragg, Dorothy Height, Judith Jamison, Eartha Kitt, Paule Marshall, Shirley Mae Williams-White, Juanita Harrison, Diana Ross, Era Bell Thompson, Isaiah Washington, Ozzie Davis, Ruby Dee, Alex Haley, Dick Gregory, Dizzy Gillespie, George Foreman, Malcolm X, John Hope Franklin, Julius Lester, Leslie Alexander Lacy, James Forman, Leon Sullivan, Phillipe Wamba, Duke Ellington, and W. E. B. Du Bois.

Era Bell Thompson's 1953 visit to multiple African countries in search of her ancestors led her to conclude that, ultimately, she was American. Isaiah Washington's 1996 visit to Namibia and 2006 trip to Sierra Leone brought him to the exact opposite understanding. Not only did Washington embrace his African heritage, but he "substantiated" his belief with DNA evidence that estimated he shared 99.9 percent of his matrilineal ancestry with Mende and Temne people. He returned to his "homeland" and was embraced by people of Sierra Leone who, with grand gesture, stooled him as Chief Gondobay Manga II in the village Ngalu. His transformation to chief was complete in the eyes of his tribesmen with his participation in a disciplinary ass kicking of a thief from his village.[6]

Richard Pryor's Africa reflections wavered between the realism of Thompson and the romantic and majestic narrative of Washington. Richard Pryor's storytelling genius and the relevance of his life-changing "epiphany" warrant extensive quotation.[7] Pryor's trip came after his therapist challenged him to see the world differently than through the eyes of a drug-induced cynicism that had come to represent his personal and professional voice:

> "What exactly about cocaine do you like?" he asked.
>
> "It fucks me up good. I like that ping it puts in my head."
>
> "Do you see how it removes you from reality? Mentally as well as physically? You spend days and even weeks isolated in your house, alone in your bedroom, getting high."

"Yea, but that's okay."

"Why's that? Why's it okay?"

"I don't see any need to be in reality because I know how ugly the world is."

He didn't buy that shit. Not for an instant. Wanted to know how I was so confident of the world's ugliness when I wouldn't venture into it and check things out. He started asking me where I'd been, the places I thought were ugly, places I thought were nice, and finally, as if setting me up, he asked how I could make such extreme statements about the world when I'd never been to the origin of the world's beauty.

Okay, I bit.

"Where's that?" I asked.

"Africa." . . .

Excited after reading Richard Leakey's and Roger Lewin's *Origins*, Jennifer and I left for Kenya on Easter Sunday, 1979. From the moment we touched down at the small airport in Mombasa, I sensed something extraordinary. Through the jet lag, I knew something was different but couldn't articulate it. Couldn't get good reception. I strained to hear a beat that was too far away. However, I realized the shrink had been right. The place really was beautiful.

My eyes were full.

It was so beautiful. It was black. Blue black. Original black. The kind of place where you go, "Black." And landing at the airport in Nairobi, it fills your heart up. You see everybody's black. And you realize that people are the same all over the world. Because people in Africa fuck over your luggage just like people in New York.

The next day we went to Nairobi, where the sensation of being in Africa grew even stronger. Something was indeed different, exciting, alive, but radically so. We took a tour of the National Museum, and that completely rearranged the cells in my brain. Did a whole rewiring trip on me. By the time I sat my ass down in the hotel lobby, I knew what I was feeling.

"Jennifer," I said. "You know what? There are no niggers here. . . . There are no niggers here, I repeated. "The people here, they still have their self-respect, their pride."[8]

Pryor would disavow the word "nigger," regretting that he ever said it. Though it took a while after the trip for the lessons he learned to sink in, he credited his inner change to experiencing the wildlife, landscape, and people of Africa. The ultimate realization was that Africa was the origin of humankind, and meditating on that fact brought him back from the brink of total self-induced annihilation where he was hospitalized for almost killing himself smoking crack cocaine. African Americans who returned "home" expressed variant layers of connection or discord with African people in the homeland, but all visitors seemed to take a valuable lesson away from the trip that connected their humanity to an increased sense of positive will far beyond what was felt in the United States.

Similarly, enslaved African Americans who ran away demonstrated an insatiable ingenuity that must be at the basis of any discussion of self-possession. William and Ellen Craft disguised themselves in gendered genius, Linda Brent hid for seven years before escaping, and Henry "Box" Brown mailed himself to freedom through the U.S. Postal Service. The desire for freedom, when grounded in the bones of one's will, cannot be quelled. Youth exposed to these stories of life-and-death escape can gain perspective for their current situations and from the fortitude of those who have mastered challenges in the past. The bootstrap mentality of Booker T. Washington who argued for economic self-sufficiency, like the desire for self-care demonstrated by Nancy Prince throughout every step of her treks through nineteenth-century Jamaica and Russia display a commitment to excel regardless of any external limitations set by society.

While personal perseverance is a running theme in the collective picture, several authors demonstrate a commitment to exposing and tearing down limiting social barriers that have systematically restricted opportunity for Black Americans. For example, Charlayne Hunter-Gault's determination to desegregate the University of Georgia laid the groundwork for her commitment to exposing lingering challenges in South Africa. Later, the protest by John Carlos and Tommy Smith on the winners' stand at the 1968 Olympics in Mexico grew to legendary status as both authors share complementary accounts of the meaning of that moment. In a world where Black male athletes dominate media presentations that heavily influence youth, narratives by athletes like Paul Robeson, Muhammad Ali, Hank Aaron, and Bill Russell can provide humanistic interventions into images of one-dimensional sports figures.

Further, Paul Robeson and Assata Shakur offer ways of understanding how African Americans fought for rights outside of the established political system. Robeson exemplifies the complexity of an individual story: at once a scholar, sportsman, actor, and political activist, his *Here I Stand*—at a narrow

121 pages—revealed a kaleidoscope of a man. Beginning with his youth in Princeton, New Jersey, the book leads readers from his own high school years where he won a 1915 scholarship essay competition, which landed him an opportunity to attend Rutgers University, to spotlighting the heroics of the 1957 high school students in Little Rock, Arkansas, who were fighting for their rights for equal education years after the 1954 *Brown v. Board of Education* ruling. Robeson's epilogue underscores his main concern in life: social justice and Black empowerment.

Robeson recalled how his White high school principal, Dr. Ackerman, presented him with "furious opposing" in every area where he might excel, be it singing, sports, or academics. Despite Ackerman's attempts to confirm and demand Robeson's submission to "Negro inferiority," he wrote the winning essay to secure a four-year scholarship to Rutgers (which was not actually his first choice). Robeson recalls, "Well, I won the scholarship—and here was a decisive point in my life. That I would go to Rutgers was the least of it, for I was sure I'd be happier at Lincoln University. The important thing was this: *Deep in my heart from that day on was a conviction which none of the Ackermans of America would ever be able to shake*. Equality might be denied, but I *knew* I was not inferior" (Robeson's italics).[9] In a similar vein, he encourages youth of the 1950s to never submit to an inferior place in society,

> In the glow of lamplight on my desk I gaze upon one of the wondrous signs of our times . . . and I smile to see in these newspaper photographs the faces, so bright, so solemn, of our young heroes—the children of Little Rock. Their names are: Elizabeth Eckford, Carlotta Walls, Minnie Jean Brown, Gloria Ray, Thelma Mothershed, Melba Patillo, Jefferson Thomas, Terrence Roberts, and Ernest Green. And to the list could be added the names of all the other Negro children in the Southland who have given us great new epics of courage and dignity. The patter of their feet as they walk through Jim Crow barriers to attend school is the thunder of the marching men of Joshua, and the world rocks beneath their tread.[10]

From his high school graduation speech on Toussaint L'Ouverture through his denial a passport and right to work overseas by the U. S. government because of his political beliefs, Robeson held fast to his conviction to fight for African American equality. The story of Solomon Northup reveals his insatiable will to gain freedom. Though enslavement is outlawed in most of the world, it still endures in many forms. In addition, representation of Black freedom of expression and movement is still alarmingly present, as can be seen with the continued persecution of Assata Shakur.

Similar convictions for Black equality and against White supremacy landed several African American political activists in trouble with the law. Whereas Robeson's passport was taken away for his political beliefs, Assata Shakur was forced into exile because she refused to live as a political prisoner in the United States. Her autobiography, *Assata*, is one of several (including Angela Davis's and Elaine Brown's) that chronicle women's leadership in the Black Panther Party and their legal persecution as a consequence. As referenced in the *Swag Diplomacy* online resource, *African American Registry* gives the following summation of the political life and trials of Assata Olugbala Shakur,

> Between 1973 and 1977, Shakur was indicted 10 times and stood trial for two bank robberies, the kidnapping of a drug dealer, attempted murder of several police officers, and the murder of a New Jersey state trooper. In 1973, on the New Jersey Turnpike, state troopers stopped Shakur, Malik Zayad Shakur, and Sundiata Acoli, two of her friends, because of a shattered headlight. The trooper said they were "suspicious" because they had Vermont license plates. Shots were fired. Not much is known about who did what, but in the end, state trooper Werner Foerster and Malik Shakur were killed. Shakur and Sundiata were charged with the death of Foerster. Their trial had many flaws, including racial injustice by the jury and admitted perjury by the trial's star witness. Shakur escaped from prison in 1979 and fled the country.[11]

In 2013, Shakur was the first woman placed on the FBI most wanted terrorist list, indicating the enduring injustice to those who dared challenge wholesale oppression of Blacks in the 1960s. Despite her experiences with numerous trials for various false charges, including a string of bank robberies impossible for her to have committed and a "shooting" that was, by medical testimony, impossible for her to have carried out, Assata's autobiography is filled with poetry:

> i understand that i am
> slightly out of fashion.
> The in-crowd wants no part of me.

Someone said that i am too sixties
Black.
Someone else told me that i had failed to mellow.
It's true that i have not
straightened back my hair
Nor rediscovered maybelline.
And it is also true
that i still like African things,
like statues and dresses
and PEOPLE.
And it is also true
that struggle is foremost on my mind.
And i still rap about discipline—
My anger has not run away.
And i still can't stand ole
el dorado.
And i still can't dig no
one and one.
And i still don't dig no
roka fellas.
And i call a pig a pig.
And a party, to my thinking,
happens only once in a while.
Anyway, i'm really kind of happy
being slightly out of style.[12]

Political identity is an extremely important topic, and the portrayal of Black political thought must necessarily represent a broad swath of approaches, including the radical approaches deemed "slightly out of style."

It is in political ideology that international memoirs truly offer a wealth of potential discussion in personal development and world view. Here, teachers can assign a comparative investigation that would reveal the differing approaches of the following authors: Elaine Brown, Stokely Carmichael, Huey P. Newton, Condoleezza Rice, George Schuyler, Leslie Alexander Lacy, Frank Marshall Davis, Edward Brooke, James Foreman, Faye Wattleton, Florynce Kennedy, Sammy Davis Jr., Jesse Owens, Colin Powell, Paul Robeson, Harry Heywood, and Robin Quivers (of the *Howard Stern Show*). From conservative right to radical left, a collective investigation into the personal ideologies of this collection would reveal how the personal is political. Starting from radical conceptions like those of Walter White, identity, experience, and ideology can then offer a tool kit from which youth could choose to craft their own opinions of the world. Part of crafting that identity must necessarily include the creative humanistic impulses as much as the social and political.

Creative Lives of Cultural Humanists: Katherine Dunham and Dizzy Gillespie

Of all the autobiographies from the Guidance Council that are useful to understanding African American narratives as a tradition of creative and Black humanist writing, Dizzy Gillespie and Katherine Dunham offer the most salient examples for the intersection between Black identity, improvisational living, and a legacy of mentoring. Each author-artist drew upon African rhythm for inspiration, studied intensively, and taught the cultures of numerous African nations, but he or she also innovated art and in doing so, developed a strong self-authenticated voice:

> [I place] Dunham into a diasporic continuum characterized by bravado, the capacity to improvise and the wherewithal to defy the status quo in environments that had found very fixed notions about the appropriate behavior of young black women. Savvy enough to challenge restrictive and often blatantly racist and sexist traditions, Dunham has used humor, grace, and strength of character to modify her surroundings to suit her own vision. A humanist in the most exalted sense of the word, Dunham still has a lot to teach us. (VeVe Clark in _Kaiso!_)
>
> But you see Dizzy [Gillespie] is a very strong person to have survived in this kind of society with all of the pressures on him. It would be on a political basis that we argue because I look into the society, and I say that some of us might not have the kind of resilience and strength that Dizzy might have . . . This is why I say Dizzy is a "fox." He is not going to sacrifice his musical integrity. . . and especially when you are dealing with black culture, because culture is such a powerful weapon. (Max Roach, in _To Bop or Not to Bop_)

Dunham and Gillespie are recognized examples of personal vibrancy on a global scale and represent career travelers, having visited more than fifty countries each.

These two narratives can be seen as models of Africana humanism in several aspects: both authors were recognized with the National Endowment for the Humanities award, both are grounded in Africa, and their autobiographies were constructed as collaborative community projects with multiple voices (a rejection of Eurocentric or individualistic "great man" approaches to defining one's life). Further, both ground their art in Africa, but they also embody a comparative national and cultural approach as evidenced by their integration of many cultures beyond Africa into their art. Their extensive global travel translated into a nonessentialized view of blackness—one grounded in a commitment to humanism above racial centrism. Gillespie had a biracial daughter, and Dunham had an interracial marriage; as such, they both exemplify the nuances of race and culture in Black art and Black artists.

Dizzy (John Birks) Gillespie

To Be or Not . . . to Bop (1979). Europe 1948; Europe 1950; Canada 1953; North Africa, Near East, Asia, Western Europe 1956; London 1965; Nairobi, Kenya 1972; Havana 1977.

> Cheeks for weeks; slick mischief maker
> Diplomatic charmer, chanting South Carolina peanut melodies
> Faithfully trumpeting Afro-mestizo vibrato jive

Katherine Dunham

A Touch of Innocence (1959), *Island Possessed* (1969). Haiti, Jamaica, Martinique, Trinidad, 1936; Mexico, London, Paris, 1947–49; South America, Europe, North Africa tour 1950–55; Australia, New Zealand, Japan 1956–58; Europe 1959–60, 1965 Dakar, Senegal; fifty-seven countries in twenty years; 1992 Haiti (hunger strike).

> "Bravo Company"
> Chi-town feet pounding Port-au-Prince clay
> Geographically sensuous, Creole initiate
> Excavating primitive technique, visionary possession.

MODEL: YOUNG LIONS AND CREATIVE LIFE-SKILLS TRAINING

Significantly, both Dunham and Gillespie were dedicated to "the good life," which can be seen as an integral element of their creative work. They each developed disciplined schools of thought and took great pains to pass those lessons on to a next generation of artists. Evidence of creative and positive work can be seen in two of their students: Saroya Corbett and Frank Moten.

Two Case Studies of Creative Mentoring: Saroya Corbett and Frank Moten

Corbett, a member of the Katherine Dunham Center for the Arts and Humanities and subsequently certified in Dunham Technique, was a member of one of the last youth classes of the Performing Arts Training Center in East St. Louis that enjoyed guidance by Katherine Dunham herself. Moten, a member of the Dizzy Gillespie All Stars music group, lived next to Gillespie in Harlem from the time he was three until he was twenty years old. Below are Corbett's and Moten's reflections on how creative tutelage of these master artists impacted their quest for an innovative and artistic life.[13]

Q and A with Saroya Corbett

Q: What is your background, education/training? What are some of the challenges you have faced and triumphs you have enjoyed?

Corbett: Currently, I am a dance artist in the Philadelphia area. My journey as a dance artist began in the place I call home, East St. Louis, Illinois (ESL). Although I have not physically lived in East St. Louis for a long time, ESL is home. Both of my parents are from the city and my family has always lived either in ESL or around East St. Louis. I spent my summers as a child in the city with my grandparents and when I got older my mother moved back to the area (we were living two and half hours north in Bloomington). My mother and I did not move into East St. Louis until I was finished with high school. As much as we feel close to the city, she never wanted me to be educated in the ESL school district. Therefore, we settled twenty minutes north of the city in the mostly White community of Edwardsville, Illinois.

I experienced my first dance class at the age of five years old during one of my summers with my grandparents. To provide me with a summer activity my grandmother enrolled my aunt and I into the Katherine Dunham Performing Arts Training Center (PATC) in East St. Louis. Katherine Dunham and her influence is a staple of ESL and several generations of the women in my family have taken classes at her schools. My experience at the PATC was only that summer, yet the experience and pleasure of dancing remained with me.

When my mother decided to move back closer to East St. Louis, I begged for her to put me back into dance classes. And that's when it began for me. I was ten years old at the time and I have been training in Dunham Technique ever since. My first year, I took classes at the PATC center, however, after doing community service at the KD museum, I learned of the KD Museum Children's Workshop and moved my main training to this center. At the Children's Workshop, Ruby Streate was the director and I trained mostly under her direction. Yet, I was still exposed to the grand master teachers (those who where a part of KD original dance company). These teachers included Dr. Glory Van Scott, Vanoye Aiken, Tommy Gomez, Walter Nicks, and Lucille Ellis. I was also taught from time to time by the group of dancers trained in East St. Louis like Theodore Jamison, Doris Bennett-Glasper, and Keith Williams.

I believe what I appreciate about my experience is that I was exposed to some amazing people and various cultural experiences at a very young age. And now as a dance artist, I carry this history and tradition with me.

Q: Please provide details of your relationship with Ms. Dunham: include in this answer the year you met, number of years and in what locations and capacities your relationship developed, how exactly you were mentored (i.e., letters, house visits, lessons, travel, writing). What are three main lessons you learned from these mentoring experiences?

Corbett: I do not really remember when I first saw Ms. Dunham. Ms. Dunham was the executive director over the Children's Workshop and most of the major artistic decisions were at least run by her. When I joined the Children's Workshop, Ms. Dunham was in her early eighties and wasn't as hands on as she used to be. Although her house was a block over from where we trained, we only saw her at special occasions like the Children's Workshop's anniversary show or her birthday, during the summer at the Dunham Technique Seminar, and when we traveled out of town with her as her resident dance company. At the time we were performing, we were the only dance company in the world regularly performing her original works and probably the only company of children regularly focused on Dunham Technique as the main movement vocabulary. Therefore, it was only appropriate that we followed her when needed.

For her birthdays before she turned ninety, we would go to her house and pile into her bedroom and eat cake and sit with her. She would show us videotapes of different things and talk about things as a young child and adolescent I really didn't retain. Yet, the lessons I remember from her occurred during her class during the DT seminar. Her class was on Monday, Wednesday, and Friday during what used to be a two-week seminar. She often talked a lot during these classes because of course she had so much to share. I remember her once discussing negative energy and people with negative energy. This went along with our time exploring Chakras in her class. She told a story once of an African village she visited and the oldest elder of the group learned to engage the energy centers above his head or his seventh chakra and he levitated. I remember her saying that she wanted to at some point of her life get there and only after years of training personal investigation had this elder been able to master this ability. Another important lesson I learned from Ms. Dunham is you never dismiss a person of knowledge no matter what their background is. I learned this lesson at one of Ms. Dunham's ninety-something birthday parties. To my surprise sitting next to her at her party was Louis Farrakhan. I knew nothing at the time of her relationship with the Nation of Islam and how they respected her. However, during that party she said one should never turn their back on a person of knowledge no matter what their politics may be. You can learn from anyone. I took that lesson to heart.

Q: How have the humanities (performing arts and liberal arts) impacted your life?

Corbett: I am who I am because of the arts. I would probably be an entirely different me if I had not engaged the arts. As I mentioned earlier, I believe I am a much more open person than I would be if I had not encountered the arts. I saw the world outside of myself at a very early age and was able to appreciate cultural differences. I don't believe my personal ambitions and aspirations would be the same either. I have always known greatness was in my horizon and my experience in the arts made me very aware of that possibility.

Plus, I grew up in an organization headed by an icon and therefore how could I not be great under that kind of leadership.

Q: What extent does cultural identity play in your life and work? Is there a global aspect of your work?

Corbett: Cultural identity plays a large part in my work. In my work, I am very aware I am speaking as a Black woman and often times a Black feminist. History and tradition [are] very important to how I conceive my work but also providing an understanding of [them] in a contemporary environment.

Q: Do you carry on a mentoring legacy? (How are you paying forward what you have been given by Ms. Dunham?)

Corbett: Well, one major way I am working to continue the legacy of what has been given is to work hard to make sure it exists for generations after me. In order to ensure this, my generation has decided to organize ourselves and to initiate change and progression in the organization. I do also carry on a mentoring legacy. As a Dunham Certified Instructor, I work toward continuing again the technique but also working for it to be relevant to the current student as well as educate the entire body in the process. Ms. Dunham is a great example of the dancer-scholar model and continuing this process with my students is important.

Q and A with Frank Moten

Q: What is your background, education/training? What are some of the challenges you have faced and triumphs you have enjoyed?

Moten: I guess you can say I am your run of the mill Black man with all the components and mixes remaining from slavery. My education is in technology and business, where I have only a technical/associate degree. Significant challenges were in childhood; as a dyslexic in the 70s very little was understood and we were treated mostly as lazy or slow. Other challenges that existed were the obvious: my father was in prison from near my eighth birthday until he passed near my seventeenth birthday. My most prized triumphs have mostly come from helping others attain their goals and dreams in life.

Q: Please provide details of your relationship with Mr. Gillespie: include in this answer the year you met, number of years and in what locations and capacities your relationship developed, how exactly you were mentored (i.e., letters, house visits, lessons, travel, writing). What are three main lessons you learned from these mentoring experiences?

Moten: I imagine I met Dizzy Gillespie near birth but my first memory was [when I was] about three years old when he brought home a poodle for his wife. The first twenty years of my life, I was fortunate enough to live next door to Dizzy so I imagine you could say I would see him three or four times a month [and] for that period of time he was like a second dad, playmate, teacher, and inspiration in my best and worst times growing up.

Q: How have the humanities (performing arts and liberal arts) impacted your life?

Moten: As a child [and] into my young adulthood performing music was the great joy of my life. Engaging music and audience was my elixir for anything.

Q: What extent does cultural identity play in your life and work? Is there a global aspect of your work?

Moten: I think cultural identity impacts every aspect of my life. I always use my own identity to understand others and this applies to almost any situation.

Q: Do you carry on a mentoring legacy? (How are you paying what you have been given by Mr. Gillespie forward?)

Moten: Dizzy asked that all of us who benefited from knowing and learning from him that we somehow return the favor. I have been fortunate enough that I have built a few businesses and many, many relationships where I can mentor, teach, and support from the very young musicians all the way through those in the twilight of life.

An additional tribute can be found on his website, Frank Moten.com:

And so, at twelve years old, Frank began his career as a musician. Over the next decade and with Dizzy's support and guidance, Frank pursued his music career, appearing at venues like Carnegie Hall, the Apollo, and the Beacon Theater. He grew up in jazz clubs in Greenwich Village. His friends were some of the biggest artists, producers, and managers in the industry. He learned the music business inside and out and still, it wasn't enough. Though his love for music was as strong as ever, Frank's passion for performing was waning, so he traded his drums for a computer and pursued a second career in IT management and consulting. During his career Frank developed and maintained software applications for companies such as Sprint, Avon Products, Revlon, Whirlpool and Universal Music.

Still, growing up with Dizzy Gillespie as a mentor was like getting a PhD. And even though Frank's IT career was going well, he was still enamored with the music industry. . . . Dizzy Gillespie once said that ". . . music is One—and therefore it's just an evolution of what has gone before." He asked Frank, and all those who learned from him and benefited by knowing him, that they find a way to return the favor, to continue the evolution. When Dizzy Gillespie died in 1993, the world lost a brilliant musician, and Frank lost a cherished friend. After Dizzy's death, Frank decided to commit his life to "returning the favor." Frank formed TeeTah and recorded Still Boppin'/Night in Tunisia in 1998. . . . After getting a creative boost Frank returned to the support of others including the Dizzy Gillespie All Stars. . . . Today Frank continues to share the magic of Dizzy. At the 2002 Chicago Jazz Festival, Frank and the National Jazz Museum presented "Reflections of Dizzy," saluting over 5 decades of Dizzy's music. In 2009 Frank joined Jazz Legacy Productions, running label operations and helping to grow the brand. JLP is dedicated to documenting the jazz art form, and to enhancing the legacy of its artists for generations to come.[14]

Saroya Corbett remembers Dunham as leaving a "legacy" that encouraged a "dancer-scholar model," to which she shows her dedication by advancing a "progression" of the Dunham technique. Frank Moten defined Gillespie's influence in terms of "inspiration," performing art as an "elixir for anything," and being charged by Gillespie to "return the favor" and mentor others. Whether by interpersonal contact or literary inspiration, legacies can be carried through the body and through the mind. These role models of creativity passed down their gifts of artistic light to scores of students and admirers.

Dunham and Gillespie offered their mentees "life-skills training" seen in the Reichert House and PACE programs, and their guidance of the children around them obviously influenced their ABC's. Theirs is a legacy of (in their own words) "humanitarianism" (Gillespie) and "self-possession" (Dunham). Seeking humanity and self in texts of those who have faced life challenges and won will certainly feed young lions as they walk their rocky paths of life and learn to tell their own tales.

Reichert House for Boys and PACE Program for Girls: Creative Life-Skills Training

The Reichert House Youth Academy for boys serves young men in Gainesville, Florida, in grades six through twelve. The organizational mission cites a goal to offer programs "where youth can learn about themselves and learn how to develop and achieve goals that will make them exemplary citizens of tomorrow."[15] The three key elements are respect, restraint, and responsibility. Much of the focus in the culture of the organization mimics the military and ROTC models. The program was founded in 1987 by members of the Gainesville Police Department and members of the Black on Black Crime Task Force. Founders desired an intervention by community members who sought to stop the flow of young Black men into the prison system. I served on the board from 2003 to 2011, and my main task was to assist with recruiting college student mentors. During that time, almost 100 University of Florida students mentored youth through my African American studies course, several of whom continued service after the class ended.

The Reichert House staff shaped the program on a "para military" structure but built curriculum on six areas of life skills focused on liberal studies:

1. Health and nutrition: eating habits, physical fitness, mental stress
2. Financial management: credit, bank statements, loans, savings, investments
3. Conflict resolution/management: "you and the law," peacefully resolve situations, anger management
4. Self-advocacy: review of resources available in the community
5. Recreational activities: organized football, basketball, track, presidential physical fitness exam, swimming, golf, tennis, equestrian
6. Social clubs: culinary, entrepreneur, art/drama, audio/video production, and drill team.[16]

As seen above, these themes of Black male development within human development are readily found in *Black Passports* texts. For example, investigations of health (including vegetarianism) can be found in the summative chapters of Dick Gregory's work and traced back to Jack Johnson's nutritional advice. Sports buffs can expand their recreational repertoire by reading Pelé's work on soccer or C. L. R. James's history of cricket. Young men might learn some economic lessons by following B. B. King through his financial difficulties despite his material success or better understand their anger after accompanying

Robert Guillaume through his struggles with anxiety and frustration, even at the height of his successful acting career.

Frederick Douglass provides a model of self-advocacy without parallel in the nineteenth century, which can be seen a century later in Huey P. Newton's manifestos written in Oakland. The countless narratives of male, Black jazz musicians offer improvisational resources, and military narratives from the Civil War (William Gould) to Vietnam (Collin Powell) can give young Black soldiers insight into ideas of duty, citizenship, revolution, and politics of violence. Further, reading experiences of Black men whose fathers were absent or difficult (Langston Hughes, Antwone Fisher, Jeff Henderson, and President Obama), whose fathers were paramount (Martin Luther King Jr. and Adam Clayton Powell), or who include reflections about the wonders of fatherhood (George Foreman, Quincy Jones, and B. B. King) deepen the sense of family. Black men's narratives lay bare a wide variety of life skills and lifestyle choices from which growing youth can learn.[17]

Similarly, young women have a unique set of life choices to make: ample texts and tailor-made community programs are available to help them navigate tricky terrain. As a key illustration, the PACE Center for Girls, Inc. (Practical Academic Cultural Education) has thirteen locations in Florida, and their Spirited Girls™ program offers life skills development, similar to the Reichert House program, and helps girls to make positive decisions and healthy lifestyle choices.

The Spirited Girls curriculum is divided by various gender-specific issues intended to create successful experiences, which will carry into a successful adulthood. Health and wellness topics cover important issues such as healthy eating, pregnancy, sexual health, body image, sexual identity, stress management, and the importance of quiet personal time. Interpersonal aspects of the curriculum review components of healthy relationships, the dangers of gossip and bullying, and how to effectively communicate and be heard in a way that is respectful to one's self and to others. Other Spirited Girls topics include cultural education and appreciation, balancing a check book, and how to create a resume.[18] Programs like PACE can benefit greatly from women's narratives listed in the *Black Passports* bibliography.

Janet Jackson's *True You* rests soundly on the relationship of self-esteem to control—also the name of her first hit record—particularly as girls deal with body image. Jackson exposes her enduring difficulties with weight, adolescent sex, and stress management, which eventually led her to focus on health and nutrition. The last part of her autobiography is a collection of recipes that she hopes will encourage young women to treat their bodies as temples by paying close attention to what they eat. Jackson's focus is on the value of discipline in one's life as a pathway to self-control, which then leads to self-esteem.

Tina Turner's narrative of domestic violence and her escape of abuse through chanting and spiritual meditation demonstrate the core values of the Spirited Girls program. Turner admits having to learn at a late age to manage independent functions—like balancing her own check book—and that these were difficult but valuable life skills, which she developed only after escaping the abuse of an all-controlling husband. Clearly, problems individuals deal with at home do not disappear when traveling abroad. Both Billie Holiday and Nina Simone wrote of fighting with or being beaten by lovers while abroad. However, following Bricktop, Gwendolyn Brooks, and Pearl Bailey overseas will show other arenas that can serve as backdrops for living as a woman abroad.

Motherhood narratives are also accompanied by difficult topics, like birthing an interracial baby (Kitty Oliver), abortion (Beneditta de Silva), infertility (Mary Church Terrell), the difficulty of raising a child in a racist world (Septima Clark), or the fight for health and reproductive rights (Faye Wattleton, the first Black woman president of Planned Parenthood).

BE A LION: SECRETS FROM DIANA ROSS AND *THE WIZ* (HOME, COURAGE, BRAIN, HEART)

Diana Ross's *Secrets of a Sparrow* can be read as a narrative of icon, professional, and relation, and can fill in the blanks for those who do not have the benefit of mentoring by someone like Dunham or Gillespie, or who may not have immediate access to neighborhood programs like Reichert House or PACE. The details provided in her memoir show her professional journey as a premiere entertainer. The book begins with the story of Ross' rained-out concert in Central Park and goes on to describe her life before and after the Supremes, include iconic photos. Ross also recounts her adventures in the deserts of Africa and climbing the Himalayas. Her story highlights her love for her children. Most of all, her story parallels that of Dorothy in *The Wiz* and how she found her way home to create an image of herself as big as the silver screen.

Diana Ross owns the movie rights to *The Wiz* and was much of the driving force behind the movie. The movie occupies three central chapters in her *Secrets of a Sparrow*: "Learning to Fly," "Strange Wind," and "Hello World." The chapters recount her life transitions that took place, very much like Dorothy's, during the rehearsal and filming of the movie. Ross was leaving Motown and

Berry Gordy in Los Angeles, getting a divorce from her then husband, Bob Ellis Silberstein, and settling her three children into a new school in New York. She recounts in these chapters that, for the first time, she was on her own and in a new world. Ross's prose reminds us that Cinderella stories involve more than just the glass slipper. There is struggle, hardship, and heartbreak. Resilience from actual tragedies is what makes comeback stories so compelling in her never-ending quest to be the best at her craft and to be recognized as such.

Ross is another classic example of how the "role model" definition is difficult: though she portrays herself as an underdog much of her life, other perspectives (like those of Berry Gordy and Mary Wilson) show Ross' story as more than a celebrated tale of struggle against the odds. Through either interpretation, it is imperative to note that her road to success was neither easy nor linear and that success, ultimately, can be defined in many ways. A case in point is the story behind the production of Ross's first movie. The Wiz opened in theaters in 1978 to horrible reviews by critics despite the all-star cast and unprecedented buildup after the seven Tony awards bestowed upon the Broadway version. The film did not gross a significant amount of money (it reportedly cost $24 million but earned only $13.5 million at the box office), and its production effort included filming of the largest movie set of the time: the eight-city-block plaza behind the World Trade Center and the (then newly developed) Astoria Studios.[19]

There were complications even in celebrating the movie, such as the bitter disappointment by fans of Stephanie Mills and others who were a part of the Broadway success but were not featured in the film version. Not everyone who was a part of the movie counted it a success: Richard Pryor mentioned the movie only once, as an example of projects he doesn't really remember working on because of his drug-induced blur; Quincy Jones also barely mentions the movie in a brisk three pages of his autobiography. In the chapter titled "Thriller" in Q, Jones wrote that the best thing to come out of the movie was developing a working relationship with Michael Jackson, and, though he had no problem with Ross and would later work with her on the 1985 "We Are the World" African benefit song track, he cited little else was good about the Wiz movie experience.[20]

Ross's depiction of the problems behind the scenes is an informative exposé that strips the shiny veneer off of the glamorous depiction of the movie star experiences, such as the problems of Michael Jackson's makeup (which may have damaged his skin), Ross's burned retinas (from looking into the lights), and the death of one of the dogs cast as Toto (from a broken steam pipe accident on the set). Success is always smoother on the outside and often appears more pleasant than the realities that lie within the full story. But as Ross herself acknowledged, we must weigh details and be grateful for the blessings in the bigger picture:

> Even with the difficulties and the places where, in my estimation, the film came up short, the end result was a good one. I made friends, I learned and I grew, I made positive life changes. My life was expanding, becoming happier and more meaningful. I was taking my power, both as a woman and as a performer. The long-suffered emptiness within me was filling up, and by the time the film was done, I, like Dorothy, had found that everything I was searching for was right there with me all along. I just had to believe in myself and set myself free.[21]

To a whole generation of children (including me during my Arizona adolescence), *The Wiz* offered seeds of inspiration that would become a monumental cornerstone of joy and purpose that powered me forward with completion of this book even through the most harrowing of times.

Much of Ross's book offers insight into her most prized role in life: mother. She reveals intimate details about her five children, lovers, husbands, and close friendships, but it is far from a tell-all. She includes personal notes to her mother and often-critical notes from her children. Through her children, she shows herself as open to critique and open to hear the voices of children.

In fact, she often seems to address a young audience. In a chapter titled "Standing Tall through It All," her words of advice are this: "I don't hold on to anger or disappointment, I just let that stuff go. . . . I don't dwell on what might have been, and I don't let the past affect me. What I want in this life is to live my vision and to fulfill my purpose on earth, to learn to master life and pursue happiness. These are the things I have learned and I always try to follow them.

1. Be true to yourself.
2. Help others.
3. Make each day your masterpiece.
4. Drink deeply from good books (learn from all).
5. Build a shelter against a rainy day.
6. Make friendship a fine art.
7. Give thanks for your blessings.
8. Pray for guidance everyday."[22]

In the final chapter, "Miracles," she reveals her secret; *the secret [to success] is . . . there is no secret*[23] Ross's assessment of her life and statements of message reflect a focus on Tucker's ABCs of self-empowerment: Attitude. Behavior. Choices, a simple yet pervasive message, regardless of the backdrop.

The types of lessons each narrative holds for youth coincide with the main lessons of resiliency covered in the "Mentoring 'At-Risk' Youth" course curriculum and agency mission statements. Carolyn Tucker's self-empowerment theory argues for a culturally sensitive model of education for African American youth and places youth at the center of their own capabilities; the *Black Passports* texts reflect a unique set of positions of special relevance to young Black women and men.

Carol Pateman's *The Sexual Contract* (1988), Charles Mills's *The Racial Contract* (1997), and their combined work, *Contract and Domination* (2007) are advanced texts useful to understanding the development of Black boys and girls in the context of the state, but regional identity also impacts identity, and a number of additional texts are relevant to shaping an understanding of life and life writing. John Inscoe's *Writing the South through the Self: Explorations in Southern Autobiography* offered a primary example of the possible uses of comparative autobiography. For instance, he presented the variant perceptions of the 1938 Joe Louis versus Max Schmeling fight by Maya Angelou, Jimmy Carter, and Russell Baker. The authors in William Andrews's *African American Autobiography: A Collection of Critical Essays* have offered several conceptual themes, including voice (Robert Stepto on Frederick Douglass), gender (Hazel Carby and Joanne Braxton on Black women, including Nancy Prince and Ida B. Wells), and group identity (Francoise Lionnet on Zora Neale Hurston). In the context of youth empowerment, the most significant theme is found in V. P. Franklin's *Living Our Stories, Telling Our Truths*, which cites vindication as a major theme in Black autobiography. The concept of overcoming negative treatment or stereotypes applies here.[24]

As the Makeda story demonstrates, gender socialization is a topic that crosses international boundaries, and it is complicated by physical appearance, religion, sexuality, and political ideology. Black travel narratives offer opportunities for young readers of all nations learn valuable lessons about gender, identity, and culture as they change and grow, even if they "still be Black." Outside of the family and social life, school becomes an important level at which to understand youth development and socialization. And the curriculum, the subject of the next chapter, is as substantive an influence on shaping identities.[25]

THREE

SCHOOL

Curriculum and Communication (Meso)

The most delightful part of geography is when we begin
teaching by journeys. . . . Keeping the moulded map of
continents before the children's eyes, they can readily trace
their way from one country to another, and tell where they
could go.
—Fanny Jackson Coppin, "How to Teach Geography,"
Reminiscences of School Life and Hints on Teaching (1913)

MESSAGE: MENTORING ACADEMICALLY "AT-RISK" STUDENTS

The *Handbook of Youth Mentoring*, edited by David DuBois and Michael J. Karcher, includes a chapter titled "Academically At-Risk Students" by Simon Larose and George M. Tarabulsy, which provides the necessary perspective for the second core area of focus in *Black Passports*: mentoring for improved school performance. Larose and Tarabulsy hypothesize that fostering three core areas impacts success in mentor guidance for academic efficacy: the mentee's feelings of competence, relatedness, and autonomy. As an overarching theme in defining self-control, competence is the theme of the following chapter. Support for autonomy was a central focus of the "life skills" issues covered in the previous section. When employing mentoring and literary mentoring for academic success, relatedness is the main component discussed here. Specifically, I suggest how students might relate narratives to school curricula in a way that enhances their interest and skill in required topics. When Larose and Tarabulsy discuss relatedness of mentor to mentee, they convey a sense of "involvement" when working with their protégée in a way that allows the mentee to recognize connections of their own interest to that of the mentor and strengthens awareness of how their interests can be identified in school material. Thus, "relatedness" involves highlighting intersections of personal interests, academic requirements, and interpersonal commitment.[1]

The mentoring organization Big Brothers Big Sisters measures "impact" in the following areas: identity, relationships, education, leading a fulfilling life, decision making, confidence, goals, and healthy choices. Further, the Boys and Girls Club measures quality in similar terms: character, leadership, education, career, health, life skills, arts, sports, and recreation. In "Academically At-Risk Students," the authors argue that interpersonal connection is important, but the ability of youth to identify skills of interest in the mentor can have a significant impact as well: "If mentoring is structured and centered on the acquisition of concrete skills that academically at-risk students want, the affective quality of the relationships with mentors may be less critical than the instrumental function."[2]

Similar to Tucker's call for self-control more than self-esteem, these authors cite a need for mentors to focus on experiences and ideas of use in *practical* academic guidance. Toward that end, providing hundreds of profiles will certainly generate an increased opportunity for a youth to identify life stories of use that coincide with a specific work or life goal. Whether through school-based, informal, or formalized mentoring, youth can gain access to life lessons through literary mentoring in a way that can positively impact their choices regardless of where they are from and where they decide to travel. The collection of such a range of options increases the chance of identifying at least one aspect of narratives that is of value to students.

A culture of high-stakes testing has too often smothered children's ability to recognize their own interests in formal learning environments. However, by utilizing autobiographies as a tool, students can connect autobiographers' life stories of learning processes to requirements of school curricula in a way that enables them to take a fresh approach to mundane or seemingly impossible classroom assignments. Toward that end, using life stories to illuminate practical skill sets in history, geography, vocabulary, and writing will enhance youths' ability to identify with people in order to master academic skills. Below, an excerpt from a college mentoring class syllabus is presented, followed by suggestions for incorporation into high school classrooms based on Georgia State teaching and learning standards.

Mentoring "At-Risk" Youth: A Course in Resilience

For those interested in teaching a college course on mentoring that engages students in community service learning, I provide a sample course description, topics, learning objectives and course texts. The full syllabus can be found online at www.professorevans.net, along with syllabi from other related courses including Black Gender and African Americans in Paris, a study-abroad course. These college courses build on cultural and intellectual development that undergraduate students may have encountered in secondary education, and the syllabi provide ample texts and contextual entry points to discussions of mentoring those who are coming up the ranks after them.

African American Studies 3915C, Syllabus Course Description

This community service-learning (CSL) course will engage students in collaborative relationships with local community organizations for which students will be able to provide mentorship to local "at-risk" youth. The course is a seminar-style practicum course that integrates lectures, appropriate reading in the humanities and social sciences, and community service assignments. Students will work through the UF Office of Leadership and Service and become familiar with IRB (Institutional Review Board) and HIPAA (Health Insurance Portability and Accountability Act of 1996) protocol to ensure professional, ethical, and enriching partnership with local agencies.

Main Topics

- Functional history of education
- Holistic teaching and learning
- (Excellence) Ecology, questions, competence
- (Ethics) Humanization, socialization, professionalization, internationalization
- Empowerment (voice)
- Identity (race, gender, class, and other indicators like age, body style, religion, ancestry, and location)
- Demographic and geographic mapping (census records as example of primary document interpretation)
- Disciplinary theories/explanations
- Adolescent development
- At-risk indicators

- Mentoring styles
- Service learning
- Experiential education
- Community engagement

Course Objectives

- To explore aspects of ecology, social location, and history by studying relationships of identity, education, and ethics
- To ask critical questions and debate central issues concerning youth who are at risk of being trapped in a cycle of poverty, crime, violence, racism, sexism, substance abuse, poor health, academic failure, social stigma, and political disenfranchisement
- To assist college students in formulating questions and finding systematic ways of gaining mentoring support, through mentoring relationships, during and after college, and to increase competence for lifelong learning
- To study how self-possession, resilience, empowerment, and mobility intersect with student experiences and issues (see Frederick Evers and theory of competence)
- To enhance competence and lifelong learning (managing self, communication, tasks, and innovation) through experiential education and community engagement
- To explore educational autobiography in a way that clarifies professional goals and guides students to disciplinary and career resources
- To meet the community-defined need of providing local at-risk youth with responsible mentors who can learn to identify students' needs and strengths; to partner with the UF Center for Leadership and Service to youth in the Gainesville Housing Authority's Reichert House and PACE programs as well as Big Brothers Big Sisters (BBBS) and Eastside High School (thirty-six hours of mentorship per student)

In essence, mentoring service-learning classes in the college curriculum can help youth see college students as human beings in an interesting sociological setting, and classes can help college students see children as human beings within complicated ecological networks. Course texts help students to unpack the multifaceted set of circumstances in which they operate. Significantly,

Michelle Dunlap's *Reaching Out to Children and Families* provides ample preparation for awkward, emotional, political, or confusing circumstances students might encounter during service. Course readings have also included *The Miracles of Mentoring* by Thomas Dortch, former president of 100 Black Men; *Sugar in the Raw* by Rebecca Carroll, a powerful collection of young Black girls' voices; and Beverly Daniel Tatum's *Why Are All the Black Kids Sitting Together in the Cafeteria?* I have shown films to enhance discussion such as *Hip Hop: Beyond Beats and Rhymes*; *The Souls of Black Girls*; *Tough Guise: Violence, Media and the Crisis in Masculinity*; *The First Year: Five First Year Teachers*; *Beauty Rises: Four Lives in the Arts*; and *Colors Straight Up: Colors United.*[3]

In the classroom, discussions run the gamut because of the interdisciplinary nature of those taking the class. African American studies is an inter-discipline, and students' undergraduate majors have spanned the humanities (English, history, religion), social sciences (political science, sociology), arts (theater, art), and physical sciences (environmental studies, engineering). Instructed to bring their disciplinary selves to the classroom and community work, student discussions have encompassed the widest range of topics:

- Black masculinity ("acting black," sagging and rap music; using the word "nigga" or reacting to the word "nigger"; boys in the library)
- Black womanhood (politics of etiquette training; makeup, hair, body image; women in sports)
- Environment (play space; health and safety; urban food deserts; school nutrition)
- Media, sports, and entertainment (are athletics a way out or a stereotypical limitation for young Black minds?; "nonblack" sports like swimming or tennis; hip hop images)
- Violence (family deaths; prison and juvenile justice systems; surviving personal or structural violence; post-9-11 reaction)
- Art and spirituality (art in healing professions; holy texts as art; art education as a tool for deconstruction of media; co-curricular or informal learning; museums)
- Identity and life purpose (career fairs; self-esteem; ethnicity or nationality in Black American relations, such as Cape Verdian, Haitian, Jamaican, Nigerian; activism)
- Education (racism and limited resources for assessment of special needs; psychology of play; identifying mentor and mentee values)

- Sex education (goals; policy; research outcomes; homosexuality; interracial dating)
- Mentoring as a strength-based action (rather than a deficit or need-based action; building trust; sustainability and dealing with realities of time-limited relationships; cross-race or cross-gender mentoring)

These and multitudes of other topics have swarmed around my classroom in the last decade, enriching my understanding of youth and the students who sign up to mentor them.

The mainstay course texts have been Geoffrey Canada's *Reaching Up for Manhood* and Joyce West Stevens's *Smart and Sassy: The Strengths of Inner-City Black Girls.*[4] These two texts complement each other nicely as they both allow a gendered investigation of adolescent development, yet the tone of each text (Canada's narrative voice and Stevens' social-worky technical prose) offers a stark contrast when alternating the two text readings from week to week. At least ten of my students have worked in the national program Teach for America and have reflected that, at the national level, child development and public education are truly enduring problems that this country ignores at its own peril. The course texts, community partners, course work, and in-class debates prepared them for continued engagement in the world of youth advocacy. As Marian Wright Edelman's work through the Children's Legal Defense Fund has demonstrated, the fight for youth rights is an uphill battle.

Geoffrey Canada is widely known for his work with the Harlem Children's Zone. His *Reaching Up for Manhood* (1998) is largely autobiographical, and he reflects on major life themes with chapter titles such as "Sex," "Drugs," "Self-worth," and "Work." Canada also focuses on what he thinks youth need, especially young men: mentors to help them develop a positive relationship with themselves and those around them. In the final chapter, "Healing," he presents a touching scene in which he works with a mentee who has been through a traumatic event: the young man witnessed a shooting in a club and was then held overnight in jail for questioning, even though he did not have anything to do with the shooting. During the scene, when his mentee is crying in the rain (the only place it seems acceptable for men to cry), Canada puts forth a wish for growth and overcoming some of the male socialization and culture of violence revealed in his first book, *Fist, Stick, Knife, Gun* (1995).

Joyce West Stevens's text is a manual for social workers and offers advanced theories of parental communication, peer influence, making choices in school and neighborhood settings, role model selection, relationship choice, and other areas where Black girls must often develop attitudes of resistance or resilience. Interviewing two sets of young women associated with pregnancy prevention or parenting classes, Stevens employs concepts such as hermeneutics (the intellectual process of interpretation) and social ecology (relationship to interlocking environmental factors) to explain Black girls' psychological strengths to those professionally assigned to their care.

Along with these two foundational books, I engage three additional texts: Carolyn Tucker; Simon Larose, "Mentoring Academically 'At-Risk' Students"; and Frederick Evers's *Bases of Competence: Skills for Lifelong Learning and Employability*. Two supplementary journal articles were assigned Kimberly Mahaffy, "Gender, Race, Class, and the Transition to Adulthood: A Critical Review of the Literature," and William Damon, "What Is Positive Youth Development?" The final required book is Charles Green's *Manufacturing Powerlessness in the Black Diaspora*, to bring the topic into international scope.[5]

With this dual curriculum in the classroom and at the agency, college students advance their understanding of the risk factors for youth violence, particularly those designated by the Centers for Disease Control and Prevention (CDC), such as violent neighborhoods or drug use by family members. However, students' personal experiences, like mentoring a youth who lost her whole family in a car accident, give a far more detailed explanation than curricula account for. Over the years, students have also raised innovative questions, like the implications of recognizing "at-risk" status as a multigenerational phenomenon.

Many of the students in my classes have come from communities that need mentoring most, so they have demonstrated a high level of interest in not only serving children, but also in understanding the causes of social inequities or violence in order to effect change at a state, national, or international level. In the process of the class, many college students have revealed their own precarious social status and used the available curricular and counseling resources to better understand their own backgrounds and face their own ongoing challenges on the path to empowerment. This collection of narratives is designed with these students in mind who struggle in environments, like the University of California system, that underestimate their value and question their ability to positively contribute to schools, university campuses, or society in general. However, the same students of color, like the Dream Defenders who are marginalized nationwide, will inevitably begin to make up a majority demographic, and will become the next generation of policy makers, educators, information bearers, and mentors. Though nationwide students face opposition to full intellectual enfranchisement, the longstanding disparity of equal access in the South warrants a close look at the region.

MEMOIRS: NARRATIVES OF EDUCATION

The *Black Passports* bibliography proves especially useful for the "Reading across the Curriculum" State of Georgia standard. Though teachers and mentors can assess the collection of memoirs, school reference and instructional librarians will have a special role to play in utilizing paper and online *Black Passports* resources by assisting teachers in helping identify co-curricular spaces to help students meet the learning standards. The reading standard states in part, "In the study of various disciplines of learning (language arts, mathematics, science, social studies), students must learn through reading the communities of discourse of each of those disciplines. Each subject has its own specific vocabulary; and for students to excel in all subjects, they must learn the specific vocabulary of those subject areas in context. Beginning in the middle grades, students start to self-select reading materials based on personal interests established through classroom learning." An excerpt of the standard reads:

SSUSRC1 Students will enhance reading in all curriculum areas by

- Establishing context
- Explore life experiences related to subject area content
- Discuss in both writing and speaking how certain words are subject area related
- Determine strategies for finding content and contextual meaning for unknown words[6]

ELAWLRC3 The student acquires new vocabulary in each content area and uses it correctly. The student

a. Demonstrates an understanding of contextual vocabulary in various subjects
b. Uses content vocabulary in writing and speaking
c. Explores understanding of new words found in subject area texts

Sample Task for ELAWLRC3

a. The student makes a list of unfamiliar vocabulary from each text, comparing and analyzing the level of complexity of the vocabulary from the two sources

b. Revisiting the texts, the student identifies the "loaded" words and evaluates how the connotative meanings produce an intended rhetorical effect

As central to the "Reading across the Curriculum Standard," the potential to engage students in expanding their vocabularies through use of autobiography is paramount. While learning words in the autobiographies, they can also use those words to help shape their own identities and life paths. Recent research in the field of education underscores the importance of vocabulary to literacy as well as the significance of vocabulary words grounded in texts that are relevant both to course content and to students' experiences, interests, and culture. In her dissertation on Florida schools, Margaret McMillen provided two examples of vocabulary's impact on students' standardized test results:

> Marzano and Pickering (2005) developed a six-step method of vocabulary instruction designed to develop students' academic language. Rather than memorize definitions of lists of terms, students described and explained new terms in their own words, reviewed them frequently in activities and games, and focused on terms important to the course content. In Ward's study (2006), Bethan Marshall of King's College in London opined that there is no substitute for what books do in terms of helping students expand their world and extend their vocabularies. The effectiveness of information and communication technologies to increase student achievement was compared to books [books showed a 15 percent increase in student scores, larger than technologies alone].[7]

Beginning in 1957, civil rights movement educator Septima Clark also used a subject-specific approach for her curriculum to develop the Freedom Schools and had similar success on literacy tests that African Americans were required to take in order to vote.[8]

Students will read books when they clearly relate to their own interests. One stark example is University of Connecticut basketball player and college graduate Kemba Walker. Walker stated in a *Sports Illustrated* interview that the only book he had read cover to cover was William Rhoden's *Forty Million Dollar Slaves: The Rise, Fall, and Redemption of the Black Athlete*. Whether or not this is accurate, Walker's choice of book title reflects that even at the college level, students want to read books that reflect their own interests, identities, and cultures.[9] McMillen's dissertation research also supported this notion:

> Harrison and Rappaport (2007), two college students, wondered why they could so easily learn all the words to rap songs, but struggled with challenging vocabulary words found on standardized tests. They began an academic rap company named Flocabulary which produced a compact disc entitled, *A Dictionary and a Microphone*. Menchville High School in Newport News, Virginia used the Flocabulary CD with juniors, and the students' average Scholastic Aptitude Test writing score improved from 420 to 477 after using the method of learning vocabulary words rap style for one year.[10]

In addition to McMillen's observations about literature and culturally relevant vocabulary, she argued for content-based vocabulary words. She provided a template of useful words in areas like mathematics-algebra ("monomial, direct function, exponent, matrix, density, algorithm, divergent, calculus, vector") and science ("cortex, cranial, torque, momentum, impulse, inertia, electric field"). In American history vocabulary words included "George Washington, migrations, self-determination, imperialism, Thomas Jefferson, Harlem Renaissance, Manifest Destiny, civil disobedience, abolition/emancipation, propaganda, immigration, *Brown v. Board of Education*, Native Americans, industrialization, space race, labor unions, Watergate, Social Darwinism, and Vietnam War." Words on world history reference were "capitalism, city-state, republic, oligarchy, apartheid, sovereignty, coup d'état, fascism, Confucius, Jesus, Cleopatra, Joan of Arc, and Julius Caesar."[11]

Below is a sample of one hundred vocabulary words I have gleaned from the twelve Guidance Council travel memoirs. This teaser list is extracted from the total list of more than one thousand vocabulary words.[12] While surely not "hip" as Cab Calloway's list at the end of his 1976 autobiography, *Of Minnie the Moocher and Me*, these words are sure to excite young minds when introduced into classroom assignments.[13]

Passport Vocabulary: An Autobiographical Lexicon

Following is an excerpt of 120 words from the 1,300-word vocabulary list. As a paradigm for state curriculum assignment, italicized words can be found in this book.

Wells	Douglass	Dunham	Gillespie
1. *agitation*	1. abolitionists	1. atrocious	1. bario
2. bedlam	2. *callous*	2. *creole*	2. bebop
3. debauch	3. dehumanizing	3. deracinated	3. descendency
4. epithets	4. *forte*	4. flamboyant	4. esoteric
5. goose quill	5. glimmering	5. indigenous	5. gumbo
6. munificent	6. incompatible	6. *metamorphosis*	6. gyrations
7. remonstrance	7. lacerated	7. myopic	7. *improvisation*
8. streetcar	8. manifestation	8. *persona non grata*	8. notorious
9. ubiquitous	9. soul-killing	9. quaquaversal	9. rejuvenation
10. yellow fever	10. *vindication*	10. voyeur	10. syndrome

Cooper	Du Bois	Willis	El-Shabazz
1. ambassador	1. aberration	1. blissful	1. *circumambulation*
2. bolster	2. antagonism	2. confluence	2. *honor*
3. *doctorate*	3. conjure	3. *etiquette*	3. industrialization
4. *esclavage*	4. disillusion	4. existential	4. inevitably
5. gracious	5. epitomize	5. caste	5. jestering
6. *intellectual*	6. imperialism	6. historical trauma	6. mosque
7. marvel	7. microcosm	7. insurmountable	7. pernicious
8. promulgate	8. peonage	8. prattle	8. signified
9. rejoinder	9. sojourn	9. *self-absorption*	9. stricken
10. thesis	10. *willy-nilly*	10. unscrupulous	10. unison

Jemison	Henderson	Davis	Obama
1. Azoic	1. *aesthetic*	1. abominable	1. affirmative action
2. Bid Whist	2. carte blanche	2. *doctoral*	2. *authentic*
3. cosmology	3. cognizance	*dissertation*	3. baobab tree
4. epicenter	4. evidentiary	3. fascists	4. bureaucrats
5. gross anatomy	5. hustler	4. indiscriminate	5. Eurocentrism
6. *Katherine Dunham*	6. immaculate	5. muster	6. hierarchies
technique	7. kosher	6. parasitic	7. jive
7. nautical miles	8. *mise en place*	7. recuperate	8. miscegenation
8. precocious	9. palate	8. squander	9. pavilion
9. radio communica-	10. think tank	9. severance	10. *soukous* beat
tion signals		10. trinket	
10. *swup-swup*			

Georgia Standards and Historical Legacies

Motivation for writing well can be found in the critical musings of the auto-biographers who made writing their profession. Stimulating professionals abound: Amiri Baraka, James Baldwin, Alice Walker, Rebecca Walker, Maya Angelou, and Michelle Duster.

With a sense of geography and expanded vocabulary, students will be better equipped to write at a higher standard. In addition, there are rich opportunities for comparing authors' tones, symbolism, point of view, and figurative language that can deepen student reading of analysis in memoirs through the discipline of history.

National and State Standards for History

Fanny Jackson Coppin advocated teaching geography through narrative journeys; in the same way, history comes alive when accessing first-person accounts of travel memoirs. The UCLA National Center for History in the Schools (NCHS) has produced U.S. history content standards while the State of Georgia curriculum (GSC) also created curricula for civil rights history. Both national and state standards demonstrate several points of potential connection for autobiography to bolster assigned topics.

National high school standards for the subject of history list the following goals for teaching in the discipline:

1. Chronological Thinking
2. Historical Comprehension
3. Historical Analysis and Interpretation
4. Historical Research Capabilities
5. Historical Issues: Analysis and Decision-Making[14]

When considering the mosaic of *Black Passports*, a general chronology enriches our understanding of historical time. Each century of United States history can be accessed through Black autobiography, and following thematic strains like religion weaves a compelling tapestry through time:

1700s

Marrant, John. *The Negro Convert: A Poem; Being the Substance of the Experience of Mr. John Marrant, A Negro* (1785).

1800s

Henson, Josiah. *The Life of Josiah Henson, Formerly a Slave, Now an Inhabitant of Canada, as Narrated by Himself; Truth Stranger Than Fiction. Father Henson's Story of His Own Life; Uncle Tom's Story of His Life: An Autobiography of the Rev. Josiah Henson* (1849, 1858, 1876).

Smith, Amanda. *An Autobiography: The Story of the Lord's Dealings with Mrs. Amanda Smith the Colored Evangelist: Containing an Account of her Life Work of Faith, and Her Travels in America, England, Ireland, Scotland, India, and Africa as an 1893 Independent Missionary* (1893).

1900s

King Jr., Martin Luther. *The Autobiography of Martin Luther King Jr.* (1998).

Owens, Jesse. *Blackthink: My Life as a Black Man and a White Man* (1970), *The Jesse Owens Story* (1970), *I Have Changed* (1972), *Jesse: A Spiritual Autobiography* (1978).

Sheppard, William Henry. *Presbyterian Pioneers in the Congo* (1917).

Steward, Theophilus Gould. *From 1864–1914: Fifty Years in the Gospel Ministry* (1921).

Thurman, Howard. *With Head and Heart: The Autobiography of Howard Thurman* (1981).

Lester, Julius. *Lovesong: Becoming a Jew* (1987, 1995).

Malcolm X. *Autobiography of Malcolm X* (1965).

Murray, Pauli. *Pauli Murray: The Autobiography of a Black Activist, Lawyer, Priest, and Poet* (1987). Berkeley (International House).

Young, Andrew. *A Way Out of No Way: The Spiritual Memoirs of Andrew Young* (1994).

2000s

Willis, Jan. *Dreaming Me: Black, Baptist, and Buddhist* (2008).

Poitier, Sidney. *This Life* (1980), *The Measure of a Man: A Spiritual Autobiography* (2000).

Walker, Rebecca. *Black, White, and Jewish: Autobiography of a Shifting Self* (2001).

In addition, Black travel history can be summarized as a topic of interest in itself. The first wave of travelers in the Colonial, Antebellum, Civil War, and Reconstruction eras (before 1900) were explorers or cowboys (James Beckwourth and Nat Love); abolitionists, or runaway slaves (Mifflin Gibbs, Samuel Ringgold Ward, William Benjamin Gould, and Harriet Jacobs); Christian missionaries (John Marrant, Amanda Smith, and Zilpha Elaw); or a combination of these categories (Nancy Prince Gardner). During the Progressive Era and between world wars, African Americans mainly traveled for culture (Sidney Bechet and Bricktop) and sport (Jack Johnson) in addition to supporting the war as soldiers or war correspondents. A few, like Anna Julia Cooper, continued patterns of study abroad, and the sense of adventure clearly lived in Juanita Harrison, who traveled to fifty-two countries, eventually settling in Hawai'i. The midwar group was followed in the 1940s, 50s, and 60s by a new wave of educators (like Dorothy Height) and, mainly, a growing number of entertainers and athletes.

However, as demonstrated in the "Exchange" case studies (chapter 6), which feature ten narratives of study abroad, chronological thinking can best be taught through a concentrated reading of select life stories that cover a century. The Delany sisters, both of whom lived to be more than one hundred years of age, offer an opportunity to create a picture of what life was like when they were born in 1889 (Sarah) and 1891 (Bessie) to their deaths in the twentieth century. Through their compelling stories, students can track major events such as wars or social movements, but also educational access and personal feelings about integration from their lens in North Carolina, in New York as students, and as tourists in post-World War I Lithuania, Latvia, Jamaica, Russia, and Estonia. The Delany sisters resemble real-life portrayals of August Wilson's *Autobiography of Miss Jane Pittman*, whose fictive autobiographical narrative of longevity unveils collective stories of marriage, childbirth, transportation, and other experiences through transitions of Black enslavement, the Civil War, Reconstruction, and Jim Crow, and the civil rights and Black power movements. This life stream is useful to help place characters in their proper location and time in relation to significant events in U.S. and world history.

The NCHS United States History Content Standards for grades 5–12, era 9, postwar, United States, (1945 to early 1970s), standard 4 mandates that students demonstrate an understanding of "the struggle for racial and gender equality and the extension of civil liberties."[15] Selectively engaging the *Black Passports* bibliography by theme is useful here. An interesting way to approach the gender question in relation to civil rights might be to assign a student query to compare women's views of the March on Washington (Septima Clark, Dorothy Height, Coretta Scott King, Pauli Murray, Mahalia Jackson, Marian Wright Edelman, Ruby Dee, Elaine Brown, Maya Angelou, Pearl Bailey, Eartha Kitt, Delany sisters, Nina Simone, Alice Walker, Mary Wilson, and Diana Ross).

Dorothy Height's participation in the 1965 March on Washington for Jobs and Freedom will give students a context in which to place the centrality of workers and other leaders in the movement beyond Dr. King. Inheriting her mandate for justice from none other than Mary McLeod Bethune, Height's autobiography lifts the façade of individual leadership and exposes civil rights activism as a collective endeavor by a group of skilled organizers, many of whom were women. The legal work of Pauli Murray and Marian Wright Edelman gives added texture to women's leadership roles, and the involvement of Murray and Florynce Kennedy in the founding of NOW (National Organization for Women) deserves closer attention. Beyond comparing several women's perspectives, students also can measure change over time in women's voices. For instance, a close reading of Septima Clark's voice will reveal a change from race-focused agitation in *Echo in My Soul* (1962) to a focus on marginalization in the race movement because of her gender, in the second autobiography, *Ready from Within* (1987). Further complicating the issue is the fact that historian Cynthia Stokes participated in writing Clark's second text, which forces students again to contemplate the role of co-authors in autobiographies.

There are numerous outstanding opportunities for students to research U.S. and international historical events through eyewitness accounts. Ida B. Wells offers an entry point into the discussion of both suffrage for African American women and the antilynching campaign, mainly relating to men. Wells' narrative, as referenced in the introduction to this book, is compelling for its detailing a long life of struggle. The debate of Black women's politics was vigorously revisited in 2008 when Black women in the Democratic Party were offered the choice between presidential hopefuls Hillary Clinton and Barack Obama. Suffrage issues are clearly of relevance to youth in this political era, given the 2013 rollback in voter rights by Shelby County, Alabama, via a Supreme Court hearing about the attempt to overturn section 5 of the 1965 Voter Rights Act. Wells' discussion of the vote will be of great use in the area of "Historical Issues: Analysis and Decision-Making."

An additional area of curricular interest in history may be the theme of school integration: William Scarborough, through his roots in classical literature and work in professional academic organizations, exposes the long history of excellent scholarship by Black academics. However, the struggle for mass integration must absolutely include Charlayne Hunter-Gault's narrative and how she took the lessons she learned in battling segregation at the University of Georgia to cover similar struggles in South Africa. Fanny Jackson Coppin and Mary Church Terrell at Oberlin were followed by Pauli Murray at Howard University and Berkeley Law School and by Lena Morton at University of Cincinnati, who led the way for Patricia Williams in Harvard Law School; integration at every level in every decade underscores the difficult paths and insightful responses from those who have endured the hard road to academic access. Reading conflicting views of authors like W. E. B. Du Bois and Booker T. Washington and controversial interpretations like Zora Neale Hurston's ultimate rejection of desegregation will provide opportunities to stage classroom debates. Researching controversial historical issues will increase students' abilities to grasp nuances of individual and institutional decisions. This is especially important in African American history. While there has been consistent dedication to increasing freedom for Blacks in America, there has been no consensus on the process by which that freedom should be attained.

Debate-friendly topics are plentiful in authors' life stories. Huey P. Newton's articulation of Black power livens up the historical discussion and challenges students to ask about the varied perceptions of the goals of integration. Contemplating the antiwar stances of Martin Luther King Jr. and Muhammad Ali compels student research into war and antiwar movements throughout time and provides vital information from which students can understand foundations of debate on the current state of the issue. Malcolm X's description of prison, Angela Davis's trial, and Assata Shakur's exile invite historical analysis of incarceration. Students can move through John Hope Franklin's narrative of living through the aftermath of Ku Klux Klan violence and the impact that had on his work as a premiere historian. Franklin's text also invites an opportunity to link scholarship with policy, as his work was central to the *Brown v. Board of Education* decision and in preparation for work as a domestic ambassador on a national discussion of race during the Clinton presidency.

Clearly, autobiographies can supplement the Georgia performance standards for grades 9–12 for U.S. history (social studies section). Here, standards of the antecedents to the modern civil rights movement stand out as important to contextualize Georgia students' basic knowledge of figures like Martin Luther King Jr. These topics are already present in the Georgia curriculum.

Georgia History Standards SSUSH22

The student will identify dimensions of the civil rights movement, 1945–1970.

a. Explain the importance of President Truman's order to *integrate the U.S. military* and the federal government.
b. Identify *Jackie Robinson* and the integration of baseball.
c. Explain *Brown v. Board of Education* and efforts to resist the decision.
d. Describe the significance of *Martin Luther King Jr.'s* "Letter from a Birmingham Jail" and his "I Have a Dream" speech.

e. Describe the causes and consequences of the Civil Rights Act of
    1964 and the Voting Rights Act of 1965.

These national and state themes can be discussed in terms of four areas of
race and gender engagement: politics (military, Civil Rights Act, and Voting
Rights Act), education (*Brown v. Board of Education*), religion (Martin Luther
King Jr.), and culture (Jackie Robinson). Each autobiography offers infinite
intersectional investigations of historical importance.

History also can be employed to investigate the intricate tapestry of
comparative perspectives by viewing relationships, lives, and deaths of central figures. Students can compare views of well-known figures to enliven
their knowledge of personalities. These figures might consist of Jack Johnson (through James Weldon Johnson and Bricktop's reflections); Hitler (Mary
Church Terrell, Walter White, Jesse Owens); Castro (Adam Clayton Powell,
Celia Cruz, Belva Davis, Amiri Baraka, Huey P. Newton, Assata Shakur, Langston Hughes on race in Cuba); Medgar Evers (Dick Gregory, Martin Luther King
Jr.), Martin Luther King Jr. (Harry Belafonte, Sidney Poitier, Roger Wilkins,
Coretta Scott, Andrew Young, Magnificent Montague, Charles Rengel, Adam
Clayton Powell, Benjamin Mays, Dorothy Height, Septima Clark, James For-
man, Mary Wilson, Eartha Kitt); Malcolm X (Maya Angelou, Muhammad Ali),
or Michael Jackson (Dionne Warwick, Quincy Jones, Janet Jackson). *Black
Passports* will fill in, complete, and give color to U.S. history curricula just as
crayons complete the bare, stark lines of a coloring book.

Mapping Memoirs: "Cultural Aspects of Geography"

The State of Georgia's geography curriculum challenges students to "describe
the interaction of physical and human systems that have shaped Africa, Asia,
Europe, Latin America, Canada, the United States, Australia, New Zealand,
and Antarctica."[16] In addition, standards require a general understanding of
subthemes that cover physical characteristics and concept of place, people,
culture, and customs.

Equally as useful as the historical assessment, geographically, *Black Passports* covers the globe. The great majority of authors traveled to Europe, especially Paris, Germany, Italy, and England, with more than sixteen exploring
Russia (including Nancy Prince, Jack Johnson, W. E. B. Du Bois, Paul Robeson, Gwendolyn Brooks, Maya Angelou, Andrea Lee, Audre Lorde, and Harry
Haywood). Almost as many trekked to Asia (Amanda Smith, Roy Wilkins, Jan
Willis, Elaine Brown, Colleen McElroy) and elsewhere: at least twenty-two to

Australia, nineteen to Canada, seventeen to Cuba, thirteen to India, and ten to China.

As stated in the "Identity" section of the previous chapter, more than sixty authors traveled to Africa, with Liberia, South Africa, Ghana, and Nigeria as the most popular destinations. We might take account of comparative impressions of South Africa by Fanny Jackson Coppin in 1906, or Magnificent Montague, Arthur Ashe, Ralphe Bunche, Leon Sullivan, and Charlayne Hunter-Gault a century later. Broad surveys of the continent such as that undertaken by Eslanda Goode Robeson's 1936 multicountry tour from Capetown, South Africa, Swaziland, and Kenya to Congo, Uganda, and Egypt or *Ebony* magazine's editor Era Bell Thompson whose 1954 *Africa, Land of My Fathers* traced their connections to Africa long before Alex Haley's *Roots*. These texts offer ripe and in-depth analysis and lessons for historical and contemporary geography on several continents.

SSWG2 The student will explain the cultural aspects of geography

a. Describe the *concept of place* by explaining how the culture of a region is a product of the region's physical characteristics.
b. Explain how *cultural characteristics* of a place can be used to describe a place.
c. Analyze how *physical factors* such as mountains, climate, and bodies of water *interact with the people* of a region to produce a distinctive culture.
d. Explain how the development of *customs and traditions* helps to define a culture and a people.

Descriptions of lifestyle and scenery abound. Most striking is the "Flora and Fauna" chapter in *The Bern Book*, which logs Vincent O. Carter's observations of Switzerland. The descriptive imagery of nature by a Black man from Detroit will expand the minds of youth living in the Motor City today:

> I was amazed when I first encountered the indigenous inhabitants of the Jura and Alp mountains, the mountain flowers! They were so small, so perfect in every disquieting detail. Sharp cold winds, like skillful knives, seemed to have shaped them into weird, intricately beautiful patterns, with colors that were extraordinarily bright and intense. Imagine on a peak of one of the tallest mountains in the world, little patches of solitary flowers, each of which is about the size

of a fly, bursting with subtle beauty, as though forces from without, as well as forces from within, had restrained them to miniature size.[17]

Carter then moves from the country mountain landscape to the city and notes the contrast in sight and sound and the impact on politically diplomatic attitudes of city dwellers. He notes, too, the impact of the vastness of majestic mountains and the effects of serenity on his sense of time and other senses: "In the city of Bern I have encountered a stillness which is as intense as the roar of the traffic of New York. There, I could not hear for the noise; and here in Bern I could not hear for the silence."[18] The ability of writing to take the reader toward alternate realities or interpretations is a principle quality of books. When physical opportunity is limited for youth, readings like *The Bern Book* offer hope of adventurous futures.

The collective travel location list is quite impressive (see appendix B). A full set of the travelers by region and continent reveals opportunities to assign research projects by location or by travel date, but even an abbreviated list reveals the magnetic potential of cartography that can be created by tracing this group's tracks:

Angelou, Maya (Marguerite Johnson). Paris, Italy, twenty-two countries 1954–55; Ghana 1960; Cairo 1960; Sweden, Paris, Ghana 1961–64.

Ailey, Alvin. Dakar 1966; Senegal, London, Barcelona, Paris 1966. Madagascar, Tanzania, Uganda, Kenya, Congo, Ivory Coast, Ghana, Senegal 1967. Germany, Sweden 1968; Russia 1970; Austria 1972; Senegal 1982; Russia 1990; Antigua 1990s.

Bragg, Janet. London, England, Paris 1955; Addis Ababa, Ethiopia 1965; Ethiopia, Dakar Senegal, Nigeria, Cairo 1972; Ethiopia, Mexico, Singapore, Sweden, West Germany, Denmark, Italy 1980s.

Davis, Ossie, and Ruby Dee. Liberia, North Africa (Ossie) 1942–45; Nigeria 1969 (Ossie and Ruby); India 1989.

Johnson, James Weldon. Venezuela 1906–08; Nicaragua 1909–13; Haiti 1920; Japan 1929.

Johnson, John H. Ghana 1957; Russia, Poland 1959; Ivory Coast 1961; Kenya 1963; Continent 1976.

Rice, Condoleezza. Iraq, Darfur, North Korea, India, China, Bagdad, Cairo, Georgia, Mumbai 2001–09.

Robeson, Eslanda Goode. London, South Africa, Swaziland,

Mozambique, Uganda, Kenya, Egypt, Basutoland (Lesotho) 1936.
Robeson, Paul. London 1927–39; Soviet Union 1934; Jamaica, Trinidad 1948; Europe, Russia 1949, 1950–58; Moscow 1959; Australia, New Zealand 1960; London, Africa, China, Cuba 1961.
Thompson, Era Bell. Eighteen African countries by 1954; Brazil 1965; 124 countries on 6 continents.
Wattleton, Faye. Mexico City 1984; Thailand, Bangladesh, Philippines, India, Kenya, Jurkina Faso, Ecuador, Bolivia, Sierra Leone, Liberia, Senegal, Zaire, Brazil, Indonesia 1980s.
Wilkins, Roger. Japan, Korea, China, Vietnam 1962–63; Algiers, Kinshasa, Dar es Salaam, Nairobi, Addis Ababa, New Delhi, Bangkok 1964; Jamaica 1969; Martinique 1970.

Geography offers a general entry point into distant places, and this historic data set can also be used to help make sense of current trends in study abroad: most contemporary students go to Europe, with a lesser number traveling to Australia, New Zealand, Latin America, Asia, Africa, North America, or the Middle East. Teachers, mentors, and a network of school and community educators can use the locations of the narratives to help today's students plan their own desired march around the world.

Reading Multicultural Literature: Finding Voice through Writing

The State of Georgia standards for writing and reading multicultural literature offer a vital entry point into the potential uses for other core disciplines in this curriculum. An additional tool for structural analysis of these narratives is *Reading Autobiography, a Guide to Interpreting Life Narratives* by Sidonie Smith and Julia Watson. Of their twenty-five options in the "toolkit" for interpretation, the three themes of "self-knowledge," "agency," and "voice" stand out as distinct areas to guide a reader toward the mentoring possibilities for texts. These tools provide language for assessing the formation of narratives in a way that parallels the literary "character development" mandate of the State of Georgia standards in the literature and arts module.

Before I entered college full time in 1994, I wrote poetry. True, it was bad, whiney and rhymey, sandwiched between anger management and pity party poetry, but I have a record of my thoughts at that time, and *What Lies Inside*, as a book of poetry remains among a favorite of all I have written. In "Classrooms" in her text *Clarity as Concept*, poet Mari Evans presents an argument for the usefulness of creative scholarship for the express benefit of intellectual and political decolonization of students. In this, she identifies community building and engagement as core values for educating Black students. *Black Passports* poems provide a model for school-related tasks as outlined in the State of Georgia curriculum.

Children use poetry as a vital entry point to develop language skills. As an extension of my love for poetry, I engaged the curricular task ELAMLRL1b as a creative challenge while writing this book: to write poems for select authors that reflect an analysis of their overall narrative and include an aspect of their international experience.

Sample Task ELAMLRL1

The student(s) chooses a literary element directly from the standards in order to analyze its use in a minimum of four works across cultures and genres (i.e., allusion, symbolism, character development, tone, voice, diction, point of view, irony, imagery, figurative language, sound devices).

The student documents textual evidence and presents the analysis to the class, choosing at least one or more of the following formats: iMovie/Moviemaker, PowerPoint, essay, *poem*, music and lyrics, artistic/visual representation, dramatic performance, oral presentation, pamphlet or brochure, trifold board, or formats based upon student choice and teacher approval [emphasis mine].

Given the state of technology today, youth can certainly get creative in their use of PowerPoint or movies, but as language is a critical area of development, poetry is a rewarding and relevant task. Thus, Appendix D offers a collection of eighty poems as examples of this assignment.[19]

The origins of African American poetry are grounded in historical poetry. Beginning with "Bars Fight" in 1746, Lucy Terry chronicled a Native American attack in Deerfield, Massachusetts. In the same tradition, in Phillis Wheatley's 1773 "Ode to George Washington," and in her account of being "brought" from Africa to America, we see the African griot tradition to mark events, places, and people through poetry.

Regardless of the circumstances of trips abroad, African American travelers are confronted, at the very least, with extraordinarily different cultural mores around sex, food, time, race classification, or any number of other variables. One of the most striking tales of Maya Angleou's several autobiographies is her recounting of how she learned the lesson of humility when in other people's homes. She narrates that while on a first visit to Senegal she repeatedly crossed a large rug in the center of the room and grew irritated that others were simply walking around the carpet. When the dinner hour arrived, the rug was rolled up and replaced because that beautiful rug on the floor was the location of the traditional meal. She became "on fire with shame," embarrassed by her own rude behavior, and took away an important lesson: pay attention to the cultural mores of those around you.[20]

The authors who have shared their lives through autobiography have rendered a supreme service to humanity: affording purposeful reflection to those who can learn the lessons without making mistakes. Writing can also show youth the viability of their own voice. After Langston Hughes won a financial scholarship to Lincoln University in Kansas because of his publishing history, he concluded, "poetry is practical." Many authors like Nancy Prince in the 1850s and Major Taylor in the 1900s attempted to sell their life stories as an explicit means of financial survival during their later years of life. Whether as a means of making a living, as an attempt at maintaining independence or retirement security, or simply as a desire to tell their side of a story, many *Black Passports* authors took seriously the craft of creative or expository prose. As revealed in *The Big Sea* in 1931, Langston Hughes consciously and explicitly committed his life to writing:

> So as yet, the big editors did not know my name, or give any sign of knowing it. And my play, *Mulatto,* was unproduced. Nevertheless, I'd finally and definitely made up my mind to continue being a writer— and to become a professional writer, making my living from writing. So far that had not happened. Until I went to Lincoln, I had always worked at other things: teaching English in Mexico, truck gardening on Staten Island, a seaman, a doorman, a cook, a waiter in Paris night clubs or in hotels and restaurants, a clerk at the Association for the Study of Negro Life and History, a bus boy at the Wardman Park in Washington. Then I'd had a scholarship, a few literary awards, a patron. But those things were ended now. I would have to make my own living again—so I determined to make it writing. I did. Shortly poetry became my bread; prose, shelter and retirement. Words turned into songs, plays, scenarios, articles, and stories. Literature is a big sea full of many fish. I let down my nets and pulled. I'm still pulling.[21]

Like Maya Angelou, youth may want to live life and keep learning, never too prideful to admit that they desperately desire to know what the world has to teach. Like Langston Hughes, they may want to live life writing. The poems included in this text are examples of creative options in that direction.

In the Oxford *Anthology of African American Poetry* (2006), Arnold Rampersad's "This Man Shall Be Remembered" pays tribute to Paul Robeson, Frederick Douglass, David Walker, Malcolm X, Mary McLeod Bethune, and Harriet Tubman. He writes, "This anthology [reserves one section] for tributary poetry, or verse by black poets which recognizes the black hero. By black heroism we mean, in particular, the actions of men and women who have dared to lead their fellow blacks toward freedom and power."[22]

The collection of poems offered in Appendix D reflects the "tributary" tradition and expands the range of heroic figures from which youth may draw insight, inspiration, or instruction. The creation of poetic sketches allowed me to address a large number of contributors in a way that moves beyond traditional biographic outlines, which are already provided in valuable resources like the encyclopedia *African American Lives*. Poetry maximizes the capacity to present the spectrum of travelers in a sufficiently detailed, individualized scope. Though I have chosen a variation of Haiku for my samples, youth can use various poetic platforms on which to build an analytical retelling of any of the two hundred characters that most interest them or that relate to an academic task at hand. Students can also experiment with various poetic structures such as a free verse poem using spoken word affects (call and response, repetition, alliteration, or cadence).

In my community programs, poetry—haiku in particular—operated as a fun and nonthreatening means of engagement. Richard Wright is known for penning hundreds of haiku. Sonia Sanchez created "Sonoku" as a variation on the traditional form; similarly, as an alteration, I created "nenoku," substituting words for syllables while keeping a general 5–7–5 frame. I have also replaced the focus on nature found in the Japanese form, with the focus on Black history and culture. "Neno" is Swahili for "word," thus the form for these sketches is "word" poems, about Black figures, specifically for the enhancement of youth's education.

W. E. B. Du Bois

Darkwater (1920); *Dusk of Dawn* (1940), *Soliloquy: Autobiography* (1968); Berlin 1892–94; Niagara Falls, Canada 1905; London 1900; London 1911; Paris 1919; London, Brussels, Paris 1921; Liberia 1923; Russia 1926; World trip 1936; Haiti, Cuba 1944; Manchester, England 1945; Paris, Moscow 1949;

[Passport denied 1951–58]; Soviet Union, Europe 1958–59; China 1959; Accra, Ghana 1961.

> "No Apologies"
> Disciplined professor. Hopes. Races Pan-Africa
> Humbly attached. Agitating against Atalanta's greed
> Vindicating human . . . Souls . . . suffering indignities

Anna Julia Cooper

The Third Step (1945); London 1900; Paris 1911, 1912, 1913, 1925.

> "One Whole Woman"
> From *esclavage* to Sorbonne doctorate
> Southern Black woman's *studere*, measuring men
> Conjoined identities, physio-conative separation impossible

MODEL: CREATING SPACE THROUGH POETRY AND TECHNOLOGY

The structure and content of Nenoku poetry are intentionally simple and build on a familiar type of cultural poetry: haiku.

1. Structure: "Epic in Seventeen Words" haiku form (3 lines: 5–7–5). Substitute words for syllables.
2. Content: Hero-Protest Narrative: African "Epic Hero" tradition: Background/Education, Battles/Victories, Life Lessons/Leadership (Caulibaly). African American *"Renegade"* protest and Black power tradition (Shockley).

As an example of the style and principles, I offer three paradigmatic poems to reflect main themes: Black history, critical race curriculum, and humanities as the basis of empowerment education:

> NENOKU: BLACK EPIC POETRY
> Lyrically, I research Black history
> Without structure, culture dissipates—heritage lost. But,
> 17 words? Legendary African references

> ILLEGAL OCCUPATION
> Arizona's HB 2281 banned race-conscious education

Like 1830s literacy "excited dissatisfaction in minds"
Precisely. "Dissatisfaction" is my job.

BLESSED BE THE HUMANITARIANS
Ellen Swallow Richards developed ecology
Dizzy's trumpet scripted improvisation; Dunham's feet rooted
Each modernized human socio-natural connections

Sonia Sanchez's use of haiku in talks with youth and young adults under-scores the use of poetry as a form of empowerment. She says that poetry is about breathing, and I encourage employing poetry in mentoring as a way to get youth to slow down, see themselves, breathe, feel, think, and meditate on life. In an interview with Elizabeth Alexander at Yale University in November 2011, Professor Sanchez expressed that form was the most significant part of poetry. Form demands discipline, though her Sonoku demonstrates that form must also have flexibility if it is to have strength.

Further, I engage Nina Turner's grandmother wit in creating nenoku poems; they are, in form and content, meditations, invocations, and memori-als of Black travelers as a source of strength to those of us still trying to make our way. See Stephanie Y. Evans's (2012) "Bone Song":

BONE SONG
Grandmother's African derivation: my birthright.
Sheba's songs vibrate, *ingrown*. Courageous *sojourn* wisdom.
Old Bones . . . under-girding *modern ambition*
I Sing of grandmother's marrow
Carrying Candace's blessings in my journey bag
Her bones . . . my tuning fork

The sample poems provided in the "Memoir" section of each chapter and the collection in Appendix B bring together life stories in numerous ways to travel beyond one's circumstances and envision oneself as a whole person, local hero, national leader, or global citizen.

Viewshare Library of Congress Online Resources

Education plays a key role in Black history and is universally recognized as a necessary stepping-stone to individual and social freedom. This principle is made clear in narratives. Whether struggling for literacy, building an

institutional haven of opportunity for others, or serving as a teacher or professor to create universes where students of all ages can embrace the value of
lifelong learning and reap the fruit of their own labor, school plays a special
part in collective autobiography. Especially rich are the comparative opportunities by those who studied overseas when they were young (Gayle Pemberton,
Pam Grier, and Barack Obama), as they offer alternative sites of elementary
education.

Education as a core value is central to Africans on the continent as well.
Of special import is the coming of age journey of William Kamkwamba who
wrote *The Boy Who Harnessed the Wind Creating Currents of Electricity and
Hope*. This young man has made a phenomenal future for himself, based on his
personal drive to learn physics, even though his only resources were limited
access to school and discarded physics textbooks from the 1970s. As with the

Fig. 3.1. *Black Passports: Black Travel Memoirs*. Online Resource. Stephanie Y.
Evans, Library of Congress, Viewshare. http://viewshare.org/views/drevans/
swag-diplomacy-black-travel-memoirs/.

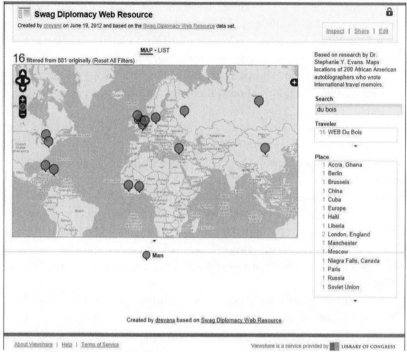

Fig. 3.2. *Black Passports: Black Travel Memoirs.* Online Resource. "W. E. B. Du Bois" search results. Stephanie Y. Evans, Library of Congress, Viewshare. http://viewshare. org/views/drevans/swag-diplomacy-black-travel-memoirs.

themes of education in early twentieth-century America, youth around the world are committed to, as the Clark Atlanta University mottos suggest "Find a Way or Make One" so that they can be a part of developing a "Culture for Service."[23]

Black Passports is constructed explicitly as a tool to enhance schooling as well as mentoring. In partnership with the Emory University Digital Humanities Center/Research Commons, I have created an online resource, which is available as a supplemental tool to this book. The Library of Congress created mapping software called Viewshare used to construct visual journeys of each of the authors. The result is an interactive online map with almost nine hundred individual plot points that can easily jumpstart youths' interest and understanding of geography.[24]

By viewing the searchable, expandable map, students can select a country and identify all of the authors who wrote about visiting that country in their autobiographies. Users can search by traveler, location, or even year. In addition to the cited location, a photo is provided as well as multiple links to online biographies that give an overview of the author's life and a link to their autobiography for reference. For instance, a search for "Du Bois" will yield a site map of sixteen international locations that Du Bois visited. By clicking on a location, additional information will pop up, including the dates and places he visited.

There are four companion bibliographic resources for this collection: blackpast.org, aaregistry.org, bio.com, and wikipedia.com, all of which offer young learners multimedia contexts for much of the material that is introduced in this volume. As Fanny Jackson Coppin wrote in her 1913 autobiography *Reminiscences of School Life and Hints on Teaching*, all education is self-directed education. Youth who have access to online resources or mentoring facilities have a unique opportunity to explore the world of travel through the universe of the Internet. However, as with any other learning tool, only those who are self-motivated to locate information about a person or place will gain full advantage.[25]

With the *Black Passports* curriculum, students in districts around the nation will benefit in that the bibliography represents four centuries, so temporal learning will be increased; the international data set provides natural opportunity to study geography; the plethora of occupations represented offers unprecedented range of choice in personal interest; the "personal interest" that Black students have will be reflected in the cultural identity of Black authors but also aid students of various racial and ethnic background by introducing several new figures for study beyond those presented during traditional Black History Month programming; and the spectrum of identities will underscore that African Americans are not a homogenous group and, in fact, have a wide array of interests, experiences, and perspectives.

Beyond elementary and secondary education, the process of gaining information literacy, defining independent research agendas, conducting research in library special collections, and submitting work for critical peer review conditions students to challenge their academic development at the highest levels. The 2010 University of Florida senior seminar course is a great example: James Haskins authored more than two hundred books for young readers, most biographies (Lena Horne and Michael Jackson) or co-authored autobiographies (Bricktop). Students in the seminar class accessed the James Haskins archives in UF Special Collections and produced a set of essays published by the UF Library.

The Haskins publication, featuring undergraduate papers, can be used as a template to incorporate young researchers into the process. The *Black Passports* vocabulary list can enhance research by conditioning new scholars to pay attention to structure as much as content when reading. By building on a stronger foundation of personal identity, enduring family challenges, and increasing their knowledge of history, geography, vocabulary, and writing, young adults will be better prepared to successfully handle career planning in their future.[26]

FOUR

WORK

Mastering Tasks (Macro)

I'm a travelin' man, movin' through places space and time
Think your life's hard workin' at your 9 to 5?
No matter what you do you can't imitate my grind
Twenty-four/seven love ain't that rough
When your career is your passion no that ain't enough
So when you hear me rappin it's like I'm makin love

I've been so many places in my life and time
And I know, this for sure, I'm a life, that's worth living
I've seen a lot of faces made a lot of moves
I'm international, because of you

—Talib Kweli, "Mister International"

MESSAGE: SELF-MASTERY AND COMPETENCE

In a *Reaching Up for Manhood* chapter called "Work," Geoffrey Canada recalls how summers gardening with his grandparents established his strong work ethic. Regardless of the work that authors have found as their calling, many narratives exemplify basic principles of excellence. What one chooses as a career matters, but the level of commitment and discipline to an area often determines the level of one's ability to sustain his or her work. Going about work in a willy-nilly fashion will unlikely produce sustainable results. The passion and commitment to a career can impact the degree to which a person's legacy in that chosen career will endure. In twenty years of higher education, I have often hated my job, but I have always loved my work. A multitude of narratives demonstrate that work can be more than a job; it can be a career if one builds one's labor on personal passions. As youth face the global economy (and the world has always been a global economy built on international trade), it is imperative that career preparation be a part of mentoring discussions.

Mastering self involves being a self-starter who is intrinsically motivated and has expectations above what others have for you. Mastering tasks means completing work within given timelines and with acute attention to detail. Mastering communication entails demonstrating written and oral communication skills to convey or exchange meaning. Mastering innovation means not only being adaptable to change and handling the stress of inevitable shifts in circumstances beyond your control, but also *creating* change around you and playing a part in moving beyond the status quo. This definition of self-mastery is infinitely useful to children who not only want to prepare for a job, but who also need to anticipate shifting circumstances in global markets and who must circumvent structural oppression in order to successfully manage inevitable hierarchies to move beyond being crushed by those markets.

This concept points to the practical outcomes of Tucker's ABCs. In *Manufacturing Powerlessness*, Green's survey of almost seven hundred children in Africa, the Caribbean, and the United States connected young people's desire to be mentored with a clear sense of need for guidance in career preparation. Accompanying this imperative is the need to more equitably manage labor markets to the benefit of the many rather than the few.

Many *Black Passports* authors made their life's work count. They practiced law to advocate for powerless clients or children (Florynce Kennedy and Marian Wright Edelman), served in politics to advance resources for their constituents (Adam Clayton Powell, Charles Rangel, and Andrew Young), and agitated for civil rights (Benjamin Mays, Dorothy Height, and Martin Luther King Jr.). Some advocated for health rights (Faye Wattleton) or advanced medical care through direct service (Rose-Marie Toussaint and Ben Carson), and some made their work in sports or entertainment also count for expanding human rights (Marian Anderson, Ossie Davis, Ruby Dee, Arthur Ashe, George Foreman, and Harry Belafonte). While some dedicated their lives to excellence, even if for their own satisfaction, many saw that it is possible to be successful as an individual and create opportunities for others to do so as well (Janet Bragg and Chuck D). Essentially, according to the six principles of business ethics by author Leon Sullivan, it is possible to "handle your business" in a way that is fun, rewarding, honorable, serious, and ethical.

Practical Guides and Useful Tools: Georgia Steppers League, Urban Debate League, Boys and Girls Club, Career Launch, Myplan.com

Organized co-curricular activities, including sports, are essential locations for youth to learn values and habits of self-discipline, communication, and leadership. The Georgia Stepper's League offers a truly unique example of a culturally based team sport that can enhance the lives of children and young adults. According to a PBS special on the topic, stepping, based on African group chants and dance, was developed by African American fraternities and sororities as a way to build brotherhood and sisterhood. The collective, rhythmic, and often-military drill-like performances employ cultural characteristics including call and response, repetition, and signification. As a Black art form that requires physical and mental discipline of individuals and a group, stepping has significant potential for developing skill sets that can ensure success in adult life.

The GSL program outline describes the league coaches for personal, physical and academic development:

The Georgia Steppers League (GSL©) is the Metro Atlanta pioneer organization dedicated solely to participants in local stepping programs where, in an accepting and nurturing environment, participants are able to build character, leadership skills, and enhance their academic performance in preparation for success in the real world. Through direct partnership with committed adult coaches, judges, mentors and educators, participating students develop qualities that will serve them all their lives, such as skills as performers, choreographers, leaders and team members while promoting healthy living through exercise and healthy eating choices. Founded in 2009 by former middle school step team coaches, the Georgia Steppers League's membership has grown from 8 founding teams and coaches in various Georgia counties, to over forty area teams boasting over 500 members throughout the state of Georgia.[1]

The GSL program emphasizes leadership and engages a popular business model of leadership mogul John Maxwell, who stresses development of character, consistency, and care for others as keys to fulfillment of one's leadership potential. GSL, like Black Greek letter organizations (BGLOs), also emphasizes service because, without a spirit of service, attempts to establish suitable leadership will fail.

The concept of leadership, or power, based on knowledge of self and character, is also presented in Susan Cain's *Quiet: The Power of Introverts in a World That Can't Stop Talking*. One of Cain's highlighted models is Rosa Parks, and she, rightly, frames Parks as a well-trained and deliberate civil rights worker who was purposeful in her participation both on the bus and in the ensuing lawsuit and boycott. At the core of what Cain identified as Parks' success was her conviction based on knowledge of self. The ability to manage one's self, particularly in hostile environments, is greatly dependent on knowledge and acceptance of self and dedication to improve the world for oneself and for others. It is conviction that powers confidence and sustainable progress. Programs like the Georgia Steppers League offer culturally based content and workplace-based structures needed for Black youth to increase probability of self-control and meaningful work options in local, national, and international contexts.

The National Association for Urban Debate Leagues exemplifies another impressive program, at the national level, also founded in Atlanta in 1985. Now operating in twenty-four cities serving 330,000 students, the NAUDL offers the ultimate in critical thinking experience through high school competitions. Trio programs, particularly Upward Bound and the Ronald E. McNair Scholars Program, which include summer research, are essential in preparing youth to think more clearly and learn about their own professions which can fuel the critical choice of a suitable future.[2]

In addition to Boys and Girls Clubs as national models for mentoring, these programs are useful resources. There are several career-planning sites available online. Boys and Girls Clubs of America offers a Career Launch resource with three features that distinguish between "job, college, and career" as points of reference. The site lists teen webinars, career interest assessments, links to connect with professionals, and search functions for career profiles. Of interest to mentors, agencies, parents, and teachers is the fact that five of eight profiles that kids loaded of themselves focused on animal care or veterinary medicine. This demonstrates a potential entry point to incorporate science into classrooms and a greater need to focus on what interests young minds: science. It also shows that there are not enough narratives about the pathways to these types of careers.

One of the most relevant and useful tools for career counselors is the Myplan website.[3] Not only is it searchable by college major or industry type, but it is also explicitly configured with portals for middle school, high school, college, and adult users. There are 902 careers defined, which contain salary information and video tutorials about each job. Utilizing the MyPlan site as a starting point for the purposes of this chapter, I list autobiographies in eight categories:

1. Politics and Law
2. Military
3. Journalism; Professional, Scientific, and Technical Services
4. Religion
5. Business, Finance and Insurance, Management of Companies and Enterprises
6. Arts, Entertainment, and Recreation
7. Health Care and Social Assistance
8. Educational Services

MEMOIRS: NARRATIVES OF WORK

Beyond a technical "how-to" guide for careers, autobiographies provide gripping portraits of intimate details involved in career choice. Below are listings of possible narratives in each profession with a brief synopsis of sample stories to pique young readers' interest.

Politics and Law: Mifflin Gibbs, Condoleezza Rice, Frederick Douglass, Barack Obama, Andrew Young, Charles Rangel, Robert Williams, John Mercer Langston, Adam Clayton Powell

Early political narratives include John Mercer Langston (great-uncle to Langston Hughes), a state representative. Langston began his life on a Virginia plantation in 1829; he was not enslaved because he was born free to a free mother. He became the first dean of Howard University Law School before serving as president of Virginia State University and, ultimately, holding office in the U.S. House of Representatives for the state of Virginia in 1890. There were significant antecedents to those of contemporary politicos like Condoleezza Rice. Rice penned a life-encompassing political tome—766 pages of great detail. In her memoir, she reveals private feelings during public moments, including her involvement in the team to secure the election of George W. Bush, her appointment as national security advisor in 2000, and her first European trip abroad as George W. Bush's secretary of state, appointed in 2005. She gives insight into her actions and reactions surrounding major international affairs from the attacks on September 11, 2001, to the 2008 financial crisis. Her singular, goal-oriented approach to securing America's place in international affairs is so encompassing, Rice reveals virtually no personal details about her upbringing, education, work at Stanford, or any significant details of her private or professional life before the White House. She reserved those details for writing elsewhere, but her professional memoir should be read carefully as a record of how to define and redefine one's labor legacy.

Rice writes at the end of her account, "As Secretary of State I was always aware of the constraints of the world as it is and resolved to practice the art of the possible . . . This is the long-term work of diplomacy. History will judge how well we did. I can live with that, and I am grateful for the chance to have tried."[4] Her attempts at diplomacy covered ground from New Orleans during Hurricane Katrina to international relations in such delicate terrain as Europe, China, India, North Korea, Iraq, Iran, the Middle East, Latin America, Palestine, and Russia, and she counts it an honor to have been a participant in such work.

The immense chasm among Black American political ideologies cannot be overstated. Black Americans' political views have run the gamut. These include communist and socialist (from Harry Heywood, Paul Robeson, W. E. B. Du Bois, and Angela Davis) and Republican conservative (George Schuyler, Pearl Bailey, Lionel Hampton, Sammy Davis Jr., Colin Powell, and Condoleezza Rice). The topic of political ideology and Black identity is, literally, an open book for students desiring an in-depth education on the subject. Regardless of the political stances Black Americans have taken or will take in the future, President Barack Obama represents the promise of democracy that civil rights activists sought to fulfill: the right to vote and hold office. Of course, political views will largely impact interpretation of players in political history.

In the area of law, authors include Edward Brooke, Florynce Kennedy, Jacqueline Regis, Roger Wilkins, Marian Wright Edelman, Pauli Murray, Barack Obama, Paul Robeson, Randall Robinson, and Patricia Williams. Several of these authors attended and taught at very prestigious law schools, including Columbia, Harvard, and Yale. They offer insight into the many types of legal work, whether traditional courtroom, nonprofit, or advocacy, all much needed primers for law students today. To contrast contemporary political participation, readers can consider the stories of Adam Clayton Powell and Colin Powell to understand the rich texture and nuanced complexity of national and international affairs. Adam Clayton Powell's *Adam by Adam* connects elected officials from the Reconstruction Era (John Mercer Langston in Virginia) to current day politicians (Charles Rangel), which will help students understand current political battles in the Harlem district.

Military: Charity Earley, Colin Powell, Charles Dryden, Alexander Jefferson, Robert F. Williams, Gail Harris, Benjamin Gould, Coleman Young, Adam Clayton Powell, Berry Gordy

One of the most compelling early military histories is Benjamin Gould's story of commandeering a ship during the Civil War, which he used to free himself and seven others. Gould escaped from a peanut plantation in North Carolina and then joined the U.S. Navy where he served until 1865. Five of his sons fought in World War I and one son in the Spanish-American War, providing a sketch of one of the earliest and most dedicated American military families.

As a political structure, the military also presents opportunities for critical observation. In particular, integration of the military and the commitment of Black Americans to serve their country can be seen through the life work of career officers like Charity Earley and Colin Powell. U.S. Army general Colin Powell's career became possible because of the military strides gained by those before him: Black veterans of the American Revolution and Civil War; Henry O. Flipper, the first Black graduate of West Point; and the Tuskegee Airmen. Interestingly, at least three Tuskegee Airmen have penned autobiographies: Alexander Jefferson (*Red Tail Captured, Red Tail Free*), Charles Dryden (*A-Train*), and Coleman Young (*Hard Stuff*).

Powell's two Purple Hearts for service in Vietnam, ascension to the rank of army general, and appointment as secretary of state is painstakingly chronicled in *My American Journey*. The details of federal decision-making processes demonstrate that there are no simple answers, especially when dealing with international conflict in Vietnam, Panama, and Iraq; political and humanitarian questions in Somalia, Bosnia, or Haiti; or lightning-rod domestic issues such as gays in the military—which he opposed.[5]

When measuring the trajectory of advancements in rights for African Americans within his lifetime, Powell noted the drastic change from his initial assignment at Fort Benning, Georgia, in 1964 to his post as a highly decorated military honoree:

The town was typical of the Old South, a part of America where we were not allowed to live in a decent neighborhood; where after fighting in Vietnam I was refused service at a hamburger joint; where a state trooper could call an Army officer "boy" and tell him to get out of town. Twenty-eight years later, Alma and I were going back to Phenix City [sic] to the dedication of the General Colin L. Powell Parkway, which intersected with Dr. Martin Luther King, Jr. Parkway. . . . I had seen a street named after me where, previously, I would not have been allowed to walk freely. We had persevered, and we had lived the American dream.[6]

Powell, who identifies himself as a Republican with a similar political position to George W. Bush's Vice President Dick Cheney, saw his military journey as one of fulfillment, and his rules for life reflect his embrace of "perpetual optimism" as a tactic in political and personal realms.[7]

Women's military service is also an area of exploration. A century after Susie King Taylor's chronicle of her role in the Civil War, Charity Earley recounts her desegregation of the Women's Army Corps during World War II, and Gail Harris chronicles her role in the navy in *A Woman's War: The Professional and Personal Journey of the Navy's First African American Female Intelligence Officer*. Following her father's path, Harris reveals her innermost reactions to a life spent on a submarine, quarantined in male-dominated close quarters. Her relationship with her father provided necessary skills and support to cope and eventually succeeded as an "only" Black woman in several ranks.

Journalism: Ida B. Wells, Belva Davis, Era Bell Thompson, George Schuyler, Frank Marshall Davis, Jake LaMar, Magnificent Montague, Claude McKay, Langston Hughes, Walter White, W. E. B. Du Bois, Alex Haley

In the tradition of Ida B. Wells and political journalism, Belva Davis's *Never in My Wildest Dreams* provides a chronological and geographic pictorial of politics from her perspective as both an insider and an outsider. Though Davis was not an elected official or military participant, her role as the first African American woman news anchor on the West Coast put her at the front lines of major national news. Her memoir gives students a significant peek at California politics through media news, and her work is invaluable for studying well-known events featuring Martin Luther King Jr. as well as the housing discrimination that baseball great Willie Mays faced when he lived in San

Francisco. Davis also broke barriers as a woman within media and communications, waging an aggressive career campaign, which landed her with impressive credentials to cover jaw-dropping news stories: Barry Goldwater and the 1964 Republican Convention; University of California Berkeley campus demonstrations for women's rights; the 1978 murder of Harvey Milk (the nation's first openly gay elected official) and San Francisco Mayor George Moscone; the 1979 trials of Black Panther Huey P. Newton and an interview with him in Cuba; an interview with Jim Jones of People's Temple two years before the 1978 Guyana mass suicide-murder; Alex Haley's completion of the television production of his best-selling novel *Roots*; Emmy-winning interviews with Fidel Castro in 1977; and international coverage of stories in Kenya, Tanzania, South Africa, Cote d'Ivoire, and Israel.

Davis's summation of her role as an eyewitness reporter to political history resembles that of Colin Powell and Condoleezza Rice: satisfaction and gratitude. She wrote, "I've witnessed so many changes in my lifetime—in the world, and in me. My Louisiana parents could not have imagined that the baby they named Belvagene would have such a full and fascinating life in front of her." Yet she sees herself as part of an ongoing story. Davis admits that she has both doubts and dreams, but she challenges readers to weigh our lives on the side of dreams: "What holds most of us back is not that our dreams are too big—it's that they are too small. Dreams and hopes of political progression are a large part of the African American experience and activist-journalists have been central to that progression."[8]

Radical Black journalism has deep roots in the works of Frank Marshall Davis and Magnificent Montague. Marshall, an editor for the Associated Negro Press, was a jazz reporter, political editorialist, and poet who moved from Kansas City to Chicago before permanently settling in Hawaii in 1948. Montague served in the Merchant Marines during World War II and then worked in Chicago, New York, and Los Angeles as a disc jockey. He began a radio show on which he would make "burn, baby burn" his call sign for smokin' hot music before it became the rallying cry for the 1965 Watts Riots. In a time before the Internet, Montague's life as a DJ placed him at the center of communication in a way easily replicated by enterprising young media hopefuls with limitless mobile Internet capabilities. Both Montague and Davis hint at the rewarding extended definitions of journalism that await young scholars who take the time to investigate off the beaten path.

Many authors wrote as correspondents for newspapers or magazines during their travel. As noted in previous chapters, Era Bell Thompson chronicled her multicountry African tour as a serial for *Ebony* magazine. Like Claude

McKay, Langston Hughes, Walter White, and W. E. B. Du Bois, Thompson's travel provided ongoing drama in several publications read by those from Harlem to Hollywood. Jake LaMar, a writer for the *Washington Post* who tired of the racism in the industry during the 1980s and chronicled his climb in the industry in his *Bourgeois Blues*, moved to Paris like James Baldwin and Richard Wright before him. He has built a career as a novelist and mystery writer, but he currently maintains his work as an international journalist, recently contributing online to outlets including *The Root* magazine, a subsidiary of the *Washington Post*.

Religion: Fanny Jackson Coppin, Jan Willis, Dorothy Height, Mahalia Jackson, Pauli Murray, Benjamin Mays, Martin Luther King Jr., Malcolm X, Zilpha Elaw, Cornel West

In the history of higher education, theology holds a respected position as a profession. Though few guidance counselors may focus on this area as a career path, religion remains deeply entrenched in autobiographical memory in interesting ways. Combining religion and education was a clear option in the life of Fanny Jackson Coppin, who was a teacher and principal at the Institute for Colored Youth in Philadelphia before accompanying her husband, Levi Coppin, to South Africa. Connections between religion and education were also clear in the lives of Howard Thurman (Howard University and Boston University) and Benjamin Mays (Morehouse College). These two towering figures are essential reading for students of Historically Black Colleges and Universities (HBCUs) in Atlanta and Washington, D.C., and hold keys to breaking the code of troubles in "urban education."

Other examples of how religion and education intersect abound in autobiography. Jan Willis turned her personal commitment to exploring Buddhism and her Baptist roots into a career as a religion professor at Wesleyan University. In a reversal of career path, Pauli Murray moved from working as a professor at Brandeis to becoming the first woman Episcopal priest ordained in the nation, presiding over services at Holy Nativity Church in Baltimore, Maryland. While many served as traditional missionaries (Amanda Smith, William Shepherd, and Zilpha Elaw), Mahalia Jackson professed her faith through gospel music and, in doing so, shone her light on the world. Jackson, a powerful female voice heard singing "How I Got Over" at the 1963 March on Washington, is thus intimately connected with others in the civil rights movement, including Benjamin Mays, Martin Luther King Jr. (at whose funeral she sang in 1968), Malcolm X, Leon Sullivan, and Julius Lester.

Of course, Martin Luther King Jr. and Malcolm X are inextricably linked in social movements in the same way that W. E. B. Du Bois is in the educational realm. However, beyond the social and political investigations, King and Malcolm X's narratives lend themselves to deep exploration of religious philosophy in the lives of African American men.

Business: William Wells Brown, Ada Bricktop Smith, Leon Sullivan, Arthur Ashe, John Johnson, Janet Bragg, Frederick Morrow, Bill Russell, Chuck D, Ray Charles, Booker T. Washington, Jeff Henderson

The narratives offer divergent business models in entertainment, ethics, and fashion that are sure to spark interest in readers. Bricktop Smith owned a nightclub in Paris and Rome, which operated as a central gathering place in the hottest time of the Jazz Age. While the Harlem Renaissance was raging in New York, Bricktop's raged in Montmartre fueling the flames of international cultural exchange and the spread of jazz globally. Her papers, housed at Emory University, surely provide primary source documents that, when paired with her intriguing story, can easily become groundbreaking research for aspiring scholars of any age.

In *Moving Mountains*, Leon Sullivan's principles connected ethical focus of religion in real-world environments. He pushed for antiapartheid business practices and divestment in South Africa, which impacted the direction of that country. The principles mandate:

1. Nonsegregation of the races in all eating, comfort, and work facilities.
2. Equal and fair employment practices for all employees.
3. Equal pay for all employees doing equal or comparable work for the same period of time.
4. Initiation of and development of training programs that will prepare, in substantial numbers, blacks and other nonwhites for supervisory, administrative, clerical, and technical jobs.
5. Increasing the number of blacks and other nonwhites in management and supervisory positions.
6. Improving the quality of life for blacks and other nonwhites outside the work environment in such areas as housing, transportation, school, recreation, and health facilities.
7. Working to eliminate laws and customs that impede social, economic, and political justice. (This was added in 1984.)[9]

As a manual for corporate codes of conduct, this text should be required reading for junior achievement programs at least but is surely needed in college business courses as well.

Last, John Johnson's empire is relevant, not only because of his use of media resulting in *Ebony* and *JET* magazines, but because his narrative ends with a story of passing his wealth and media institutions to his daughter Linda. Johnson's detailing of his daughter's education (a degree in journalism at University of Southern California and an MBA from Northwestern University) and her marriage (encouraged by him) to a Goldman Sachs stockbroker cries out for analysis from young readers who seek to understand class in America. Johnson boasts about the elaborate nature of the wedding, which offers insight into discussions of intergenerational wealth, but also hints to his philosophy of expansion into markets such as beauty projects (Ebony Fashion Fair), which bolstered his initial magazine business. These discussions of ethics, culture, entertainment, and capitalism—when read together—provide yet another exciting opportunity for comparative reflection and practical, professional preparation.

Arts and Entertainment: Singers (Pearl Bailey, Marian Anderson, Billie Holiday, Diana Ross, Mary Wilson, Chuck D, Nina Simone); Dancers/ Theater Artists (Judith Jamison, Katherine Dunham, Cholly Atkins, Zora Neale Hurston, Celia Cruz, Sherly Verrett, Maya Angelou); Athletes (Althea Gibson, Arthur Ashe, Willie Mays, Hank Aaron, Willie O'Ree, Bill Russell, Lisa Leslie, Gabrielle Douglass, Wilt Chamberlain, Jeff Commings); Actors/ Entertainers (Ozzie Davis, Ruby Dee, Angela Bassett, Courtney Vance, Paul Robeson, Sidney Poitier, Pam Grier, RuPaul); Artists (Faith Ringgold)

From Major Taylor, a world-class cyclist in the 1900s, to Wilma Rudolf, an Olympic track star of the 1950s, athletes have struggled to keep their careers financially solvent. Any would-be athlete who does not wish to retire with fewer resources than when she or he was at the top of the game will necessarily read the history of economics in Black sports.

Of sports memoir genres, boxing clearly has the most contributors: Jack Johnson, Muhammad Ali, Joe Louis, Joe Frazier, Sugar Ray Robinson, Laila Ali, Mike Tyson, and George Foreman. These clearly deserve close comparison and can excite young audiences, especially those in all male settings like the Florida Reichert House program for boys. Yet there are less popular sports that cover unconventional ground but are equally exciting. Sports figures are prominent within the genre of autobiography, so Jackie Robinson's story is surrounded by a constellation of voices that will undoubtedly resonate with youth who are often more connected with the sports and entertainment world than with adults. Building on the cavalcade of "firsts" like that of Jackie Robinson, struggles against racism when desegregating "America's" sport in 1947, baseball players like Willie Mays and Hank Aaron show the extended struggles of Black athletes to enter certain sports. When Hank Aaron approached the home run record of Babe Ruth, instead of enthusiastic support from the baseball world, he and his family received hate mail and death threats.

Willie O'Ree, a Canadian and one of the first Black players in the National Hockey League, struggled through such public humiliation as hockey fanatics throwing bananas and a black cat on the ice during games. This narrative offers an inside look at international racism while simultaneously opening doors to a virtually undiscovered world of opportunity: hockey. Similarly, tennis and swimming figures are excellent areas of sport study, particularly via Arthur Ashe and Jeff Commings. Arthur Ashe is not only required reading for his dominance of the sport of tennis, but he also studied the history of sport and produced three volumes on African Americans in sport that is a must read for any serious program looking to combine interest in sports with increased academic competence. Ashe also overtly connected his sport to political agitation in complicated ways. He rallied for antiapartheid demonstrations but then also became a health activist when he was diagnosed with AIDS after heart surgery. His health issue forced him to learn about race and AIDS, and he became a crucial ally in the fight against homophobia. On the heels of Arthur Ashe's advocacy for not equating AIDS with homosexuality and not discriminating against gay and lesbian athletes, Jeff Commings's *Odd Man Out* breaches new and necessary terrain. Commings is not only a professional swimmer and Olympic hopeful, but a gay Black man who insisted on participating in the sport on his own terms.

The entertainment industry offers as many dramatic tales as the sports world. Opera singer Marian Anderson's most well-known challenge came when she was scheduled to sing at Constitution Hall in Washington, D.C., on Easter Sunday, 1939. The Daughters of the American Revolution, who controlled the scheduling of the hall, refused to let her sing there, as the policy stated that only White performers would be allowed to appear. Anderson's manager Sol Hurok worked with First Lady Eleanor Roosevelt and Secretary of the Interior Harold Ickes so that she could appear before a crowd of seventy-five thousand people on the steps of the Lincoln Memorial. She remembered little of that day because she was overwhelmed with "a feeling that a great wave of good will poured out from these people, almost engulfing me."[10]

Marian Anderson's fight against discrimination has been well noted in her famous concert on the Washington Mall in 1939, but she fought through many indignities before that famous day: when arriving to seek an application to an unnamed music school in Philadelphia, she was simply told, "We don't take colored."[11] In a chapter titled "Shock" she wrote,

> There were other shocks to come. Though I was prepared for them, so I thought, the contact with reality never ceased to have its disturbing impact. Mother had grown up in Virginia and we had friends who had come from farther south, so I had heard about Jim Crow, but meeting it bit deeply into the soul. I was still in high school when I took my first long trip to participate in a gala concert. . . . At Washington we changed trains, and this time our bags were taken to the first coach—the Jim Crow car![12]

Anderson notes the separate waiting rooms and eating facilities, exclusion from hotels (even when she received the "key to the city" in New Jersey), and policies requiring segregated audiences.

She recalls being disrespected by venue owners who addressed her by her first name when others were granted respect by use of family names. All of these things grated on her sense of justice, and though she would decline the title "activist," at the Lincoln Memorial concert, in her final chapter, "Looking Forward," she presented a challenge to America to overcome the racist practices of segregation and discrimination that had cast a shadow over most of her life, despite her great success. The most biting comment of the narrative is her unyielding sense of loss, "Things are changing in our country, and I am hopeful. But I cannot suppress a private regret. I still wish that I could have gone to music school."[13]

Anderson insists that her contralto voice should be remembered as much as the spaces cleared by the use of her voice. She makes special note that she eventually appeared several times at Constitution Hall . . . because she is an artist and appearing at venues is what artists do. Also in position as the first African American to sing with the Metropolitan Opera in New York on January 7, 1955, she consistently walked through barriers with grace and a marked measure of gratitude. Though she presented herself as a person who did not do "hand to hand combat" for civil rights, with her dignified persona she created opportunities for those who came after her to be duly recognized in the United States and abroad (both Leontyne Price and Diana Ross listed her as an inspiration).[14]

In a *Secrets of the Sparrow* chapter called "Down and Dirty," Diana Ross recalls the profound impact Emmett Till's 1955 murder, portrayed in *JET* magazine, had on her understanding of the violent racism of the American South. The message was hammered home when a relative of hers from Bessemer, Alabama, was found dead: "To this day, we all believe that my cousin Virginia Ruth was murdered by the Ku Klux Kan. We thought that she had been in a car accident, but there were no skid marks, no marks on the car—just her body on the side of the road." Ross also recalls touring with the Supremes and not being able to eat at restaurants or stay in certain hotels, and when they tried to integrate a concert hall in Macon, Georgia, a sniper shot up the tour bus: "When we got far enough away for our hearts to stop pounding, we saw that the shots had gone right through the metal, hit the glass window, and the entire front of the bus was full of tiny shotgun pellets."[15]

Outside the United States, musicians gained much ground. Dizzy Gillespie's jazz legacy is one of an ambassador for the United States. In 1956 Gillespie led a State Department-sponsored tour, and his nonstop international touring schedule is a prime example of the geographic possibilities of tracing the globe through one person's life. He toured Europe four times in his early career and was constantly touring from the 1940s to the 1990s. In 1988, he gave three hundred performances in twenty-seven countries, appeared in one hundred U. S. cities and thirty-one states and Washington D.C., and headlined Carnegie Hall in 1992 for his seventy-fifth birthday, his thirty-second appearance there. But Celia Cruz's narrative complicates international issues even further.

Cruz, born in Cuba, might not usually be addressed in discussions of "African American" culture and thus presents a salient opportunity to discuss nation and definitions of race in the United States. But beyond the citizenship and race discussion, Cruz's life and work promise students a deeper understanding of the term "diaspora" because of the conduit of Cruz's culture: salsa music. Salsa, as an intermingling of African, indigenous American Indian, and Latin American rhythms, maps itself onto the spirit of Celia Cruz. Maya Angelou wrote the introduction to her autobiography, so we see that cultural connections run deep in unexpected places.

While Chuck D and Sandy Denton will resonate with aficionados of the hip hop generation, the fact that hip hop has evolved much since the 1980s means that these narratives are very much "history" for the youth of the second decade of the new millennium. Chuck D's *Fight the Power* includes a deeply touching comment on the impact of his visit to Africa: much like Richard Pryor a decade before, he understood for the first time the way that use of the word "nigger" spreads like a virus to places unseen and can deteriorate the very humanity of Black people far off American shores.

Health: Rose-Marie Toussaint, Susie King Taylor, Janet Bragg, Faye Wattleton, Claudia Lynn Thomas, Ben Carson, Mae Jemison, Jeff Henderson

Ben Carson has, for numerous youth, come to represent the epitome of self-discipline and the heights of educational possibility. The reverence for his work in the field of medicine is widely recognized and brings the thrill of science into clear focus at a time when it has been stated as a national priority. Carson worked in a postresidency program in Australia and learned quite a bit about international medicine when he perfected his brain surgery skills during his tenure at Gardiner hospital in Perth. He anticipated some resistance to his work, given the apartheid-like history of Australia, but he actually received access to opportunities to participate in intensive surgeries, which helped to hone his neurosurgical craft, that he would have never gotten in an American hospital.

Carson's national and international training resulted in his taking on ever-increasing risky surgeries. After years of work in pediatrics performing hemispherectomies and separating *cranio pagus* conjoined twins (joined at the cranium), Carson even delivered his second son at home.

A public figure on Carson's level, Mae Jemison is well known as an astronaut. Yet, few focus on her medical degree. In her narrative, *Find Where the Wind Goes*, she recalls growing up in Chicago and stating explicitly, as a young girl, "I want to be a scientist."[16] Like the teacher's negative reaction to Malcolm X when he said he wanted to be a lawyer, Jemison was subject to discouraging remarks. She remained determined to study science and eventually decided on the medical field. Adamant that she had no intention of becoming a nurse, Jemison graduated from medical school and pursued her every professional whim from serving in the Peace Corps to becoming the first Black woman astronaut, holding nine honorary doctorates and even making a cameo appearance on *Star Trek: The Next Generation* in 1993. Like Jemison, Dr. Ainissa Ramirez of Yale University carries a passion for science to young audiences. She is a material scientist who continues her research agenda, but who also tours the country as a science evangelist turning kids on to the wonders of science. She grounds her cultural self in her intellectual self: her Twitter name is @blkgrlphd, and she, like Jamison, also cited Nichelle Nichols, the *Star Trek* character Lt. Uhura as a childhood idol.

Dr. Ronald E. McNair, a laser physicist and astronaut who was killed in the *Challenger* space shuttle tragedy, had a love for science, and his legacy lives on through the McNair Program to prepare minority college students for graduate school. Thousands of college students are studying to earn a PhD and follow in his footsteps. I was a McNair scholar as an undergraduate at California State University-Long Beach, and like I say in several talks with college students preparing for graduate school, if you work for McNair, the McNair Program will work for you. Dr. McNair's family is carrying on his legacy and name, ensuring that the opportunity remains available and, in addition to the TRIO programs highlighted in the previous chapter, is a component of youth being informed of careers outside the normative or popular work areas. Regardless of the chosen field youth decide to explore, hard work is mandatory for sustained success. As two exemplars show, whether in the kitchen or in a spaceship, attention to detail, passion, and perseverance will be required. Whatever your work, bring your "A game."

.*. .*. .*.

Jeff Henderson

Cooked. From the Streets to the Stove, from Cocaine to Foie Gras (2007). Mexico, 1986.

"Twelve Steps Away from Ten Years of Hard Time"
56-grams of sugar tastes sweeter
Than 56-grams of coke at Mexican boarder
And, though expensive, costs less

Mae Jemison

Find Where the Wind Goes: Moments from My Life (2001). Liberia 1983–85; Space 1992.

NASA afros and African science
Sporting Chi-town smile. Migrant dancer-doctor commands questions
*Endeavor*ing: finding the real thing

Jeff Henderson and Mae Jemison's life stories show that control of self, communication, tasks, and innovation can take you deep inside the human brain or to the far reaches of space. It is essential to stress that even those, like Henderson, who do not have a linear path to success can rise and lift others through focused, strategic, and determined decision making about controlling one's own labor. As Geoffrey Canada stated and Jeff Henderson's rise from a prison cell to Caesar's Palace head chef demonstrates, work ethic is a principle element to success. But the ultimate cornerstone is education. In terms of "grind," two of the most inspiring examples are Jeff Henderson and Mae Jemison. Making a living doing what you love is a blessing in life, and those like Nat Love, James Beckourth, Mathew Henson, Nancy Prince, and Juanita Harrison, who chose to be self-employed, adventurers, or social advocates give being an entrepreneur a new twist. However, the mainstream approach to sustainable success most often requires a path through higher education.

Education

As indicated in several chapters, many authors chose to be educators and are responsible for the growth of generations of young scholars. As teachers, administrators, and college professors, Angela Davis, Colleen McElroy, Booker T. Washington, W. E. B. Du Bois, Reverend Morgan Latta, Robert Moton, William Sanders Scarborough, Septima Poinsette Clark, John Hope Franklin, and Samuel Kelly groomed their students to excel. As demonstrated through their mentees in the first chapter, Katherine Dunham and Dizzy Gillespie also formalized the teaching of their crafts, connecting structured learning outside of school walls.

One of my mottoes is "grind *then* polish." Too many people focus on the surface façade of their image and miss the need to stay on task at all points of a career, no matter how high you ascend up the ladder of your field. Here, as with the course syllabi provided online, I offer my writing in the profession as an illustration of life as a university professor to assist those in secondary education who are seeking a bridge to college. As a person who chose education as a career, I share my ideas about the profession.

Model: A Memoir of Lifelong Learning, Research, Teaching, and Service

Anna Julia Cooper earned her doctoral degree from the Sorbonne University in Paris at the age of sixty-five, and in a ceremony at Howard University commemorating that 1925 event, she wrote that everyone has a "right to grow." Like Cooper, I have chosen a life of learning and continued growth through higher education. Accordingly, I have engaged many authors in my definition of the three pillars of academia: research, teaching, and service. I did not know anyone with a PhD when I was growing up, so hopefully the glimpse of writing below will compel others to consider a career in the life of the mind. At the very least, the trivium of research, teaching, and service will offer insight into the driving force behind my compulsion to collect and codify two hundred Black travel memoirs.

An Empowerment Education Research Philosophy

Here, I submit reflections on "research" written for the McNair Scholars Program, summer 2007 course on which I have built my professional investigations: It seems to me that "research" is a combination of art, science, and policy. The researcher's cultural identity, values, and ethics are implicated in each step of inquiry, from forming the question and defining terms to selecting data and interpreting results. Given this observation, my personal definition of research is based on propositions from the following sources: James Baldwin, Zora Neale Hurston, and historic Black women educators like Anna Julia Cooper, Mary McLeod Bethune, and Willa Player.

Research as Art—James Baldwin

In "The Creative Process" (originally published in 1962), Baldwin wrote:

> Perhaps the primary distinction of the artist is that he must actively cultivate the state which most men, necessarily, must avoid: being alone . . . the conquest of the physical world is not man's only duty. He is also enjoined to conquer the great wilderness of himself. The precise role of the artist, then, is to illuminate that darkness . . . so that we will not, in all our doing lose sight of its purpose, which is, after all, to make the world a more human dwelling place. . . . The artist cannot and must not take anything for granted, but must drive to the heart of every answer and expose the question the answer hides. . . . I am really trying to make clear the nature of the artist's responsibility to his society. . . . It is for this reason that all societies have battled with the incorrigible disturber of the peace—the artist. We become social creatures because we cannot live any other way. . . . And we cannot learn this unless we are willing to tell the truth about ourselves, and the truth about us is always at variance with what we wish to be. The human effort is to bring these two realities into a relationship

resembling reconciliation. . . . The dangers of being an American artist are not greater than those of being an artist anywhere else in the
world, but they are very particular. These dangers are produced by
our history . . . [W]hoever cannot tell himself the truth about his past
is trapped in it. . . . Societies never know it, but the war of an artist
with his society is a lover's war, and he does, at his best, what lovers
do, which is to reveal the beloved to himself and, with that revelation,
to make freedom real.[17]

I see three main similarities in how Baldwin describes the artist and how
I imagine the doctoral and professional researcher. Truly original thought
requires solitude. Though the best research is collaborative, a productive collaboration will require that each partner bring unique perspectives to the
work. This original intellectual production is hard, much like the tortured
poet or painter attempting to make a new statement.

Second, researchers who are producing work that unsettles the status quo
(particularly those that challenge White or male supremacy) are often perse-
cuted, as are artists. I think of Galileo's monumental fight against the Catholic
Church. I think of the innumerable metaphysical, mathematical, and medical
solutions that were lost when Alexander "the Great" and his European succes-
sors burned, destroyed, and dismissed the valuable research of Egypt, Timbuktu, and many other African nations. As in the past, we see today, through
examples of Mali and Timbuktu, that to attack a culture, invaders will seek
to denigrate a country's women and then decimate its libraries. I think of
the retaliation women receive when producing scholarship that challenges the
"conventional" wisdom of male thinkers. And yet, we must write, as artists
must create—alone in many ways, if speaking truth to power, or when simply
speaking truth.

A final comparison of art and scholarship lies in the potential of scholarship to help free its society from excessive prejudice, discrimination, and
malice. I believe that the academy cannot produce social solutions any more
than political leaders can—only the general public made of all professions can
create a just society. Certainly, much of the best writing happens *outside* of formal educational institutions. However, the academy is a critical site that offers
space and time to engage ideas useful to the general public. Research, when
contextualized by an honest assessment of social, political, and national pasts,
has the ability to advance the cause of universal human freedom and much-
needed social justice. However, without a critical look at historical antecedents

that have produced today's problems, researchers will be powerless to come up with answers that provide a viable or sustainable future.

The creative process of research—as art—represents infinite possibilities. Research, as art, can be as beautiful, sensual, grotesque, and moving as human beings ourselves.

Research as Science—Zora Neale Hurston

In my book *Black Women in the Ivory Tower*, I consider Hurston's work as a scholar. A graduate of Barnard College and a graduate student at Columbia University, she is often only regarded as a novelist. I write:

> Anthropologist Gwendolyn Mikell rightly observed that because Hurston did not finish her [doctoral] degree, she is generally recognized for her literary production instead of for her formal research. This trend ignores her scholarly processes. "Research," Hurston explained in *Dust Tracks*, "is formalized curiosity." While collecting stories, she was insatiably conscious in her approach, recorded discrepancies with expected results, and formulated unique methodological strategies; she was well read, well trained, and focused; yet her writing was regarded as more hapless than scholarly. Regardless of how she revered [her advisor Franz] Boas for his objectivity, her methodology for communicating with locals was what later scholars would call "subjective ethnography" and "reflexive" study. According to Hurston, the more a researcher related to the content of the study, the more accurate and rich the analysis. Conventional practice—scientific objectivity—ran counter to this approach. After gathering data in Florida, Haiti, and Jamaica, Hurston's excellent artistic product (most notably *Their Eyes*) proved the value of her scholarly process.[18]

Hurston's practice of research allows us to understand that a subjective approach to data collection and interpretation can, in fact, be organized, valid, and formal. Ultimately, there must be a balance of subjective and objective aspects of qualitative and quantitative approaches. Formal inquiry requires rigor; it does not, however, require rejection of any association to the object under review.

As the authors of *Practical Research: Planning and Design* note, "the scientific method" involves identifying a problem, positing a hypothesis that may resolve the problem, gathering data, then analyzing and interpreting the data to see if they support the hypothesis in solving the problem.[19] Scientific processes involve the following:

Consistency and discipline
Survey of relevant literature and prior research
Methods that can be replicated and repeated
Relational measurement
Evaluative measurement
Position or argument that others can verify

Some of these aspects are present in art, but science, unlike art, requires validity and reliability. Art too requires a certain type of validity—the audience must validate art—but, for some artists, that part is optional. In contrast, science demands verification: in natural, physical, and social sciences, formalized process of review is integral. Though science is kin to art in the end of social applicability, it is measurably different in its means: artists must originate ideas internally; scientists must originate ideas relative to other scientists. Good researchers will find the balance and use the creative forces of both art and science in their work.

Research as Policy—Historic Black Women Educators

In my publications, I argue that "Anna Cooper, Mary Bethune, and their contemporaries articulated educational philosophies that had four central themes: demand for applied learning; recognition of the importance of social standpoint and cultural identity in scholarship; a critical epistemology that both supported and resisted mainstream American ideals; and moral existentialism grounded in a sense of communal responsibility." Because of Black women's subjugated position (based on the intersection of race and gender which limited their economic class), their ideas were more likely to be dedicated to alleviating social disparities. There was a tension between the elitism inherent in academic endeavors and the democratic current driven by their community identity, yet historic Black women researchers provide a model for connecting scholarly research to social justice.[20]

Though contemporary researchers must ultimately decide on their own disciplinary, philosophical, theoretical, and methodological approaches, it is essential that each scholar understand the political implications of research. No matter how remote the lab or abstract the idea, a researcher's production will impact social mores, practices, or policy. Scholars must recognize the potentially damaging application their work might have and formulate their ideas with politics in mind. Either your work will be used to further social disparities or to alleviate them . . . as Howard Zinn has said, "you can't be neutral on a moving train." There is no such thing as apolitical research.[21] If researchers do not love humanity more than themselves, their findings will be deadly.

For me, research is an individual creative process, a formal approach to asking and answering questions, and a means to improve the quality of social and civic life. Academic and intellectual work provides scholars an opportunity to connect the innermost mind with all that exists in the past, present, and future.

I believe a scholar's existence—reading, thinking, writing, *and* acting to apply ideas toward improving the quality of life—is a merciful consolation for the significant limitations of our human condition.

An Empowerment Education Teaching Philosophy

My approach to teaching derives from my research agenda. As a historian who studies African American women's educational and intellectual history, I have melded my personal experiences in the college classroom (since I began in 2001) with the insights gleaned from Black women educators like Fanny Jackson Coppin, Anna Julia Cooper, Mary McLeod Bethune, and Septima Clark. These four women in particular, whom I studied for my dissertation, were educators between the 1860s and 1960s who were effective, efficient, and dedicated. Reflecting on their pedagogical wisdom was essential in translating and transforming my own teaching. Katherine Dunham, a scholar-educator-activist, identified four essential aspects of creative teaching and provided a roadmap for what I call "empowerment education": humanization, socialization, professionalization, and internationalization. These four core elements encompass my views on how and why I teach.

Humanization

Historical and cultural identity, as seen in my scholarly research focus, is deeply embedded in my appreciation for Black women's history. As a first-generation college student, I traveled widely with military parents, but I did not attend college until I was twenty-five years old. I did not have grounding in African American educational history while growing up. When I found out that the first Black woman to graduate from college did so in 1850, it made me realize how much having role models would have meant to me as a young student. No one I knew who looked like me went to college, so I didn't think I could. In my classroom, I infuse the content of my research to spread the knowledge that race and gender stereotypes of learning are simply myths perpetuated by a void of historic knowledge. Historic Black women attended college and formed a teaching force that made a significant impact on the illiteracy rate of the 4 million freedmen after the emancipation of 1865. Their legacy of a passion for teaching and learning lives in my courses. By humanizing Black women, I seek to make connections to the many disparate ways of knowing—especially those of marginalized peoples.

I embrace humor in my work. Humor allows people to see that even in dramatic situations, comedy can enable one to more easily embrace connection and compassion. One of my favorite jobs before going to college was waiting tables at a comedy club. There is nothing like a room full of people laughing. Though my teaching style is nowhere near that of a stand-up comedy act, I have a great deal of fun teaching and encourage my students to actually en-JOY the learning process. Teaching in African American studies and women's studies, the subjects are often painful, controversial, grim, frustrating, and disheartening. Racial and gender oppression, subjugation, coercion, and discrimination are serious topics. However, my work deals with activism as well as oppression, so I find inspiration from those who historically and contemporarily fight for equality and social justice. Enjoying the learning process, as a scholar-activist, comes through in my teaching. When I'm in the classroom, I would not rather be anywhere else. I try to make the topic interesting enough so that the students have a great time learning and feel the same way.[22]

Socialization

For me, the greatest teaching tools are discussion and debate. I very rarely give straight one-hour lectures. I try to present a clear set of learning objectives and begin classes with a series of questions. This way, students learn to be ready to discuss the reading, offer an opinion based on evidence, and hold each other accountable for alert interaction. I design my lesson plans with pairs and small-group discussion in addition to open dialogue; this assists in allowing everyone a voice and balancing those who are very talkative with those who are initially hesitant to participate. The discussions are required to be grounded in the course materials, and I continually refer to and ask for page numbers in order to keep from devolving into simple opinion or conjecture.

In most of my survey classes, about twice a semester, I organize formal debates. Each student has a chance to be in a debate and then to judge as an audience member. The topics are generally controversial, and students work in teams but do not get to choose their sides. Each member of the team is expected to present a part of the argument, and the discussions that ensue after the debates are fruitful because students get to address whether or not they agreed with the side that they were assigned to argue. The debate guidelines call for professionalism and respect, and I use Wayne Brockreide's "Arguers as Lovers" for a theoretical frame. This article situates the act of debate as a love of learning rather than a quest for power or domination. The students seem to enjoy debating and take seriously the responsibility of judging the rounds. Judges are expected to sound off after they choose who wins, and that, again, provides entrée into the complexities of historical, theoretical, or political discussions. The peer-learning process exponentially solidifies the questions, themes, topics, and concepts that I present in the class. Though I rarely give traditional quizzes, when I have, students seem to digest and deconstruct the concepts more convincingly with examples provided by discussion and debate with other students.

This approach is essential in critical race, gender, and intersectional studies. Questions of identity flowed into my teaching and into my administrative leadership of the African American Studies Program at UF and CAU because even though it may be "inconvenient" for those who oppose advances in social justice, self-definition is an essential part of Black intellectual heritage and women's academic traditions. African American history and culture are crucial ingredients of the American experience, so training in African American studies enhances the minds and lives of all students, regardless of their racial, ethnic, national, or cultural backgrounds.

Professionalization

Frederick Evers' offers a clear guide to the type of engaged learning and professional development I set as goals for my class. My ultimate job is to train scholars, and I strive for academic excellence. Though means were often meager in the late nineteenth- and early twentieth-century classroom, dogged determination and an attitude of gratitude fueled young scholars to achieve heroic academic feats. I let my students know that I have high expectations because I genuinely believe that every student can learn, with the right attitude, tools, and time. I spend much time preparing for class and honing my pedagogy. I hold myself to the same standards of excellence that I expect of my students because, given the proof of historic intellectual growth, high-quality measurable learning is possible and should always be the goal. Not everything I do in class works; I allow myself, as I allow my students, accidents and failures. What I do not excuse is lack of attempt or sustained practices of mediocrity.

I am transparent in my work and like to avoid what I call "fuzzy teaching." As an African American woman in U.S. higher education, I am used to being underestimated, questioned, and challenged based on racist and sexist presumptions. Students have, on occasion, taken liberties to inform me that they strongly disagree with a grade or comments on their paper. Because I rarely offer my own opinion, students do not often challenge me ideologically, but some have compared me, unfavorably, to the popular perception of a "real" professor (White, male, and "objective"). After clarifying my course and learning objectives, reiterating my grading criteria, and sometimes after they have consulted other professors, those students who have challenged my academic capacity usually have been satisfied and enlightened by the process. I do not teach or grade in a "willy-nilly" fashion. I strive to be clear in my course syllabus, but especially clear about grading. I am known as a "tough" grader, but not randomly so, and I feel no great joy when some students (inevitably) perform poorly in my class. Students who earn As in my classes have been plentiful, but those who have received that mark know they earned every point! Ultimately, I hate grading. At St. John's College, where I studied my first year of college, we did not get "grades"; we got comments from the professors, and that changed the entire focus of the student/professor interaction. However, since grades are required, I take the duty seriously. I see this as preparation for future professional endeavors; you will not always see eye to eye with those with whom you work, but you must find a way to be productive and be responsible for producing an excellent portfolio regardless of the attitudes of those who supervise you.

I engage students in learning and assessment definitions to underscore my practice: though pure objectivity is impossible, fair and standardized evaluation is assured. Students are given exam and final paper grading criteria in plenty of time to prepare. The rubrics simultaneously function as an assurance of my competency, a concrete guide for assignment expectations, and an equitable measure of papers that are sometimes as different as apples and oranges. As my teaching has improved over time, my dedication to transparency has strengthened, and both the students and I seem to like the flexibility that such a strict rubric actually allows.

I bring theories, models, examples, and worksheets into class so that students can see there is more than one way to conceptualize the material. Through various approaches, I capture the wide range of material in a women's studies or African American studies class and provide students with points of entry to the multitude of information provided in the course text. Students know that regardless of the topics, which range from African enslavement to women's health debates, they have a paradigm to frame the issue. They will employ historical and contemporary lenses, bring in their own chosen major for scholarly perspective, read the text through their cultural identity, and form their own questions about the material.

Internationalization

In an online editorial titled "Between Truths and Indulgences," writer Wole Soyinka illuminated the murky grounds that exist in the often-oversimplified portrayals of race and critical race studies. He wrote, "What constitutes a disservice to our faculty of judgment, however, is to place obstacles in the way of assembling truth's fragments, remaining content with a mere one- or two-dimensional projection where a multidimensional and multifaceted apprehension remains open, accessible and instructive."[23] As someone who has traveled internationally for much of my life, I am keenly aware that transnational experiences shift identity over time. I teach study abroad classes, write about Black women's travel, and in many ways my work reflects a construction of self that has been enriched by multiple settings. Part of my teaching practices rest on challenging students to recognize and demonstrate that their educational experiences happen within a global setting as do their identities, beliefs, and careers. The world is a complex place, and without due attention to global matters, one cannot truly be educated.

Conclusion

Teaching has allowed me to learn at a deeper level, and I am thankful for an occupation where I can be a lifelong learner. Ultimately, my teaching philosophy returns to information gathered by historic Black women educators. I reflect this history through my involvement in community service learning, teaching in race and gender studies, and encouraging debate in my classroom, and also by telling my students I care about them. In my teaching, I try to make the impossible a reality for my students, my ancestors, and myself.

··•· ··•· ··•·

EDUCATIONAL PHILOSOPHY CONCEPT MAP

A Plan for Lifelong Learning:
Carrying Forward the Tradition of Regeneration
Stephanie Y. Evans

What: Guidance for Sustainable Success

Message   Strong Bones = Wishbone, Jawbone, and Backbone (Inez Emerson, Grandmother Wit)

Wishbone	Goal Setting	Game Plan	(Sociology of Sports)
Jawbone	Speaking Out	Information Literacy	(Library Science)
Backbone	Perseverance	Competence/Innovation	(Business)

Goals   Develop Functional Philosophy of Education (Good—History), Address Engle's Problematique (Legal Studies) Ontology (Being), Epistemology (Truth/Knowing), Axiology (Values/Doing) Relate Intrinsic and Extrinsic Motivations to Seek Wisdom (Makeda/AACU)

Connect Educational Philosophy (Muzzolo) to Information Literacy (ALA)
Create Timeless Knowledge

So What: Information Literacy Is Essential for Sustainable Learning

Locate / Information

Attitude   Push/Pull Factors of Learning (Love and Fear); Fear: Intellectual Freedom ("Emancipate Yourselves from Mental Slavery"); South Carolina Negro Act of 1740; Historical Arguments of African American's and Women's Mental Inferiority; Love: Positive Psychology and a Strength-Based Foundation; Lifelong Love of Learning (Elders Reading with Mind and Heart); Empowerment Ed: Bwms Phil. Intellectual History; Approach: Positive Regeneration

Behavior   Dr. Cooper and Roots of Regeneration: Learning Is "Timeless" (Look Backward, Look Inward, Look Forward); BWIT, ASCM; Positive Regeneration—Find Joy (Nieto) in Past, Present, and Future

Choices   Self-Empowerment Theory (Self-Control over Self-Esteem, ABCs); Modeling Strength: Joyce West-Stevens (Smart and

Sassy: Strength—Context—Hope); Appreciative Advising and Career Advising (Positive Questions); Social Foundations to Social Justice Education; Role Models

Evaluate/Knowledge

Regeneration as an Educational Threshold Concept

Models of Regeneration

Look Backward (Dr. Cole)   Look Inward (Dr. Painter)
                               Look Forward (Dr. Rockquemore)

Use/Metacognition

Interdisciplinary Models of Lifelong Learning

Game Plan   "Unlock Creativity in a Purposeful Way" (Community Art)
Info Literacy   Work-Learn Project in Senegal (Digital Information Studies)
Competence   Practical Skills (Engineering)

Create / Wisdom

Case Study: My Love of Learning from Sankofa to Afrofuturism

Restrospection   *Black Women in the Ivory Tower, 1850-1954: An Intellectual History*

Introspection   *African Americans and Community Engagement in Higher Education*

Prospection   *Black Passports: Travel Memoirs as a Guide for Youth Empowerment*

Research = LL/*BWIT* 410/483 "Benchmark" (Hine); Haskins, Du Bois, Hilliard, Interdisciplinary Love Studies

Creative Literacy/Websites: NIA, ProfEvans, Du Bois, Byrd Wedding; *Chronicles of the Equator Woman*

Now What: Develop Creative Literacy (Regeneration)

Scholar-Activist Tradition (UMass Du Bois Department of Afro-Am); Problem-Solving through Philosophy of Education: What? So What? Now What? Combines Experiential Education with Social Justice Education

Problem to Solve: Expand Horizons for Myself and Others

Solution: Creative Literacy: Look Back, Inward, and Forward for Ways to Advance Love of Wisdom and Add "Creating Knowledge" to Benjamin Bloom's *Taxonomy of Educational Objectives*; Locate/Information, Evaluate/Knowledge, Use/Metacognition, and Create/ Wisdom by Teaching and Learning ABCs and Advance Black Women's Traditions of *Living Legacies*

Service and Social Justice Philosophy: Humanizing Science

An Open Letter to Professor Stephen Hawking:
With All Due Respect, Your Calculations Don't Add Up[24]
April 27, 2007
Dear Dr. Hawking,

I just learned of your recent weightless flight and took great joy at the news. Though I do not study space science I have taken an interest in your personal story (since the 1990s) and have enjoyed your commentary on the origins, nature, and future of the universe. Surely, your 2009 time in space will be infinitely satisfying and stimulating. However, when I read of your comments about humans' need to flee our planet, I was more confused than ever. You see, I am a Black woman who studies history, and you may understand the scientific Earth, but I understand the social Earth: not everyone is going to get a ticket into space and there is a high probability that those who will be left behind will be poor people of color.

While I encourage exploration of space (I was a Ronald E. McNair Scholar in college after all), I reject the notion that we should just abandon ship without trying to fix the damage we have done to it. We have a responsibility to change and to improve the quality of life, even as we develop plan B. The threats you cite, "global warming, nuclear war, a genetically engineered virus or other dangers," are all man made. And here I stress man made. As the shootings at Columbine, Virginia Tech, Denver, Newtown repeatedly demonstrate, men (regardless of race) are addicted to violence. Masculinity is too often defined as domination; the violent notion of masculinity is a social disease. To suggest that we don't need to fix this human problem and that we may simply move to another planet is to ignore that, without active intervention, the problems will persist there too. Wherever you go, there you are.

Instead, I suggest that we consult alternative experts. Perhaps, Dr. Willa Player, an exemplar who in 1959 wrote:

> Today we are dangling in an uneasy balance between world deliverance and world destruction. These circumstances have come about so rapidly that we have not had time to close the ever-widening gap between scientific discovery and moral commitment. Although our colleges are desperately re-examining their goals and re-appraising their values, we have not yet found the solution to the problem of how to establish the appropriate organic relationship between the search for truth and the moral responsibility inherent therein.[25]

Dr. Player's solution for institutional improvement was deceptively simple: love was her answer to the crisis academics faced. But the love she advocated was not a "Pollyanna" panacea; it required physical, moral, and intellectual rigor:

> We desperately need a leadership of inclusiveness. May I say that this is possible in proportion as we are able to put our love of humanity above the love of self. Responsible leadership must be characterized by love. . . . We need desperately a leadership of intellectual integrity. We have to say this over and over again—for we are prone to want the world at too cheap a price, and nothing really worthy is ever achieved except by hard, intellectual effort, and the development of the power of straight thinking.

Dr. Player was the president of Bennett College, a historically Black woman's college in North Carolina. She challenged researchers to admit and ensure the right of all living beings to grow instead of academics taking the more often traveled road of dominance, arrogance, exclusion, and hatred —or escape.

Dr. Player's address, titled "Over the Tumult—The Challenge," was given at her alma mater, Ohio Wesleyan University, as a powerful post–World War II entreaty for the redirection of institutional research. Her admonition to maintain a strong link between scientific inquiry and ethical action exposed the failings of technological advancement and limitations of nationalism. Her comments—referencing the wake of the August 1945 bombing of Hiroshima and Nagasaki—ring eerily true as the United States orchestrates a "War on Terror" in the twenty-first century and explores space to Pluto and beyond.

Dr. Player's story, excerpted here from my newly released book, *Black Women in the Ivory Tower, 1850–1954: An Intellectual History,* offers but one example of how African American women have contributed to critical academic and imperative social thought. It can no longer be said that Plato's dialogues are "universal" while Black women's writings are merely simple or particular. Though originating from a unique standpoint, Black women have spoken to themes of universal human interest at least as much as Greek men. Additionally, without reading Black women's and other marginalized scholarship, one may very well miss a full appreciation of the enduring relevance of the Pyramid Texts, the implications of the Phaedrus or the Republic, or the philosophical significance of "The Beginning of Time." Black women complicate ideas of innocence and judgment found in ancient Egypt; they embody the relationship between love and written word and challenge ideas of citizenship or freedom in Plato's dialogues; and they engage Stephen

Hawking's assessment of impending forward motion of time in ways that give deeper meaning to these and other stories.

Black Women in the Ivory Tower exemplifies the best of scholarship: activism. Historically Black women's views of education offer a foil to Machiavellian models that don't provide a sustainable future for the country or world. I offer black feminist approaches to higher education, but not to assert all black women are genius or saints (trust me, we're not). Rather, I argue that by researching black women's academic history, we may find hints on how to alleviate inequalities through humane research, culturally sensitive teaching, active learning, and informed service. Colleges and universities in the United States have increasingly become central to defining cultural, political, and economic reality on a global scale. For those interested in ensuring that the academy does not continue to reify impenetrable social hierarchies, history is instructive. I pray that this story helps create more equitable and ethical institutions as time, technology, and circumstance reconfigure the international human landscape.

Surely we must advance study of space, but not without also advancing research in race, gender, humanities, social science, and peace studies. I write to you with humility, respect, and admiration. But I also write with a sense of duty. In the spirit of Dr. Mary McLeod Bethune, I believe if we can build a better space ship, that we can—and must—also try to build a better world.

Best regards,
Stephanie Y. Evans

·•· ·•· ·•·

A job is different than a career. Common advice given to college students faced with choosing their major for career preparation is simple: follow your heart. The memoirs in this chapter reveal an incredible depth of possibilities for youth to choose their professional life path. They also demonstrate the difficulty in achieving and maintaining competence in any chosen career. Acknowledging what Harvard University professor Howard Gardner calls "multiple intelligences," in his 1983 groundbreaking book *Frames of Mind*, adults who mentor students must steer youth to better understand the various capacities they have for excellence and the learning styles best suited to realizing their full potential in a range of areas. Just as standardized tests do not measure intelligence, not all career placement guides present the full range of a person's vocational choices. If I had been asked what I wanted to be in high school, I would not have chosen "professor" because I did not know anyone who did this work. However, with the proper encouragement in college I was able to realize my passion for reading and writing and create a career doing what I love.

My educational philosophies and experiences create a professional memoir and provide a glimpse of my career development. The road to my work as a professor has been long, which I make clearer by the personal memoir in the final chapter. I argue that work does not simply reflect personal interest; it also speaks volumes about personal values and the impact guidance has had on shaping a professional self. Katherine Dunham's model shows us that personal and professional selves take place in a global context. A close look at international exchange and the connection with identity development is warranted.

FIVE

EXCHANGE

*Insubordinate Minds, Border-Crossing Bodies,
and Innovating Change (Global)*

So can I get a window seat?
Don't want nobody next to me
I just want a ticket outta town
A look around and a safe touch down
—Erykah Badu, *Window Seat?*

MESSAGE: BLACK HUMANISM

Joyce A. Joyce offered a fundamental paradigm for understanding ethnic studies: *Black Studies as Human Studies: Critical Essays and Interviews*. Dedicating her work to the student activists who pressured San Francisco State University to incorporate race studies in the curriculum, Joyce celebrates the legacy of the 1960s movement, which resulted in campuses moving beyond physical integration toward intellectual integration. As the student movement rhetoric argued, diversity is excellence; this adage bears weight when considering that what became known as the Ivy League were campuses where integration of racially diverse students first took place. However, long before general integration of predominantly White campuses, Historically Black Colleges and Universities (HBCUs) produced effective scholar-activists who well understood that excellence in scholarship required serious study of diverse human cultures. This study, by necessity, had to make serious inquiry into the spectrum of experiences and philosophies of Africans in America and the diaspora. Thus, what came to be known as Africana studies is elemental for quality scholarship, and any study of humanity without this perspective is simply incomplete. However, as exemplified by Jan Willis and Malcolm X, Africana studies includes a multitude of African and non-African cultures.

In *Existencia Africana,* philosopher Lewis Gordon underscores the need to seriously investigate Black human existence and provides a deep intellectual history of the Black existential tradition: "It is clear that without the contributions of Africana thinkers, reflections on such concerns as existence, ethics, aesthetics, politics and human studies exemplify, at best, a false universal. . . . For people of African descent, we need, then, an emancipation of ideas in which we can engage, without subordination, thoughts that we can treasure far into subsequent generations. A task faced by our generation is the liberation of such ideas. . . . Africana humanism is a tradition indicative of the human tradition because of its 'antipodal status in Western civilization.'"[1] In sum, it is imperative to begin with Black experiences and ideas as comparative points, to bring out nuances within the race. To truly appreciate the human-ness of Black people and take advantage of the richness that comparative studies represent, Black narratives in the diaspora are essential points of comparison. Gordon lists the following thinkers as his historical base: David Walker, Maria Stewart, Martin Delaney, Frederick Douglass, Alexander Crummell, Edward Blyden, Anna Julia Cooper, W. E. B. Du Bois, Alain Locke, Marcus Garvey, Pagent Henry, Joseph Owens, Richard Wright, Ralph Ellison, Leopold Senghor, Franz Fanon, James Baldwin, William Jones, Cornel West, Joy James, and bell hooks—all intellectual or ideological role models to many in the field of African American philosophy. To get a real sense of the intellectual possibilities, we must begin with the supposition, as did W. E. B. Du Bois in *Black Reconstruction* (1935), that Black people are, in fact, human, and humans are complicated.

Complex difficulties of travel and identity are deep and long-standing. Nat Love provides another example of the problematic interpretation of Black travel history. He is hailed as an adventurer and exhibited a compelling desire for "sweet" freedom: "I wanted to see more of the world and as I began to realize there was so much more of the world than what I had seen, the desire to go grew on me from day to day. It was hard to think of leaving mother and the children, but freedom is sweet and I wanted to make more of the opportunity and my life than I could see possible around home."[2] However, although

Love sought adventure as a cowboy in the "Wild West" and learned to speak Spanish, part of his experience in the Western Territory involved shooting Native Americans in the genocidal "expansion" of post–Civil War "Manifest Destiny." Black identities and international relations are certainly complicated, especially around war: many Native American nations sided with the Confederacy because of promises of land. Conversely, thousands of Black soldiers were active in the Indian wars and Black "Buffalo Soldiers" (six regiments of Civil War veterans) actively participated in the killing of Native Americans, including on the Oklahoma "Trail of Tears," and earned the Medal of Honor for their killing in "frontier cavalry." These questions of war linger still as the Middle East launches into a new era of shifting Islamic leadership. This complicates Black nationalist views of places like Egypt as a cultural center, and Africana scholars are accountable for the task to reconcile ancient empires with contemporary realities.[3]

Regardless of time and place, international relations present constant need to reassess one's position vis-à-vis the host country. In chapter 2, I explored author reflections on Africa in order to learn more about African Americans' views on how they did or did not fit into culture on the continent—especially given the idea of travel to Africa as a "homecoming." James Baldwin's report of the September 1956 Artist and Writers Congress at the Sorbonne University in Paris offers another relevant lesson when considering complex Black humanity. His report erased the illusion that all Black people around the world have the same culture. Baldwin skillfully recorded the contrasting language, tone, social practice, political agenda, economic ideologies, and religious assumptions of conference attendees. Participants gathered from the African continent, the Caribbean, and the Americas. Although the participants were all Black men, their perspectives were vastly different, and the debates revealed significant national rifts that were argued loudly in the Amphitheatre Descartes. The agenda for the congress and resolutions did not reach consensus because of the cultural and political clashes. The meeting added an impressive new chapter to the 1955 Asia-Africa Bandung Conference held the year before in Indonesia, which Richard Wright and Adam Clayton Powell both attended. In his Bandung report, *The Color Curtain* (1956), Wright focused on using the conference as a tool to criticize European powers. However, Baldwin's focus reported that the Paris exchange revealed the intricate fault lines of international conflict within leadership of the African diaspora itself. Though there are areas of comparative cultural convergence based on relatively parallel experiences, there is no static Black worldview.[4]

Diaspora Narratives

The State of Georgia standards on multicultural literature highlight the intended notion of comparative humanities: to enrich youths' understanding through ethnic, national, and cultural diversity. Beyond homogeneous representations of blackness, curricula should include voices from the diaspora. Thus, it is not enough to read African American narratives; a clear sense of Black life can only be conveyed by including memoirs by natives of different nations. A short list of fascinating autobiographies by Black authors outside of the United States or Caribbean should contain:

Australia: *Murawina: An Authentic Aboriginal Message* (1993); Rita Huggins and Jackie Huggins, *Auntie Rita* (1994)

Brazil: Benedita da Silva, *An Afro-Brazilian Woman's Story of Politics and Love* (1997); Pelé, *My Life and the Beautiful Game* (1977); *Pelé: The Autobiography* (2006)

Britain: Kelly Holmes, *My Olympic Ten Days* (2004)

India: Bama, *Karukku* (Dalit Writing in Translation, 1992)

Jamaica: Barbara Blake Hannah, *Growing Out: Black Hair and Black Pride in the Swinging Sixties* (2010)

Kenya: Wangari Maathai, *Unbowed: A Memoir* (2007); Auma Obama, *And Then Life Happens: A Memoir* (2012)

Liberia: Ellen Johnson-Sirleaf, *This Child Will Be Great: Memoir of a Remarkable Life by Africa's First Woman President* (2009); William K. Reeves, T*he Native Boy: An Autobiography of a Man from Myaake* (2004)

Malawi: William Kamkwamba, *The Boy Who Harnessed the Wind: Creating Currents of Electricity and Hope* (2009)

Nigeria: Olaudah Equiano. *Interesting Narrative of the Life of Olaudah Equiano* (1789); Chinua Achebe, *Home and Exile* (2000); *Education of a British Protected Child* (2009); Dympna Ugwu-Oju, *What Will My Mother Say? A Tribal African Girl Comes of Age in America* (1995); Wole Soyinka, *Aké: The Years of Childhood* (1981); *You Must Set Forth at Dawn* (2006)

Rwanda: Marie Beatrice Umutesi, *Surviving the Slaughter: The Ordeal of a Rwandan Refugee in Zaire* (2004)

Sierra Leone: Ishmael Beah, *A Long Way Gone: Memoirs of a Boy Soldier* (2008)

Somalia: Waris Dirie, *Desert Flower: The Extraordinary Journey of a Desert Nomad* (1992)

South Africa: Nelson Mandela, *Long Walk to Freedom* (1994); Mark Mathabane, *Kaffir Boy: The True Story of a Black Youth's Coming of Age in Apartheid South Africa* (1998)

Sudan: Menda Nazer, *Slave: My True Story* (2003)

Trinidad: C. L. R. James, *Beyond a Boundary* (1963)

Useful questions here mirror earlier themes: How do native Africans represent education, health care, or culture in their countries? What does a comparison of the presidencies and autobiographies of Liberia's Ellen Johnson-Sirleaf and South Africa's Nelson Mandela reveal? How is violence portrayed by Africans on the Continent? What skin color, hair, or body image politics are at play in narratives? In which areas does gender converge and diverge in writers' perspectives? These narratives will assist us in understanding global challenges in Black life as well as the contributions to Black humanist traditions.

MEMOIRS: NARRATIVES OF EXCHANGE

One of the most important study abroad narratives provided within an autobiographical text is that of W. E. B. Du Bois. In *The Autobiography of W. E. B. Du Bois: A Soliloquy on Viewing My Life from the Last Decade of Its First Century*, his final life narrative, Du Bois begins with a chapter titled "My Fifteenth Trip Abroad." Writing about his extensive travel in the Soviet Union, China, and Europe, he grounds his ninety-five years of life in a narrative of constant transatlantic transit. Location plays a significant part in his racial identity development as he grows from a boy in New England to a young man in the South to an adult in the wide world. Region is clearly an impactful force on his sense of self, which unfolds in chapters about studying at Fisk University in Tennessee and serving as a faculty member for twenty-three years at Atlanta University.

Du Bois fully engages the topic of racial identity in his 1950 autobiography, *Dusk of Dawn: Autobiography of a Race Concept*, but it is in his final life reflection that he most fully reveals the locations where he formed his understanding of self and race. A critical turning point happened while he was in Germany. While abroad on a Guggenheim Fellowship in Berlin, Du Bois celebrated his twenty-fifth birthday alone, listening to Schubert in a candle-lit room. There, he penned a manifesto that guided his actions in his nineties through the epic battle to retain his freedom—and his passport—in the United

States. The battle ultimately ended with his retiring to Ghana and choosing life as an eternal expatriate rather than a citizen of a country that had criminalized and pathologized blackness. Like numerous other eureka moments that take place abroad, Du Bois's time studying in Germany impacted the rest of his life and his view of self in the world as he related the oppression of Black people in the United States to oppression of Africans all over the world.

Other Black men participated in learning abroad. Claude McKay came to the United States to study because of the legacy of Booker T. Washington. Phillipe Wamba, born of African and African American heritage moved to Tanzania in 1980 and pursued education on both continents, which clearly expanded his understanding of himself as a global citizen. Tragically, after graduating from Harvard University, he died in a car crash while in Kenya. He returned to Africa several times, signaling his extended sense of African connection that he explored in the narrative *Kinship*.[5]

However, educational concept moves far beyond study abroad when we study the example of Malcolm X. When considering the spiritual and social awakening as a result of his Hajj to Mecca, we see the power of international exchange as a source of irreplaceable learning:

> Never have I witnessed such sincere hospitality and the overwhelming spirit of true brotherhood as practiced by people of all colors and races here in this Ancient Holy Land, the home of Abraham, Muhammad and all other prophets of the Holy Scriptures. For the past week, I have been utterly speechless and spellbound by the graciousness I see displayed all around me by people of all colors. I have been blessed to visit the Holy City of Mecca. I have made my seven circuits around the Ka'ba. I drank water from the well of Zem Zem. I ran seven times back and forth between the hills of Mt. Al-Safa and Al-Marwah. I have prayed in the ancient city of Mina, and I have prayed on Mt. Arafat.
>
> There were tens of thousands of pilgrims, from all over the world. They were of all colors, from blue-eyed blonds to black skin Africans. But we were all participating in the same rituals, displaying a spirit of unity and brotherhood that my experiences in America had lead me to believe never could exist between the white and non-white. America needs to understand Islam, because this is the one religion that erases from its society the race problem. Throughout my travels in the Muslim world, I have met, talked to, and even eaten with people who in America would have considered "white"—but the "white"

attitude was removed from their minds by the religion of Islam. I have never before seen sincere and true brotherhood practiced by all colors together, irrespective of their color.

You may be shocked by these words coming from me. But on this pilgrimage, what I have seen, and experienced, has forced me to re-arrange much of my thought patterns previously held, and to toss aside some of my previous conclusions. This was not too difficult for me. Despite my firm convictions, I have always been a man who tries to face facts, and to accept the reality of life as new experiences and new knowledge unfolds it. I have always kept an open mind, which is necessary to the flexibility that must go hand in hand with every form of intelligent search for truth. During the past eleven days here in the Muslim world, I have eaten from the same plate, drunk from the same glass, and slept in the same bed, (or on the same rug)—while praying to the same God—with fellow Muslims, whose eyes were the bluest of blue, whose hair was the blondest of blond, and whose skin was the whitest of white. And in the same words and in the actions and in the deeds of the "white" Muslims, I felt the same sincerity that I felt among the black African Muslims of Nigeria, Sudan and Ghana.

We were truly all the same (brothers)—because their belief in one God had removed the "white" from their minds, the 'white" from their behavior, and the "white" from their attitude. I could see from this, that perhaps if white Americans could accept the Oneness of God, then perhaps, too, they could accept in reality the Oneness of Man—and cease to measure, and hinder, and harm others in terms of their differences in color. All praise is due to Allah, the Lord of all the Worlds. Sincerely, El-Hajj Malik El-Shabazz (Malcolm X).[6]

In his search for Black humanity, El-Hajj Malik El-Shabazz also found White humanity. In a similar vein to Malcolm X, Alex Haley also "studied abroad" while conducting research that formed the foundation of *Roots*. His search for family heritage led him to discover intimate details that, when the published book and television show were released in the 1970s, impacted an entire generation of African Americans. As Richard Pryor's visit intimated, Black people in the 1970s rediscovered Africa and life outside of the United States in a way reminiscent of the first and second world wars. But before *Roots*, a multitude of students found the world an ample textbook, including a fascinating group of women.

Why study a group of women travelers? Because women's physical movement has been hindered by gender roles (i.e., child rearing and family caretaking expectations) and what movement women have been able to experience has been absent from the historical record or in the shadow of male "explorers, adventurers and pioneers." Elaine Lee's *Go Girl!*, a 1997 anthology of Black women's travel writing, was a significant intervention in this area. As a prime example of traditional exclusion, James Baldwin's report of the 1956 Artist and Writers Congress at the Sorbonne raises an important question about the relative lack of documented travel by Black women. Only one woman was present in the official photo of more than fifty participants, and she was only identified as a "Madame" without her full name.[7] This chapter's focus on Black women's study abroad gives a purposeful nod to African girl-child movements by those like innovator Beverly Bond's "Black Girls Rock" project and *Essence* magazine's former editor Susan Taylor's National CARES mentoring movement.[8]

In her dissertation "'Conceived in Transit, Delivered in Passage': Travel and Identity in Nineteenth-Century African-American Women's Narratives," Cheryl Williams interprets this group as "recharging" travel and identity. Their travel represented a breaking away of dichotomies (home/away, roots/routes, self/other, black/white, and native/traveler). In relation to research on Black men and White women travelers, Williams further argues that Black women's narratives like Nancy Prince's activist travels to Jamaica and Russia "function as figurations of a laboring mobility," which effectively counters historiographical interpretation of a male-centric American Jim Crow history of movement.[9]

Black manhood studies are essential, and such works as Mark Anthony Neal's *New Black Man* and Daniel Black's dissertation "Dismantling Black Manhood" and novel *Perfect Peace* are among the many resources available. Yet, Black women's studies in the global context are a necessary area to politicize Black gender and movement. A close look at primary sources in autobiography reveals that Black women have been avid travelers, but not nearly as much as men. The one area where women have documented their travel memoirs more than men is study abroad narratives. This is important because today, Black women study abroad at a much higher rate than Black men. This is a trend across race where, nationally, women study abroad at about 66 percent and men at 34 percent, an issue that offers a prime data set for investigation.[10]

Unfortunately, not all women who studied abroad left full-length autobiographies of their travels. For example, Flemmie Kittrell (Hampton University, BS 1928; Cornell University, MS 1930, PhD 1936) researched nutrition practices in West Africa, India, Japan, Hawaii, and Thailand. Though her dissertation focused on infant feeding practices in North Carolina, she traveled widely to do comparative surveys. When Black women traveled abroad to study, their professional development in later years often retained an international character. Dr. Kittrell headed the Home Economics program at Howard University and also helped to set up the College of Home Economics at Baroda University in India.[11]

Grounded in (grand)mother wit as much as in formal intellectual history, these narratives can prove useful in mentoring young women and girls who aspire to move their education beyond narrowly prescribed national, cultural, or gender boundaries. The ten women featured below surely are the immodest and unembarrassed nomadic daughters of Makeda, and their insights are narratives of backbone, wishbone, and jawbone in transnational contexts. Their guidance through some of the world's most interesting places is priceless.

Ten Memoirs: Blackness Is a Journey, Not a Destination

> My passport would make me to some degree *persona non grata*. I counted on color to offset this, but then there was to offset *that* my sex and class—the student class, very hard to place. . . . As the situation presented itself, I seem to have wavered or capitulated from mulatto to black, elite to peasant, intellectual to bohemian, in to out, up to down, and tried hard to keep out of trouble but did not succeed.
> —Katherine Dunham, *Island Possessed* (1969)

Of the hundreds of African American women who have penned autobiographies, ten offer global memoirs of college or university study: Mary Church Terrell (Paris and Berlin, 1884), Anna Julia Cooper (Paris, 1911), Katherine Dunham (Haiti, 1935), Zora Neale Hurston (Jamaica, 1937), Colleen McElroy (Europe, 1953), Marian Wright Edelman (Paris, 1959), Lena Morton (England, 1956), Angela Davis (Paris 1963), Gayle Pemberton (England, 1965), and Jan Willis (Tibet, 1967).

Mary Church Terrell's 1884–86 trip to Europe, recorded in her autobiography, *A Colored Woman in a Black World* (1940), is one of the earliest known Black women's study abroad reflections. Terrell (Oberlin College, BA 1884, MA 1888) studied in France, Germany, Italy, Switzerland, and England after her college graduation, and after marrying, she continued to travel for pleasure. Terrell also traveled to participate in international activism around peace and women's rights in 1904 and 1919.

Anna Julia Cooper's first international voyage came in 1900 when she spoke at the first Pan-African Congress in London, but she began her formal study abroad in 1911 and worked numerous consecutive summers in Paris researching her topic at the *Guilde International, Bibliothèque Militaire*, and the national archives of France. Under threat of losing her teaching position at Dunbar High School in Washington, D.C., she completed her dissertation in time for defense and, when she arrived in Paris, "burned out a devastating number of candles" making extensive adjustments and corrections to her manuscript. She published a reflection of the dissertation and defense process in *The Third Step* in 1945.[12]

Katherine Dunham traveled to the Caribbean (Haiti, Jamaica, Trinidad, Martinique) in 1935–36 on Rosenwald and Guggenheim fellowships while studying at the University of Chicago. She founded a dance studio and continued her travels in 1947–49 to Mexico, London, and Paris, and to Senegal in 1956 and visited fifty-seven countries in twenty years. A generation later, in her autobiography, *Dancing the Spirit*, Judith Jamison would offer tribute to Dunham as a founder of African diaspora-influenced jazz and Black modern dance, which laid the groundwork for the Alvin Ailey Dance Company. However, before traveling as a performer, Dunham traveled as a researcher. Dunham's first autobiography was published in 1959, *A Touch of Innocence*, but the international account of her study was recorded in *Island Possessed* (1969) a decade later. Paired with Dunham, Zora Neale Hurston is most recognized as a novelist, yet before penning her highly regarded novel *Their Eyes Were Watching God* (1937), she too conducted field research in Jamaica and Haiti while taking graduate courses in anthropology under Franz Boas at Columbia University. Hurston wrote *Their Eyes* while in Jamaica traveling on a Guggenheim Fellowship, much of which is recorded in *Tell My Horse* (1938) and patchwork reflections of which appear in *Dust Tracks on a Road: An Autobiography* (1942).

In the tradition of researchers like Dunham and Hurston, Colleen McElroy began as a study abroad student in 1953 to Munich, Germany, and developed her work portfolio as a scholar-traveler while she was a Fulbright and Rockefeller fellow in the 1970s and 1980s, venturing to Mexico, Yugoslavia, and Japan. Her lyrical travelogue is recorded in *A Long Way from St. Louie* (1997), one of the most creatively written travel accounts of the group. Though some authors engage poetry, McElroy's entire work is written as a collection of image-saturated sketches and patchwork of scenes, often engaging concrete or shape poetry as much as a chronological account of her travel or in-depth presentation of her research.

Though Lena Morton did not travel while studying at the University of Cincinnati (BA 1923, MA 1925) or while at Western Reserve where she earned a PhD in English (1947), she attended a summer session at the University of London in 1956 and traveled throughout Europe after graduation. Morton's autobiography, *My First Sixty Years: Passion for Wisdom* (1965), details her travels to England, France, Scotland, and Switzerland in addition to her Literature and Art in England, 1750–1850 summer course.

Marian Wright Edelman studied abroad in 1959 while a student at Spelman College. Her summer-long trip included visits to Ireland, Scotland, and the Soviet Union as a Lisle fellow; the account is given in a chapter entitled "Europe" in *Lanterns: A Memoir of Mentors* (1999). Angela Davis also studied abroad in 1963 in Paris while in her third year as an undergraduate at Brandeis University. She continued her study in 1965–67 in East Berlin at Humboldt University to earn her master's and PhD. Her travel and study memoirs are recorded in *Angela Davis: An Autobiography* (1974).

Stretching beyond Europe, Jan Willis began studying in Tibet during a summer program in 1967 while a student at Cornell University in a program administered through the University of Illinois and the University of Wisconsin. Her travelogue appears in *Dreaming Me: Black Baptist and Buddhist* (2008), where she chronicles visiting Tibet, then Nepal, in 1969. There, in secluded shrines and temples, she began her sustained curriculum of Hindi and Buddhist philosophy, poetry, and music, which she continued to develop in her academic preparation for a professorship in religion, which she currently holds at Wesleyan University.

Of the ten case studies, Gayle Pemberton offers one of the most recent accounts of international memoir within a full-length autobiography. Her 1965 study abroad trip to England closely mirrors Terrell's expression of anticipation, freedom, and mobile defiance in terms of her reflection of her travel. In *The Hottest Water in Chicago* (1992), she recounts her own trip but also contextualizes her travel within the larger meaning captured also by her sister's study abroad experience in France. Pemberton stands out because she traveled as a high school student.

Whether writing about the joy of human curiosity, frustrating displacement, freedom of movement, thrill of new audience, discomforting difference, spiritual mission, or political insurrection, Black women's international public lives demonstrate that self-education and global quests have been soul-moving and mind-shifting endeavors.

As Katherine Dunham suggested in her reflection of entrance into Haiti, a Black woman *student* traveler was someone who was "hard to place" and, she argued, "unpredictable," which meant she would inevitably run into "trouble." A Black woman's place was at home—or at least in her home country—not in an international setting of higher learning. *Persona non grata* status was inevitable, but it was exactly their ability to disregard or overcome expectations that make these ten women models of self-efficacy. They were, at core, socially *insubordinate*. Insubordination is the foundation for quest and voice; thus, defiance is the cornerstone of Black women's intellectual history because it is the grounds for Black women's survival and, ultimately, their self-creation.

Codifying Study Abroad Narratives: Embodying Empowerment

In her characterization of Ida B. Wells, Patricia Schechter writes that "the survival of women like Wells . . . demanded self-possession, self-defense, and 'talking back.'"[13] Most closely attributed to bell hooks, the concept of "talking back" closely relates to self-mastery. Self-possession, self-determination, and self-definition are the very characteristics that Nina Turner's grandmother encouraged her to develop. Back talking, is ever present in early memoirs.

Self-Possession (Backbone): Katherine Dunham, Angela Davis, and Jan Willis

A vital part of self-possession or owning the self is the ability to formulate a positive *self*-concept, especially in the midst of a negative environment that insists on your degradation and dehumanization. Dunham articulated that the first step in an empowerment curriculum was "humanization," and in her research, she articulated a phenomenon of "self-examination" necessary for a student to actively engage in a process of intellectual agency.[14] In the field of anthropology, Dunham pioneered international dance studies at the University of Chicago while conducting research in Haiti and several other Caribbean countries. After working with Melville Hertzkovitz from Northwestern University and earning a Guggenheim Fellowship, Dunham wrote her master's thesis (for a degree at University of Chicago, 1938), "Dances of Haiti: Their Social Organization, Classification, Form, and Function," which was subsequently published in both French and Spanish. Adjacent to her research on dance, Dunham published an account of her field studies, titled *Island Possessed* (1969). Her pioneering studies of anthropological dance involved her induction into Haitian religion of voudun and initiation into spiritual beliefs including marriage to Damballa.[15] Dunham's research abroad, both objective and subjective, intimately paired with her self-exploration as revealed in her feelings about exposing some secrets of the initiation, while keeping others confidential:

> I have no feeling of guilt or punishment or mystic retribution should I disclose these secrets. If any one of my readers could receive satisfaction or find the end of a quest in what I have experienced I would be more than happy at some time to make these revelations. But if a curiosity is for neither scientific records nor self-examination, these things are best left within their sacred environment where for those who experience them they represent truth.[16]

Halifu Osemare, alumnae of Dunham's school and associate professor of African American and African studies at University of California–Davis, argues that in the burgeoning field of anthropology, Dunham's explicit participation in the fieldwork research crossed more boundaries than even Zora Neale Hurston, who was also immersed in anthropological field research in the mid-1930s.[17]

Clearly, immersion in the Haitian culture and voudun practice permeated Dunham's being, and she used the lessons learned abroad to shape her self-concept. She spoke in the intimate first person more than in the tone of an objective researcher; she often was more participant than observer. This feeling of connection with Haiti would endure throughout Dunham's life even though she would eventually find home bases in East Saint Louis and New York. Many years after she became an initiate, Dunham continued to reflect a Haitian embodiment when, in February 1992 at the age of eighty-two, she went on a forty-seven-day hunger strike to protest the United States Coast Guard's treatment of twelve thousand Haitian refugees after the ousting of President Jean-Bertrand Aristide. For Dunham, travel abroad created a transnational identity grounded in a fight for human rights, a fight built on spiritual reflection, Black humanization, and a life of dancing one's culture.[18]

Activist Angela Davis would engage classic European philosophy and Jan Willis, Eastern philosophy to create an understanding of self that could also more effectively ensure their ability to interact with and shape their worlds. As a philosophy student, Angela Davis epitomized the legacy of self-possession. In her autobiography, she presented a contemplative account of her study in Paris, France, and Humboldt, Germany, mainly under the influence of Herbert Marcuse. In her writing, she references the profound impact that social events had on her studies in the 1960s. These events included hearing Malcolm X speak; being distraught by the church bombing and murder of four of her friends in a Birmingham, Alabama, church on September 15, 1963; the assassination of President Kennedy; and the Watts rebellion. However, she articulated that it was her desire to understand philosophy that internally satisfied her and that prepared her to have a deeper involvement in activist struggles for social change:

> Although I was on the verge of receiving a degree in French Literature, what I really wanted to study was philosophy. I was interested in Marx, his predecessors and his successors. Over the last years, whenever I could find the time, I read philosophy on the side. I didn't really know what I was doing, except that it gave me a feeling of security and comfort to read what people had to say about such formidable things as the universe, history, human beings, knowledge. During my second year at Brandeis, I had picked up *Eros and Civilization* by Herbert Marcuse and had struggled with it from beginning to end.[19]

Marcuse had taught at the Sorbonne, then at Brandeis before moving to California. Though Davis could not officially enroll in his classes during her senior year because of their popularity, she attended every session:

> One day, shortly after the semester began, I mustered up enough courage to put in a request for an interview with Marcuse. I had decided to ask him to help me draw up a bibliography on basic works of philosophy. . . . [By reading an independent study list of authors foundational to the field of philosophy,] I had acquainted myself with their thought, which was collectively known as Critical Theory. . . . Poring over a seemingly incomprehensible passage for hours, then suddenly grasping its meaning, gave me a sense of satisfaction I had never before experienced.[20]

After Brandeis, Davis earned her master's in Frankfurt but ultimately returned to the United States to complete her doctorate under Marcuse at the University of California–San Diego. "I wanted to continue my academic work," she said, "but knew I could not do it unless I was politically involved. The struggle was a life-nerve; our only hope for survival. I made up my mind. The journey was on."[21] For Davis, answering large, enduring philosophical questions gave her a personal sense of her vibrant humanity, but it was only through the application of the philosophical principles of critical theory that she felt her humanity could be fully realized.

Jan Willis provides an interesting contrast to Angela Davis's study abroad experience. Also faced with questions posed by the Black power movement of the 1960s, Willis too chose philosophy as her answer—albeit Eastern spiritual philosophy instead of Davis's Western political philosophy. As an undergraduate student at Cornell University, Willis was faced with the typically harrowing choice of deciding on a major and settled on philosophy, which led her to explorations of Buddhism. As she discusses in her book, *Dreaming Me: Black Baptist and Buddhist*, her choice of philosophy and her study abroad experience in 1967 in India irreversibly shaped her reaction to the Cornell Black Student Alliance uprising in April 1969. She describes a march and rally on campus as a reaction to a cross burning on the lawn of a house where twelve Black women lived. Following the rally, Willis found herself in the midst of a potentially violent conflict between the 260 Black students (up from 8 enrolled during her freshman year) and administrators, campus visitors, students, and local residents. The two-week incident did not escalate to violence but did push her to a fork in the road.[22]

After her 1969 graduation ceremony, she jockeyed for position at the front of the line with another student involved in the struggle, their fists held high. After graduation, Willis recalled:

> I had to make the most important decision of my life: whether to join the Black Panther party or return to the Tibetan Buddhist monastery in Nepal. After the experience at Cornell, I was convinced that as a thinking black person in this country, I was left no choice but to join the party; to lay my life on the line for my beliefs and for my people's freedom. Making the choice troubled my every waking moment and invaded my nights.[23]

To make the decision, she journeyed to Chicago where she met Fred Hampton at a Black Panther rally, then to Northern California to arrange a meeting with the Huey Newton–led Panthers. After contemplation, she "bolted" and chose not to go through with the Oakland meeting, but rather to take an opportunity as a graduate student in philosophy, which would include a year beginning back in Nepal:

> My whole being—mind, body, and soul—bolted. And even though doing so made me feel like a coward and chickenshit deserter, I had

to turn away from it. "To thine own self be true," the saying goes, and my sister, San, had always said, "Trust your first mind." I decided not to meet with the Panthers. I didn't know where the path of Buddhism would ultimately take me, but it seemed to offer at least the possibility of peaceful transformation. I told myself that it offered the best opportunity for clarity—about personal as well as political strategies. . . . I would go back to Nepal. Only a few months passed before I saw the article about Hampton's death. My heart was saddened to think of him, cut down in his shining prime. But I had made the right decision.[24]

This reflection, in a chapter titled "Decision Time: A 'Piece' or Peace," precedes a chapter titled "Choices" and demonstrates how Willis used Buddhist philosophy to guide her in her struggle to design her own additional self-concept that in turn governed her behavior and choices. Continuing her pattern of discovery, she hitchhiked through Europe during the fall of 1969, traveling through Paris, Chalon, Milan, and Istanbul on the way back to New Delhi. The remarkable complexity of her identity formation can also be seen in the book's title: even though she claimed Buddhism as her religious path, as a self-proclaimed child of the South, she did not give up connection to her Baptist roots.

These three examples demonstrate that Black women's identity development is indeed diverse and complicated. Coming to a place where one has a stable sense of identity—backbone—is a difficult process filled with twists and turns of what Joyce West Stevens calls "intersubjectivity." Cultural environment heavily influences one's adulthood identity formation process, race and sex role commitment, and role model formulation and therefore the ability to make one's own choices regardless of potential backlash. Shifting environments and international ecologies mean Black women's sense of a transnational self is not static. Claiming a unique self in the face of rigid inter- and intra-racial expectations requires willful visibility, but belief in the ability to bring to fruition one's own desired destiny and defining a self-motivated journey require an applied self-determination. Terrell, Morton, and Edelman offer relevant models of creating a life of willful physical mobility.[25]

Self-Determination (Wishbone): Mary Church Terrell, Lena Morton, and Marian Wright Edelman

Twenty-five years before any one of her other study abroad cohorts, Mary Church Terrell shamelessly blazed her path as a single woman in Europe. Her ability to travel Europe in the 1880s was a direct result of her economic class, a privilege that Anna Julia Cooper, a classmate of hers at Oberlin who was born enslaved and had meager financial means, did not enjoy. Travel was a family affair, and though Terrell's father accompanied her across the Atlantic, he returned without her, granting her graduation wish to study abroad for a year. Terrell recalled that while her father was saddened and worried, she was elated:

> As he stood in the station waiting for the train, Father begged me to return with him. Although he rarely showed how deeply moved he was about anything, his eyes filled when he kissed me good-bye and left me alone in Paris. Not a tear was in my eye, however, for at last the time had come when I could do the work which I had planned so long. I was the happiest girl on earth. I am sure I felt as Monte Cristo must have felt when he exclaimed, "The world is mine." Here I was in Paris. I could study French, visit the wonderful galleries to my heart's content, learn something about art, and attend the theaters. In short, here at last was the realization of those radiant dreams which had filled my heart for years. Father promised I might study abroad a year, and I knew he would keep his word. There was nothing to worry me. Not a care in the world, bubbling over with enthusiasm and youth![26]

Not only did Terrell enjoy her stay in France, but she defied her father's mandate to stay put by traveling to Switzerland without his knowledge and stretched the one year into two by traveling in London and Paris, then staying in Lausanne and ultimately moving on to Munich, Dresden, and Berlin, Germany. She had the luxury of travel without worry of finances, and when her mother and brother visited at the end of her stay, she chronicled that their shopping, jewelry, and fashion rivaled Parisians' tastes for extravagant living.

Eventually, Terrell would turn to social activism, and the seeds of her commitment to causing social unrest can be found in her early social critique. The focus of her writing, like Lena Morton's after her, was largely a social observation that condemned American behavior and touted Europe as an enlightened environment. She contrasted her experience as a *Colored Woman in a White World* in the United States (filled with racist encounters and limited opportunities) with her favorable experiences in more "civilized" countries. Whereas she revealed close friendships with European women and no less than three marriage proposals by European men, she exposed the long arm of White American racism. She shunned the pervasiveness of American racism by exposing and condemning two White male students from Massachusetts, staying in the same boarding house in Germany, who tried to get her thrown out of the house because she was Black. In her relatively stable station as one of the few Americans—of any race—who could afford leisurely travel, Terrell leaned heavily on her economic and educated class and benefitted from her relatively light skin, which on at least one occasion enabled her movement through Europe without alarm. She wore her finances and education as badges of superiority that she imagined Americans, even those living outside of the states, were bound to respect. Though the world was White, her autobiography and travel memoirs demanded room to move in her own way without restriction.

Desiring the same type of upward mobility enjoyed by Terrell, Lena Morton and her family sought opportunities for education and social status that could only be realized outside of the American South. Raised in Kentucky, Morton's family moved to Ohio during the World War I northern migration so that Lena could attend an accredited high school, something she could not do in segregated Winchester or Lexington.[27] Morton's autobiography includes pages from her academic diaries as well as original poems titled "Chase the Muse," "Admonition to America," "A Little Lower Than the Angels," "To Teach or Not to Teach (Apologies to Shakespeare)," and "Courage for the Times," among others. Though much more of a chronological autobiography, Morton's work solidifies the tradition of embedding poetry within different genres.[28] Her text also contains social commentary in which she took both Blacks and Whites to task for behaviors that contributed to the "commotion in America" caused by racism.

As if to mercilessly goad Americans, Morton wrote glowingly of her travel abroad, "I have the kindest remembrance of Europe. Not once did I have a significant unpleasant experience. I was accepted everywhere—not only accepted, but warmly received. Even in countries where I could not speak the language, the natives made primitive signs of friendship."[29] Of significance here is her emphasis on the "civility" of Europe juxtaposed with the barbarism and standard rudeness of citizens in the United States. Like Terrell, Morton uses her travel diaries to shame Americans for their lack of culture. As part of her enrollment in the Literature and Art of England course, she recorded visits to the British Museum, Windsor Castle, Eton College, the Tower of London (to see the Ceremony of the Keys), Hampton Court Palace, Westminster Abbey, the Houses of Parliament, St. James Palace, Oxford University, Stratford-on-Avon, Cambridge University, and Canterbury, England (home of Charles Dickens). In addition to emphasizing the elevated nature of these locations, she stressed the hospitable nature of Europeans by relating the following stories: an Englishman hailed her a cab; an American Express agent in Paris loudly and repeatedly referred to her as "Doctor" in exaggerated but sincere deference; a Scottish woman personally escorted her to the post office after shopping at Woolworth's; another Scot assisted her across a dangerously busy traffic circle; and an Italian woman on a train offered her cherries, though neither was able to speak the other's language. Morton's message was simple: Europeans would not stoop so low as to discriminate against African Americans, and, therefore, Americans needed to clean up their behavior deficits and get with the program.

By the publication of *My First Sixty Years*, Morton had taught for four decades, fifteen years of which were at the college level, mainly at HBCUs. As indicated in the book's subtitle, *A Passion for Wisdom*, Morton was determined to pursue her education at any cost and hell bent on fulfilling her "three eminent goals" of earning a doctorate, studying abroad, and earning a degree from Harvard University. Having done so, she dedicated her life to the profession of education to ensure the ability of her students to fulfill their goals as well.

After Terrell and Morton, Marian Wright Edelman also followed her heart to Paris while an undergraduate at Spelman College. Wright's experiences of relative freedom in France, Spain, Ireland, Scotland, and the Soviet Union, in semester courses at the Sorbonne, and in a summer class at Oxford University laid the groundwork for her involvement in the civil rights movement upon her return from the fifteen-month trip. She subtitled her autobiography *A Memoir of Mentors* because it is a tribute to those who enabled her to surpass the low expectations and limited opportunities historically afforded to Black women. On the eve of her trip, Edelman recalled "Howard Zinn was always there with a bottom-line question: How will a position help or hurt others or bend the universe close to justice? . . . Like my daddy, [Dr. Benjamin Mays, Charles Merrill, and Howard Zinn] reinforced in me a sense that I could transcend the world I lived in and help transform it into the world I wanted to see."[30]

In her story, Edelman recounted her initial excitement: "[I was] nineteen and on my own—free—for the first time in my life." When awakening to look for the first time out her bedroom window at the "teeming crowds on Boulevard St. Michel below and the beautiful Luxembourg Gardens across the street," she "jumped up and down and yelled" with excitement. Her feeling of joy was initially a reaction to breaking the restrictions of Spelman and any adult supervision but, in addition to finally claiming adulthood status, her delight soon turned to resolve her newfound social freedom. Fortunately, her interaction with American Whites abroad in 1959 was more positively engaging than in Terrell's time:

In Paris, I engaged in long, honest interracial conversations with southern White students who like me were seeking to reconcile the chasm between America's professed principles of equality and freedom and its actual practices. In Europe, wellsprings of long-suppressed rage bubbled up within me against the confining prison of segregation my native South and country had imposed. I knew I'd never return to that prison again either as a Black citizen or as a woman.[134]

Upon her return, she became very active in the civil rights movement and would become an especially powerful advocate for youth through her development of the Children's Defense Fund. Fittingly, her autobiography reads like a policy manual, offering specific suggestions for creating social change to impact the physical health and mobility of children.

Edelman's feeling of freedom in international contexts is a common theme; however, not all authors defined mobility in terms of social status. Though all autobiographies featured here involve women's ability to create their voice, four in particular offer relevant examples of how those who possessed themselves and claimed physical space could then produce inspirational, self-conscious writing. Anna Julia Cooper, Zora Neale Hurston, Collen McElroy, and Gayle Pemberton used their ability to travel to redefine themselves in enduring ways.

Self-Definition (Jawbone): Anna Julia Cooper, Zora Neale Hurston, Colleen McElroy, and Gayle Pemberton

In the single-most powerful demonstration of Black women's intellectual legacy of study abroad, Anna Julia Cooper *defined her self* by choosing the word "slavery" as the first word of her dissertation. When in her sixties, Anna Cooper completed her dissertation, "L'Attitude de la France a L'Egard de L'Esclavage: Pedant La Revolution," about French attitudes toward slavery during the Haitian revolutionary era.[32] Cooper's memoir about her graduate studies abroad tells how the doctorate, what she called the "third step," came at the end of a long but fruitful journey. She discussed her doctoral experience with triumphant imagery, especially because the writing process represented literary freedom, most significant for someone born into chattel slavery and a U.S. legacy of antiliteracy laws.

In her dissertation, Cooper argued that the cause of France's downfall was greed, then she presented clashing ideologies between the "Friends of the Blacks" and the power mongers who advocated enslavement during the revolutionary eras of Haiti (1791–1804) and France (1789–1799). Cooper's personal history as someone enslaved certainly influenced her scholarly interest in international power struggles over race, economic development, and attitudes influencing dehumanization of Africans in the diaspora, but her commitment to write a dissertation in French demonstrated a commitment to not only redefine her own personal history as being born enslaved in the United States, but also to claim definition over the institution from the perspective of strategic linguistic shores. When accepting her recognition at a ceremony at Howard University, she claimed that her triumph was not hers, but belonged to all of her race. She determined that her "voice from the South" would be heard worldwide.

She faced a formidable final battle because Celestin Bouglé, one of her committee members, forcefully opposed her thesis and challenged her philosophical framework. For her dissertation defense, she quickly had to decide what to change, what to keep, and how to rationalize her findings to a native French-speaking senior scholar with whom she fundamentally disagreed:

> I had but one short week to think it through. Besides and more emphatically I was frankly afraid of Bouglé. My French ear seemed duller than ever when he spoke and my tongue stupidly stuck in my throat. Madame told me that he was Breton which explained his variation from the more accustomed Parisian. But to make matters worse, I found myself on the opposite side in some pronouncements from his own thesis in Égalité, and when I gave out my opinion to Madame she said: "That will not help you. Bouglé is atheist."[33]

Cooper was on opposite sides of the table from her committee members both in social standing and in social thought. Underneath her controversial content about French slaveholders and abolitionists, her philosophical framework directly challenged Bouglé's. He claimed that the rights of man were an invention of Nordic man and therefore granted by man. Cooper countered that the rights of man were granted by God and could be neither granted nor taken away by mere humans.

Despite these challenges, on March 23, 1925, she successfully defended the dissertation that she had so diligently researched and carefully written and championed her beliefs of freedom, race, nationality, and divine origins of human rights. When Cooper reflected on her defense twenty years later, she remembered the process fondly, despite the tension and ideological dispute:

To me this discussion was both significant and informative. I realized, not unpleasantly that a soutenance was not a test [or] "exam" to be prepared for by cramming and cribbing the night before and brazened through by bluff and bluster the morning after by way of securing a "passing" mark. . . . Rather and most emphatically a soutenance "sustaining," supporting, defending if need be, an original intellectual effort that has already been passed on by competent judges as worthy a place in the treasure house of thought, affords for the public a unique opportunity to listen in on this measuring of one's thought by the yard stick of great thinkers, both giving and receiving inspiration and stimulus from the contact.[34]

Cooper wrote that, though Bouglé took exception to her activist tone—which he called "partisan pleading"—she passed her defense with his grudging approval and apparent respect, and when she was called "Docteur" she successfully rewrote ideas of possibility for herself and those Black women to follow.

Cooper was not the only writer to connect her voice to broader communities of race and gender. Zora Neale Hurston was at once a brazen individualist and an audible representative of Black culture. Hurston's work in *Dust Tracks on a Road* and *Tell My Horse* set her apart as a folklorist who narrated the stories of voodoo possession in Jamaica and Haiti and spoke of cultural or spiritual belief, but from a more distanced, "double-voiced" strategy of signification.[35] While Dunham's autobiography, *Island Possessed,* also traces a personal experience as an initiate of Haitian voudun possession, Hurston's writing does not focus on herself as an initiate or practitioner. Further, variant subjective and objective viewpoints permeated Hurston's study, down to the spelling of the practice: voodoo (Hurston) or voudun (Dunham).

Hurston's internal experience of possession was often mediated by an irony-filled voice that largely acted as master narrator about other people's possession. Amy Fass Emery argues, "Critics have identified self-reflexive strategies of ironic distancing—of signifying—in works by Hurston such as *Mules and Men* and *Dust Tracks on a Road*, but readers of *Tell My Horse* have been strangely literal-minded."[36] For example, Emory cites that both Dunham and Hurston interviewed Dr. Reeser, a White man who "practiced" voodoo in Haiti and that both found the man "flawed." While both interviewed him, Hurston presented Dr. Reeser as a symbolic caricature in her critical observation of voodoo culture, but Dunham presented him in critical contrast to her own, more studied, practice. Typically, Dunham's "voice" was her own body, while Hurston's voice was translation of communal experiences.

Emory writes, "Hurston's sense of her own vulnerability is mirrored in that of the folk from whom she collects folktale; throughout her career, she searched for a style in which to convey the richness of Black folklore as performance in writing without draining it of its dynamic, creative spirit of its living voice."[37] In contrast to Dunham's concentration more on her individual transformation, Hurston uses her voice as a traveling scholar to shape herself as a folklorist of Black culture: she shapes her voice through presenting the voices of Black people in Florida, Haiti, and Jamaica.[38]

Hurston's self-definition via Black folklore and personal voice through communal voice is clearly seen in her reflection about her fiction-writing while in the Caribbean: "I wrote *Their Eyes Were Watching God* in Haiti. It was dammed up in me, and I wrote it under internal pressure in seven weeks . . . the force from somewhere in Space which commands you to write in the first place, gives you no choice. You take up the pen when you are told, and write what is commanded. There is no agony like bearing an untold story inside you."[39] The story that Hurston bore inside of her was a story of "her people." Yet, Hurston refrained from romanticism in favor of presenting a complicated view of race, class, religion, and culture within Black American experiences:

> I maintain that I have been a Negro three times—a Negro baby, a Negro girl and a Negro woman. Still, if you have received no clear cut impression of what the Negro in America is like, then you are in the same place with me. There is no The Negro here. Our lives are so diversified, internal attitudes so varied, appearances and capabilities so different, that there is no possible clarification so catholic that it will cover us all, except My people! My people![40]

Not only did Hurston's work show that Black people vary as individuals, but her nomadic portrayal of her own life over time demonstrated an interesting evolution that defies easy definition. It was Hurston's quest to capture folklore in Florida that led her to expand her research to international travel to find origins of the stories she grew up with in Eatonville.

Just as Hurston spent time excavating the Black world in order to find the best way to tell her own story, Colleen McElroy found new dimensions of her Black self in faraway places including European countries like Germany and France, but also in other lands like Japan, Yugoslavia, and Mexico:

> Stateside education had not prepared me for the likes of Alexandre Dumas, Leopold Senghor, or Aime Cesaire. I'd only heard of two

kinds of black folks—those in Africa and those in America. (Speaking the Spanish of Central American and the Caribbean was not enough to place anyone of color outside of those categories, and African languages were depicted as a gumbo mixture of grunts and gestures straight from Hollywood.)[41]

McElroy credited her grandmother with igniting the fire of curiosity in the wider world. Her grandmother played Josephine Baker records on the family Victrola, but also warned the young Colleen, "Don't you go acting like Josephine Baker . . . took herself over to Europe and didn't come back. No telling what went on over there."[42] Of course, this guaranteed that McElroy would pay special attention to the life of Baker and eventually leave for Germany in 1953 to see for herself what all the fuss over Europe was about. McElroy made friends with a German girl she met in a museum and, by her second year abroad, had collected friends from Germany, France, Italy, Senegal, and Turkey, which she called an impromptu version of Josephine Baker's "Rainbow Tribe."[42]

McElroy's autobiography stands out in this study because, like Dunham, all but two chapters of the entire book take place internationally. However, where Dunham's *Island Possessed* goes into detail about one place, McElroy's writing takes the reader to Malaysia, Turkey, Yugoslavia, Yucatan and Nogales in Mexico, Lima and Machu Picchu in Peru, fishing in Belize, and deep water scuba diving off the Fiji islands, all while discussing everything from language and romance to taxi drivers and toilets. McElroy's account reminds one of the extraordinary nature of Nancy Prince's 1850 *Odyssey* travelogue of Russia and Jamaica. McElroy's dizzying breadth of geography hearkens to a time when Black women's independent travel was truly unfathomable; she covers "far and away" more than anyone else in the group, so her reflections of transnational Black womanhood are real gems. She ends the book in Australia, assessing reactions of locals to her not-quite-Aboriginal blackness. From beginning to end, regardless of the exotic places she found, McElroy wrote herself into existence *as a Black woman* but not confined to a narrow definition:

> Even in a group, I can manage to travel alone. In fact, as a black woman, that's easy to do. Most often I'm the lone black female on a trip—sometimes making folks rethink the notion that black women never travel except to Africa and the Caribbean, sometimes an uncomfortable reminder of America's racial history. . . . I've done a lot of traveling alone. Sometimes on purpose, sometimes inadvertently.

For a black woman, traveling alone can be an awakening, a way of defining myself that is not dependent on the American system of color coding. I know the traps are out there, the biases set for race, religion, and gender, but skin color is no longer an absolute measure on that thin line between black and white.[44]

McElroy ends the book mulling over the duality between a color "trap" and feeling of blood relation that she experienced with other Blacks in Mississippi, Chicago, St. Louis, Goree Island, Peru, and Australia. Ultimately, the maps she found on her grandfather's shelf as a child in St. Louis would be the key to defining herself at home as a Black woman in the worlds that lay outside of the segregated Missouri of her birth.

The final narrative in the collection, by Gayle Pemberton, offers yet another take on self-definition. Pemberton was raised in various parts of the United States but ended up in a relatively privileged part of Kansas City where she attended the well-resourced Central High School. Pemberton described the school as "a powerhouse of academic self-confidence and athletic prowess. And although there were other black integrated schools in the city," she explained, "we felt that we were in the best of all possible places. We went so far as to avoid those teachers who we thought weren't good enough for our college plans."[45] Attending this school eventually led to her enrollment in not only college, but graduate school and her appointment as an English professor by the young age of twenty-five.

Talk of college among her peers was normative and so was participation in the yearlong Americans Abroad Program, through which she earned a scholarship to study in England from 1965 to 1966. During her year at Bradford Girls' Grammar School (BGGS) in London, she noted the advantages of the American "smorgasbord" approach to education and acknowledged the positive impact that range can have on revealing possibilities for college. However, she felt the British concentration on rudimentary and fundamental aspects of academic skill-building clearly prepared her European classmates at a higher level than Americans.

As with most study abroad experiences, Pemberton stated that the most important parts of her educational experiences took place outside the classroom. She not only learned how to live in another culture where everything was unfamiliar, but found that to her dismay, "race and habit retarded a teenager's discovery of her own character and mettle." She found that growing up in the American Midwest had constricted her development and placed her in an unenviable position of competitive learning for which she was ill prepared:

I will never forget my first day at BGGS, when a girl who later became a fairly good friend asked me to define and defend U.S. policy in Vietnam. I knew better than to say we were protecting the world against communism, but other than that, I could come up with nothing intelligent at all. I was embarrassed and shocked at my ignorance, at my failure of intellectual curiosity and citizenship. . . . And from my first day at school, and that difficult question, I began to realize that one of racism's aims is to keep black people intellectual and emotional provincials. The necessity of concentrating on surviving in black skins saps the energies; not only does it keep real political and social power in the hands of the whites, but it makes the self no more than a sociological fact, dancing marionette-style, to a degrading tune.[46]

Pemberton felt travel had emancipated her from both a mental ghetto and an environmental one, and when in England, she said, "I felt free for the first and only time in my life." Freedom was the main point of her story. She wrote to construct the story of her father. Thus, her feeling of freedom in Europe was, in her book, only relevant to the extent that it allowed comparisons to her father's experiences as a Black man growing up in America. In fact, the premise of Pemberton's autobiography is her finding three yellow pieces of paper that would have been her father's autobiography, had he not died before completing more. In the final chapter, titled "Where I Lived, What I Lived For," she ended where the book began: attempting to write the autobiography of her father they had intended to write together . . . undoubtedly centering on his life of activism as a "race man" fighting against segregation in the Midwest.

Like Hurston defining herself through Black folktales, Pemberton grounded her narrative in the life of her father and frames the book in terms of Black literary history, including W. E. B. Du Bois's *Dusk of Dawn* and Richard Wright's *Native Son*, in addition to *JET* magazine's feature of Emmett Till and Alice Walker's *The Color Purple*. In order to understand her father, Pemberton spent time learning about Black narratives, one part of which was her exposure to life and critical analysis outside of the racist United States. The root cause of her effort for self-definition was to write the story of her father and, in doing so, she defined her self in terms of her family, a relationship narrative, preserving their story as she articulated her own.

Creating a three-dimensional lens through which to interpret these ten study abroad memoirs does not mean that any of these stories fit simply into one component of identity development. However, entries from these books offer concrete examples of the way in which Black women shaped their own ideas, movements, and legacies. Samples of those legacies are explored in chapter 6, where I include select reflections of young Black women who traveled with me to Paris for a study abroad short course.

With an extensive data set of narratives in the *Black Passports* bibliography, research opportunities for personal or academic growth are limitless. The explication of this chapter's theme, women's study abroad narratives, provides one small example of the types of rich research topics awaiting scholars of all levels. Most impressively are those who took formal study to the next level in foreign countries, but whose formal study expanded beyond school.

Though school and standardized curriculum represent a central location of learning, personal growth is the core process of lifelong learning. Examples of this growth and autonomous education are found in Malcolm X and Jan Willis's stories.

.⁕. .⁕. .⁕.

Jan Willis

Dreaming Me: Black, Baptist, and Buddhist (2008). Tibet 1967; 1970s.

"Luminous Choices"
Putting down guns at Cornell
Non-violence: not a dream, but a journey
Mother's rainbow on Buddha's robe

Malcolm X

Autobiography of Malcolm X (1965). United Arab Republic, Sudan, Nigeria, Egypt, Mecca, Iran, Syria, Ghana 1959; Germany, Mecca, Saudi Arabia, Sudan, Egypt, Nigeria, Ghana, Liberia, Senegal, Morocco, London, Ethiopia, Kenya, Tanzania, Paris 1964; Canada, London, refused entry to Paris 1965.

"The Witness Rests His Case"
Setting out . . . prosecuting false realities
Smiling with conviction, indicting *all* spiritual liars
Interrogates even his own definitions

MODEL: ETHNIC STUDIES FOR GLOBAL COMPETENCE (HB 2281)

The impetus for this book originates at the crossroads of my personal and academic story. I grew up in various environments, some privileged, some violent, but none which provided a strong sense of cultural identity. Whether in predominantly White or Black environments, I internalized messages that my blackness was a deficit. This can most clearly be seen in my formal education: I attended middle and high school in Tucson, Arizona. Though I attended secondary school in the 1980s, contemporary events reflect the hostility to racial differences in that desert region that resulted in my cultural disorientation. Despite my participation in activities like the NAACP ACT-SO competition and the Miss Black Teenage Arizona pageant, I found that consistent reinforcement of positive Black voices in school was nonexistent.

In junior high, through a program called Reading Is Fundamental (RIF), my seventh-grade class was allowed to scour mounds of books scattered across the library and choose a free book to keep. Frustrated with my inability to find one book that satisfied me (I wanted them all), I chose my first dictionary. I figured it had all of the words the other books had, so I clung to that. When I read *The Autobiography of Malcolm X* over ten years later, I was profoundly touched that his first serious study of books also began with the dictionary. In high school, the book that resonated with me most was Chaucer's *Canterbury Tales* because I enjoyed stories of travelers. Although my senior English teacher suggested that I find works by James Baldwin, none were ever assigned in regular coursework, so it would be a decade before I would find my way to him.

In April 2010, Arizona passed SB 1070, a regressive anti-immigration law, which was quickly followed by a law against teaching ethnic studies in schools: HB 2281, signed into law by Governor Jan Brewer. The law defines ethnic studies as a "course or classes that: 1) promote the overthrow of the United States government; 2) promote resentment toward a race or class of people; 3) are designed primarily for pupils of a particular ethnic group; or 4) advocate ethnic solidarity instead of the treatment of pupils as individuals."[47]

These two related bills narrow views on citizenship and nation, and they reject any attempt to educate students on the topics of racial identity. I view this approach as a calculated miseducation designed to keep students ignorant of racial differences in order to prevent solidarity or even empathy for those historically oppressed by the White dominant culture because of their race, ethnicity, nationality, language, or similar characteristics. The listing of over sixty *Black Passports* authors who provide memoirs of travel in Africa is included to encourage a nuanced view of how African American travelers describe African countries in terms of Christian missionary work (Fanny Jackson Coppin), popular culture (Chuck D or Diana Ross), or political education (James Baldwin, Pauli Murray, or Leslie Alexander Lacy)—far beyond a static definition of race identity.

The education away from cultural guidance and therefore away from paradigms of self-knowledge, self-definition, and self-determination is reminiscent of the antebellum era. From the 1740 South Carolina antiliteracy law to 1960s battles for Black studies, education has represented a battle for freedom in Black life. Libratory education has always been, in the words of author Roland Williams, a "quest for freedom," and, for African Americans, freedom has been grounded in literacy. Thus, in addition to presenting a bibliography that highlights a wide range of narratives, I argue for an increased focus on how words are used to construct historical lives. Offering a student a random set of words will not be nearly as effective as encouraging students to investigate words in literary context and contemplate the meaning of words in their own life writing.

Mary McLeod Bethune lamented being denied literacy when she was young, and Ida B. Wells explicitly railed against the limitation of appropriate materials: "I had formed my ideals on the best of Dickens's stories, Louisa May Alcott's, Mrs. A. D. T. Whitney's and Charlotte Bronte's books, and Oliver Optics's stories for boys. I had read the Bible and Shakespeare through, but I had never read a Negro book or anything about Negroes."[48] The imperative of Black studies prevails as a pathway to critical consciousness.

African American studies programs have gained popularity and are growing at the graduate level across the country (though much more slowly in the South, of course). Notable people have majored in Black studies including cartoonist Aaron McGruder (University of Maryland), author Gloria Naylor and actress Angela Bassett (Yale University), pediatric surgeon Claudia Thomas (Vassar College), astronaut Mae Jemison (Stanford University), and First Lady Michelle Obama (Princeton University). Though under attack by conservative pundits, the interdiscipline is gaining the academic attention it richly deserves.[49]

Arizona obviously still has a long way to go in this area, with its violently provincial curriculum keeping its children behind nationally and internationally rather than taking full advantage of strengths in cultural diversity. Africana studies, like Chicano-Latino studies, Native American studies, and Asian

American studies, offers a unique opportunity to infuse much-needed human-ism into national education. The outcome of such study will be an essential understanding of one's self, the body, and the interaction with the world.[50]

Identity Development Takes Place in Global Contexts: Black Body

Race scholarship is vital and in Africana studies, theoretical frames are instruc-tive. As a prime example, Radhika Mohanram interrogates Black women's life stories in *Black Body: Women, Colonialism, and Space*. Her multidisciplinary analysis changes the interpretation of a story's character as the relationship changes to a story's setting. Her interpretation of Black women foregrounds *place,* and she argues that location is as important in a story as the characters themselves. She insists that in life, each character's identity—thus each charac-ter's rendition of her story—shifts with location. A person tells different stories when in different settings. Mohanram demonstrates this argument by tracking her own shifting experiences of "blackness" as an Indian woman in India, the United States, and New Zealand. *Black Body* is an exploration of the changing meaning of women's blackness in relation to nation. The author unveils Black women's stories to contrast identity characteristics of "black" and "woman" in various settings and challenges readers to redefine their notion of identity in terms of geography.[51]

Black Body consists of three parts: first, a theoretical exploration of terms such as "native," "body," and "nation"; second, a historical situation of "native" and "settler" in the Antipodes (New Zealand and Australia); and third, a trea-tise to dislocate Black identity from static Western binary interpretation. This work is a rejection of simplistic interpretations of Black identity as "Other," which is the premise in much post-colonial discourse.

Mohanram convincingly argues that blackness is a shifting part of identity construction, not static as some have supposed. She demonstrates that black-ness is not concrete as implied in "African diaspora" because "diaspora" clashes with thorny indigenous debates, conflicts between members of a supposedly homogenized "Third World," and ignores realities of historical miscegenation. Mohanram complicates notions of universal Black identity. However, her com-plication of Black identity does not totally negate the reality of blackness as a universally regarded "Other." While challenging a singular fixed meaning of blackness, she shows the varied settings in which women's blackness impacts their ability to tell their own stories. Including her own story, she explains that blackness is at once an indicator of oppression and a means of resistance.[52]

Just as there are many stories, and many ways to tell a story, there are many ways to study how stories are told. Anthropology, psychology, and sociology are ways of studying characters, character attributes, and social relations. History is a way of studying motivations, events, plots, and conflict. Black studies researchers work from an assumption that Black people are main characters, not just supporting characters in White stories. Likewise, women's studies voices assert that women are main characters, not just supporting characters in men's stories. The implications of Mohanram's arguments impact the disciplines of psychology, anthropology, history, literary criticism, and political economy as well as Black studies and women's studies. Hers is an important contribution to the discussion of the impact of geography on identity development. Complicating one's identity is the first step in having honest discussions about cultural exchange.

Black female and male international narratives physically and figuratively embody complex exchange. In addition to study-abroad narratives, cultural clashes in sporting arenas offer infinite intrigue. Accounts by Olympic and world-class athletes are yet another area beyond education or religion that offers rich ground for future study of race, identity, and nation. Young women seeking to understand positive possibilities of their Black bodies can look to women athletes for narratives of victory and power. In the tradition of Nubian woman queens, named Candace or *Kandake*, women athletes who have penned narratives include Althea Gibson, Venus and Serena Williams (tennis), Wilma Rudolph and Jackie Joyner-Kersee (track), Layla Ali (boxing), Lisa Leslie (basketball), and Gabrielle Douglass (gymnastics). These books can be placed alongside Arthur Ash, Bill Russell, John Carlos, and Tommie Smith to better understand how strong Black bodies move in the world.

Black life, school, work, and movement hold much for those interested in studying humanity and social systems. As Zora Neale Hurston said, "you got to go there to know there" and cultural exchange, whether through formal study abroad or informal travel to fulfill personal, professional, or spiritual goals, gives us a "window seat" to the world. Interactions with global communities and a close look at intersections can educate young and old alike and can enhance both our swag and our diplomacy—by re-inscribing Black humanity.

SIX

Conclusion

Our Swag Is Worldwide, Wisdom Is . . .
Writing Your Own Freedom Papers

I was parading the Cote d'Azur,
hopping the short trains from Nice to Cannes,
following the maze of streets in Monte Carlo
to the hill that overlooks the ville.

A woman fed me pate in the afternoon,
Calling from her stall to offer me more.
At breakfast I talked in French with an old man
About what he loved about America—the Kennedys.

On the beaches I walked and watched
Topless women sunbathe and swim,
Loving both home and being away from it.

At a phone looking to Africa over the Mediterranean,
I called my father, and missing me, he said,
"You almost home boy. Go on cross that sea!"
  —Afaa M. Weaver, "My Father's Geography" (1995)[1]

MESSAGE: WISDOM IS CREATIVE CHOICES FOR SUCCESS
"EXPAND YOUR HORIZONS"

As academic mentors, we must lead youth to resources that increase their self-mastery. Self-mastery and global competence can bring balance to one's life. Wisdom, the combination of guidance, control, and ethics, is ultimately about self-creation. Our mothers' and fathers' geography can guide us home, but we must develop our own sense of direction. Books deepen all areas of that creative process and exemplify virtues of excellence.

Of all texts ripe for literary mentoring, the library of research, poems, short stories, and autobiographies by Dr. W. E. B. Du Bois is solely qualified to offer expansive instruction. His fifteen trips abroad and his "broader sense of humanity and world fellowship," found when he studied abroad in Germany epitomize a lifelong quest for wisdom, and his breadth and quality of production are unparalleled. I highlighted this when creating the Clark Atlanta University Du Bois Legacy Project. The project consisted of a 2012 yearlong seminar series featuring fifty panelists and covering monthly themes from art and literature, church and family, crime and health, to business, education, autobiography, and major publications including *Souls of Black Folk* (1903) and *Black Reconstruction* (1935).[2]

The project concluded with a 2013 conference to commemorate the fiftieth anniversary of his passing that was held over four days culminating on February 23 with a dedication of a bust of Dr. Du Bois to the CAU campus. More than 150 panelists participated in the conference, and Du Boisian scholars from California and Colorado to Texas, New York, and Massachusetts offered an unprecedented reflection on the premiere scholar-activist of the twentieth century. From this event, I learned lessons that have been percolating throughout my life and are present in each of the *Black Passports* chapters.

Keep Seeking Wisdom: The Never-Ending Journey to Expand Horizons

Dr. Du Bois wrote hundreds of books, articles, and opinion pieces, but the takeaway messages on which I constantly meditate are the two interlocking ideas of memory and legacy: "[T]here is no dream but deed, there is no need but memory" and "The worker must work for the glory of his handiwork, not simply for pay; the thinker must think for truth, not for fame."[3] These quotes connect our past with our future. Essentially, we must contemplate the legacy that we will leave, even as we go about the business of making our life. My goal, with documenting Black women's intellectual history, Black autobiography and travel memoirs is to identify enduring truisms of use to those who historically have had the least amount of power.

During the 2013 Wings of Atlanta commemorative conference, Dr. Gerald Horne delivered a paper titled "Du Bois and the Failure of Contemporary Black Intellectuals and Scholars," in which he argued that today's intellectuals fall short of our potential and purpose when we fail to produce scholarship that engages global connections and prepare the next generation to deal effectively with international economy. Essentially, the failure of today's intellectuals, which echoes Green's *Manufacturing Powerlessness*, is the inability to wield interdisciplinary texts as tools for youth's global competency. More than ever, we need to underscore the value of what Anna Julia Cooper identified (ten years before Du Bois's 1903 *Souls of Black Folk*) as "expanding horizons."

In "Postgraduate work in sociology in Atlanta University" (1900), Du Bois wrote, "The truly educated man is he who has learned in school how to study and in life what to study." However, rather than emphasizing only words from Du Bois, I will end with words by Dr. Anna Julia Cooper because, as a woman, she has received much less recognition that Du Bois, and much reclamation of her legacy remains ahead. Cooper left salient insight about the power of education and intellectual development:

> Her horizon is extended. Her sympathies are broadened and deepened and multiplied. She is in closer touch with nature. Not a bud that opens, not a dew drop, not a ray of light, not a cloud-burst or a thunderbolt, but adds to the expansiveness and zest of her soul. And if the sun of an absorbing passion be gone down, still 'tis night that brings the stars. She has remaining the mellow, less obtrusive, but none the less enchanting and inspiring light of friendship, and into its charmed circle she may gather the best the world has known. She can commune with Socrates about the *daimon* [deity/spirit] he knew and to which she too can bear witness; she can revel in the majesty of Dante, the sweetness of Virgil, the simplicity of Homer, and the strength of Milton. She can listen to the pulsing heart throbs of passionate Sappho's encaged soul, as she beats her bruised wings against her prison bars and struggles to flutter out to Heaven's aether, and the fires of her own soul cry back as she listens. "Yes; Sappho, I know it all; I know it all." Here, at last, can be communion without suspicion; friendship without misunderstanding; love without jealousy.[4]

Cooper earned her PhD at the age of 66, and lived to be 105 ½. She wrote poetry well into her hundreds, so hers is another key narrative that epitomizes the powerful connection between lifelong learning, international communication, and quality of life. Yes, education is the journey of extending horizons and communing with texts is an essential first step of that journey to wisdom. My eighth-grade teacher was one of the first to expand my horizons. For me, the journey has been arduous, but definitely satisfying.

Figuring it Out: Dr. E's Memoir

Empowerment is a journey. The journey to success and self-efficacy is long and winding. I was nine years old when the movie *The Wiz* was released in 1978, and it had a lasting impact on me. Growing up in a household that loved music, I memorized all of the songs, danced the musical numbers in the living room, and carried these images with me throughout my life. My favorite performance was "He's the Wiz" with the kids from Munchkinland on the playground running around with skateboards, kazoos, and hula-hoops. Of course, I adored the Emerald City sequence—that became my guide for how to stroll with sophistication at events sponsored by my Mu Upsilon Omega chapter of Alpha Kappa Alpha Sorority, Incorporated (skee-wee). Exploring Diana Ross's memoir has helped contextualize my own experience.

As a young girl trying to find her swag, I watched *The Wiz* repeatedly—almost obsessively. The vibrant colors and energy of the dance scenes on the screen carried me from my Arizona bedroom to a New York-Hollywood-Oz (complete with twin towers), a location where the right song could get you out of any situation. I loved going to Oz, since my bedroom was not always a safe place to be. When Thelma Carpenter's Miss One character sang, "Sweet thing, let me tell you 'bout the world and the way things are" to Diana Ross as Dorothy, it seemed she was singing directly to me and schooling me on how to defeat the evil in my life, find answers to my problems, and always get back to "running my business." At the end of the story, Lena Horne's revelation, as Glenda the Good—that everything you need is already inside of you—gave me a sense of peace, direction, and hope to hang onto when things got rough. Those are memorable scenes of the movie that had lasting impressions, and every day I quest internally to find, maintain, and share my inner balance.

My husband calls me Yoda. He alludes to my relatively peaceful nature, which has been hard won. In the fall of 1994, as I entered college for the first time at twenty-five years old, I experienced several anxiety attacks and developed a bleeding ulcer. Since that time, I have made peace with many of

my insecurities that caused my fears to bubble up and develop into excruci-
ating physical consequences. At the time of this publication, I am forty-five
years young, and I have finally made peace with the fact that—on a regular
basis—the world and people in it are prone to let me down, piss me off, or
otherwise get on my very last nerve. *C'est la vie.* Cherryl Arnold, a long-time
mentor, recently introduced me to Millicent St. Claire's concept LIGMO: "Let
it go! Move on!" and I have enthusiastically *embraced* letting go (contradiction
intended).[5]

Coming to terms with my emotions over the uncertainties or disappoint-
ments in life—and accepting my emotions—has gotten me closer to a mindful
equilibrium. It seems I never quite achieve balance, but taking every day as a
journey in itself has become a habit that I seek to pass on to those wanting to
trek a similar path. Just like with the *Star Wars* guru, mentoring work is not
simply about telling someone, "May the force be with you." For me, mentoring is about tapping into the force within yourself and then helping others
find their own source of power and light. But sometimes wicked warriors give
in to the dark side and you have to face these enemies head on. As always,
self-discipline is the shortest path to enlightenment, as thought leaders like
Morihei Uesheba, founder of the Aikido martial art, wrote in *The Art of Peace.*
Above all, I have found I am happiest when I give up trying to control other
people and focus on maintaining my own self-possession. That is what most
impacted my successful entry into academe and what has proven most useful
in my advancement, and reading Susan Cain's book *Quiet,* has given me more
fodder for feeling at peace with my introvert tendencies.

Since 2001, I have taught roughly one thousand students in my mentoring,
introductory or advanced research, higher education, race, gender, autobiography, or study abroad courses. In the later years of the mentoring course, I
developed a "NIA Statement" assignment in which students used haiku to
introduce their educational autobiographies. My haiku reflected my interest in
race, gender, intellectual history, and international problem solving:

> Black women's ideas
> Can help solve global problems
> At least, they solved mine

Black women's intellectual history was my guide, and in writing *Black Women
in the Ivory Tower,* I created a manual for my academic career. The text also
revealed my traveling childhood, as I sought to "act as a cartographer" and
created visual maps from the data provided by researchers who traced college

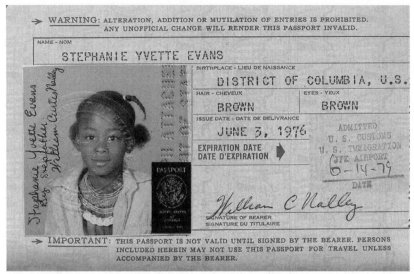

→ WARNING: ALTERATION, ADDITION OR MUTILATION OF ENTRIES IS PROHIBITED. ANY UNOFFICIAL CHANGE WILL RENDER THIS PASSPORT INVALID.

NAME - NOM

STEPHANIE YVETTE EVANS

BIRTHPLACE - LIEU DE NAISSANCE

DISTRICT OF COLUMBIA, U.S.

HAIR - CHEVEUX — BROWN

EYES - YEUX — BROWN

ISSUE DATE - DATE DE DELIVRANCE — JUNE 3, 1976

ADMITTED U. S. CUSTOMS U. S. IMMIGRATION JFK AIRPORT

EXPIRATION DATE DATE D'EXPIRATION ▶ 6 - 14 - 79

DATE

SIGNATURE OF BEARER SIGNATURE DU TITULAIRE

→ IMPORTANT: THIS PASSPORT IS NOT VALID UNTIL SIGNED BY THE BEARER. PERSONS INCLUDED HEREIN MAY NOT USE THIS PASSPORT FOR TRAVEL UNLESS ACCOMPANIED BY THE BEARER.

Fig. 6.1. Stephanie Y. Evans. 1976, Passport Photo, Author's Collection.

attainment between 1900 and 1938: Anna Julia Cooper, W. E. B. Du Bois, Augustus Dill, Charles Johnson, and Harry Greene. This fascination with mapping continued in my review of the ethnicities in the state of Florida and clearly led to my creation of online resources.[6]

Throughout my adult life, I would draw on the imagery of *The Wiz*, especially when reflecting on how powerless I felt during much of my early career as a Black woman in academe. At the end of my first published monograph, I equated my feelings of professional frustration and intellectual insecurity to Michael Jackson's rendition of the scarecrow. In graduate school and as a new faculty member, I often felt, "You can't win, you can't get even, and you can't get out of the game." Over the years, I have met hundreds of people who felt the same insecurities when attempting to scale the walls of the Ivory Tower or who have simply struggled to make it over the gargantuan hurdles of adolescence. Survival is a virtue.

Like many children labeled, "at-risk," when I was young, I had many difficulties navigating through challenges like identity development, safe social choices, and how to establish solid, immovable personal values within shifting environs. My environment shifted often: Washington, D.C., where I was born; Albuquerque, New Mexico; Edwards Air Force Base, California; Hessisch Oldendorf, Germany; Chanute Air Force Base in Rantoul, Illinois; and Tucson, Arizona, all before I became a teenager. Moving regionally and internationally shaped my perception of the world and my place in it by granting me several opportunities to create and re-create myself.

Part of my childhood was very privileged: I saw much of the best things that the world had to offer through precious moments with a loving family and lived abroad for three years from ages seven to ten, which opened my eyes to the wonders of food, language, education, and culture outside of the United States. The other part of my childhood was filled with sexual violence and neglect by a not-so-loving, extended "family," lack of awareness or abandonment, failed efforts of protection from my caretakers, recurring psychological terror, repeated attacks in my young adult life, incidents of domestic violence during my twenties, and a sinking feeling that the world held for me only danger and pain. Reading Pam Grier's explicit recollection of rape at age six and again in her college years stunned me because my own attacks occurred at similar ages. But, I lived and live still. I had help in the form of a role model teacher and, when personal attention was lacking, I made books my salve.

Fortunately, my eighth-grade dance teacher at Utterback Jr. High School in Tucson, Pam Copley, acted as a vital intervention. She provided me with tools that I would carry throughout my life that would get me through more difficult times in my young adulthood. She tucked life lessons inside of dance lessons: like how to shape my own self-worth; to value and respect others regardless of how awful people could sometimes act; and how to hold myself to high academic, personal, and professional standards even when others' expectations for me were low. She masked life survival tools within *pliés*, *pas de-bourrées*, and *tour jetés* and gave me a soundtrack for my own life. We performed dance numbers to George Benson's "On Broadway," *Chicago*, and *All That Jazz* musicals, and even Nipsey Russell's "Slide Some Oil to Me," in Copley's DAZE REVIEW productions in Tucson, Arizona, as if it *were* Broadway. We did a roller skating number to Cool and the Gang's "Celebrate" in gold lame capes. When it came to talent, no one could touch Copley's kids.

Ms. Copley's classes in musical theater allowed me to develop a loving relationship with my body, project a joyous spirit, have serious *fun* in demanding learning environments, and envision a future for myself that surpassed my sometimes-unbearable circumstances. At a crucial moment in my life, when I was contemplating suicide in high school after a run-in with a long-time abuser, one fortuitous phone call to Ms. Copley reminded me that I could indeed persevere and dance myself into a new reality. Pam Copley was my "Miss One," and the whole gang of "Copley's kids" that she saved could indeed fill a large playground in Munchkinland. Let's be clear: teachers and mentors save children's lives.

It was her example that I have followed in broadening my understanding and guiding others to do the same.

Wandering the World, Looking for the Sweetest Spots

After high school and during young adulthood when I moved to Nevada and California, books fed my spirit. Memorable favorites were *Johnathan Livingston Seagull* and *Illusions*, both by Richard Bach. The focus on independent spirit and acceptance of persecution for that independence allowed me a resolve and conviction to be my weird self, no matter how others judged me. Books understood me if no one else did, and that offered me solace and a will to "keep it moving" past the naysayers who literally spit in my face and told me I "wouldn't ever be shit."

Emboldened to survive, I eventually found my way to college full time and continued the world travel I had begun at age seven. Working with a faculty member on a research paper combining my work in cultural studies and her focus on sports, I traveled to Rio de Janeiro, Brazil, in 1999. Later, as a first-year faculty member in Florida, I gained support from the Paris Research Center Scholar in Residence program and spent ten days in Paris tracing clues of Anna Julia Cooper's time at the Sorbonne, which resulted in collaboration with the creators of the Virtual Montmartre and Jazz Age Paris project.[7] After giving a paper at a Cambridge University conference in 2005, I studied for one month at the University of Dar es Salaam, Tanzania, in 2006. In the East Africa library, I surveyed master's theses and dissertations by or about African women. The results, published in the *Journal of Black Women, Children, and Families*, debunked the myth of a lack of African women's scholarship,

Fig. 6.2. Stephanie Y. Evans. 1987, Palo Verde High School Prom, Tucson, Arizona, Author's Collection.

Fig. 6.3. Mr. and Mrs. Byrd. 2011, *La Coupole* Restaurant, Paris, France, Author's Collection.

created a map of higher education on the African continent, and presented a complicated picture of nationality, race, gender, and research focus as scholars of different African countries documented widely divergent questions, data sets, and topics.

Celebrating the completion of my book, I took a wine tour of Bassana de Grapa, Valpolechella, Verona, and Venice in Italy in 2007. Highlights of that excursion included tantalizing food, "Old World" wine, breathtaking country-side and vineyard dining, and a tango lesson from a *sommelier* named Roberto. The good life indeed. Italy was certainly a "sweet spot," but I was somehow still haunted by all of the African gold on display, treasures stolen from Ethiopia. Unlike when I was a child, when I travel as an adult, there is now always a criti-cal awareness that has grown out of my education in race and gender studies. While I definitely enjoy and partake, I also habitually interrogate and critique. But I keep going, and my journeys have been especially satisfying since 2009, when I married Curtis Byrd, my travel partner for life, as we began our adven-tures honeymooning on the islands of Grand Turk, Grand Cayman, and Ocho Rios, Jamaica, on my first (but not last) cruise.

In my autobiographical narrative archetypes, to a much greater extent, I am a survivor, but I am also an insatiable seeker. Like Makeda, I have an enduring curiosity and desire to find treasures. As Michael Franti of the music group Spearhead sings, reviving an old spiritual, "I'm just a poor, wayfaring stranger." As in the "Work" chapter, much of my personal life intersects with school and my professional life; so part of my memoir necessarily includes some of the work of my students. Below I share how a section of University of Florida students processed a study abroad class. In 2007, 2010, and 2011 I taught African Americans and Paris, and some of the reflections are certainly reminiscent of the narratives encountered from the previous "Exchange" chapter. It highlights the pleasure of sharing world travel with my students, and these have been some of my favorite trips abroad. While being a professor has allowed me to do my own thing, my career path has also allowed me to "do what the world needs done."

WISDOM IS COMPETENT BEHAVIORS

In the last chapter of *Soliloquy*, "My Tenth Decade," on the occasion of his ninetieth birthday, Du Bois gives advice to his great-grandson, Arthur Edward McFarlane II (then an infant). I have had the pleasure of meeting and working with Arthur, and when visiting my classroom, he emphasized Du Bois's message and underscored his life work in health can speak to us as well:

> As men go, I have had a reasonably happy and successful life, I have had enough to eat and drink, have been suitably clothed and, as you can see, have had many friends. But the thing which has been the secret of whatever I have done is the fact that I have been able to earn a living by doing the work which I wanted to do and the work that the world needed done. . . . Income is not greenbacks. It is satisfaction; it is creation; it is beauty.

Du Bois advised to do work you love, do work to advance the world, in his writing to Nkruma, so that Africans can "be free to live, grow, and expand." Expansion takes a lifetime, and growth is contagious.

To help others "expand," I have had the joy of taking forty students to Paris in my spring break to study abroad classes, so I can attest to the intellectual and academic confidence that increases when students, particularly those from disadvantaged backgrounds, are afforded the opportunity for international study. Travel engenders competence: by moving and communicating in a foreign country, these students gained a greater sense of their ability to navigate micro, meso, macro, and global locations.

UF Study Abroad Narratives

Reflections from travel memoirs can excite a new generation of young scholars who are awakening to their culture and global selves, eager to walk in the footsteps of Terrell, Cooper, Dunham, Hurston, Morton, Edelman, Pemberton, McElroy, Willis, Davis, and others who have written about their time in Paris. Paris is an especially fascinating site because of the gateway airport to Africa and the colonial history in the Caribbean. The result is a never-ending contrast of possible reactions to blackness. The most recent example, musician Ahmir "Questlove" Thompson demonstrates the point: In one chapter about hip-hop at the turn of the twenty-first century, he recounts his awful experience, which amounted to a stop-and-frisk:

> I remember how the cops in Paris would come at you if they thought you were African and then, once they saw you were American, let you go. That was routine. Once, maybe around 1999, 2000, I was walking down the street. The cops drove past on the sidewalk and then backed up and ran up to me. I pulled my passport out, but this

Fig. 6.4. University of Florida Students: "TEAM," 2007. UF Paris Research Center, Reed Hall, Paris, France, Author's Collection.

motherfucker stuck his hand in my pocket. I had a teeny bit of weed in there, which he found, and then he handcuffed me and drove me down to the precinct. I had dreads and people were shouting at me as I went in: 'Bob Mar-lee! Bob Mar-lee!'[21]

This passage substantiates observations by authors James Baldwin and Angela Davis that African Americans are given a wider berth than Blacks from Africa or the Caribbean. Questlove's experience underscores that a Black man with dreadlocks is *perceived* to be Caribbean enough to not warrant a pass, even with a United States passport. On my first arrival in Paris in 2003 to conduct research on Anna Julia Cooper at the Sorbonne, I too noticed the African diaspora and was aware, including in the *Black Girl In Paris* novel by Shay Youngblood, that the disparity of treatment by Blacks by nationality is widespread and well understood.[9]

On three occasions, I traveled to Paris to teach, African Americans in Paris: Identity, Politics, Culture, and Education.[8] Students and I have hunted for definitions of blackness in the *arrondissements* of *Montparnasse, Montmartre*, the Latin Quarter and *St. Michel*, and in the churches, cemeteries,

Fig. 6.5. University of Florida Students: "CHUUCH." 2010, with Ricki Stevenson, Alexandre Dumas Monument, Paris, France, Author's Collection.

Fig. 6.6. University of Florida Students, "JEWELS." 2011, Place de la Sorbonne, Paris, France, Author's Collection.

universities, shops, street markets, metro stops, museums, restaurants, and gardens of Paris. For one intense week at the UF's Paris Research Center (mostly Black female) students have been exposed to the history and culture experienced by Carter G. Woodson, Anna Julia Cooper, Marian Wright Edelman, Angela Davis, and others.

Guest speakers for the class have included Ricki Stevenson (founder of Black Paris Tours), Bob Swaim (dean of the Paris Film School and director of *Lumieres Noires*, a documentary about the 1956 First Assembly of Black Writers and Artists), and Jake LaMar (Black mystery novelist). These speakers were all Americans who have lived in Paris for at least a decade, and their lectures exposed students to a greater sense of African diasporic history and culture. In addition to American speakers, a personal reading by Martiniquan poet Daniel Maximan provided a living sense of Caribbean contributions to creative intellectual life in the Black diaspora.

Site visits included a tour of the Sorbonne (including the Amphithéâtre Richelieu where Cooper defended her dissertation and Amphithéâtre Descartes, the meeting room of the 1956 conference), the monument to Alexadre Dumas (author of the *Three Musketeers* and *Count of Monte Cristo*), the Grand

Fig. 6.7. University of Florida Students, "Sally's Daughters." 2007, with Thomas
Jefferson Portrait, *Hôtel Langeac*, 92 *Champs-Élysées*. Author's Collection.

Hotel (site of the 1919 Pan-African Congress), and the Scribe Hotel, where
Josephine Baker used to stay and the location of a breathtaking larger-than-
life fifth-floor pictorial tribute. While on the Champs-Élysées about midway
between the Arc de Triumph and the Louvre (both locations visited during the
class) an apartment building was a special point of interest: Hôtel Langeac, 92
Champs-Élysées where Sally Hemings stayed with Thomas Jefferson, as they
began their alleged "affair" and where it is argued that one of the founding
fathers of the United States began raping a teenage girl who would bear him
five children and from where, though technically "free" in France, she chose to
return to Monticello in Virginia. While the question of paternity remains one
of contention, Jefferson's owning of slaves while proclaiming rights of equality
deserves sustained meditation. This historical site elicited critical contemplation from young Black women on the trip who imagined what decisions they
might make in the position Hemings was faced with.

Other sites of interest included the Présence Africaine bookstore and publishing house (the central gathering site for Black intellectuals of the Caribbean, Africa, and the United States). These experiences certainly have been
transformative journeys for most of the students: in the 2011 class three of

the students had never been on an airplane, and only six of the total number students over the years had traveled internationally prior to the class. Student reflections in the final papers showed an increased understanding of the concept of race and the shifting interpretations of "Black" in international contexts, especially given the multivariate history of Africans, West Indians, and African Americans in Paris.

Student reflections from the 2011 class parallel observations of historic travelers. One key moment during the 2011 trip was getting to meet Madame Christiane Mame Yandé Diop while at *Présence Africaine*. The fortuitous meeting happened in March as she was heading to the airport to give a talk about International Women's Day. The students commented on her great stature and humble nature and how meeting her made them re-evaluate their identity and the political power of Black women and reflect on latent power within themselves that they may have previously overlooked or underestimated. Students also commented on ways the trip impacted their self-perception, particularly gaining a better understanding of the variant possible ways to experience race, ethnicity, time, nation, and privilege.

In the same way McElroy had no knowledge of Alexandre Dumas, Leopold Senghor, or Aimé Césaire, these students were introduced to a wider understanding of historical blackness fifty years after McElroy's Parisian visit. The prompt question for student reflection was as follows: What three moments in Paris had the most impact on your considering or reconsidering the meaning of your identity?

Student Responses

1. When I first arrived to the airport in Paris, an African taxi driver seemed very hesitant to approach me and asked me if I needed a ride; however, a European taxi driver did not hesitate one bit and seemed extremely comfortable. This situation definitely boggled my mind, not the fact that the European driver approached me, but the fact that that African driver was so hesitant. At this moment, I realized that I would be treated as an African American as opposed to just being Black.

2. Bob Swaim's film *Lumieres Noires* definitely had an impact on the way I considered the meaning of my identity as well. The way all of my people gathered together, regardless of political ideology, religion, sex, and other barriers, they met for the greater good of them all. They were not Caribbeans and African Americans and

Africans, etc. No, they were all Black and members of the African
diaspora. It is not fair of me or anyone else to just limit myself to
being African American anywhere. Yes, that is my ethnicity, but it
is only one part of it. If I am really trying to better the world for
my people, it should not matter whether I'm African American or
Caribbean or whatever.

3. The last moment that had the most impact on me considering
   the meaning of my identity was definitely getting a chance to
   encounter Madame Diop. Her words, "It's International Women's
   Day," were simple, but they had a very large impact. I have always
   identified with being a woman, but she confirmed that I am a
   part of something bigger. That something is womanhood. I am a
   woman of the African diaspora.

4. The three moments in Paris that had the most impact on
   considering and reconsidering the meaning of my identity are
   summarized by (1) realizing my rushed spirit, (2) understanding
   my humanitarian views of the treatment of those with less money,
   and by (3) truly appreciating my race. Our first trip to the Sacre
   Coeur [church] was quite beautiful and peaceful. Although
   there were tons of people, the melodious music from the harp
   was playing in the background. As I sat and listened to the live
   musician, I couldn't help but realize that I don't spend much
   time soaking in life. . . . Understanding my humanitarian views
   stemmed from a trip to Little Africa. Apparently bargaining down
   pricings was quite common. I felt uncomfortable bargaining past a
   point of no profit to the seller. I figure that since these people are
   trying to make a living, if I have the means to give "generously,"
   why not make their day? If I was in their shoes, I wouldn't mind
   someone doing that for me. On the topic of truly appreciating my
   race, during an educational tour by Ricky Stevenson, I learned
   about how strong, perseverant, and brave my ancestors were,
   especially in the Caribbean. When I was younger, I felt that the
   black race was naturally inferior to the Whites. I was made fun
   of when I wore my hair in its natural state, an afro, mostly by
   affiliates of my own race. I believe that many Blacks do not have
   respect or appreciation for their race. They do not understand that
   we are truly unique; no other race has the same history that we
   do. This lack of appreciation, in my opinion, thrives from the fact
   that there aren't many classes where African Americans, Africans,

and Afro-Caribbeans are statistically exposed in a positive light. I remember feeling so insecure while sitting through Human Growth and Development classes because the teacher would use "statistics" to "reinforce" the disadvantage of blacks. I absolutely detested this because while Whites would discretely be praised, Blacks would be blatantly scorned. At least this was the image that was painted in my head during these lectures. After this study abroad course, I learned about the struggles that these Afro-nations had to endure in order to be accepted.

5. The top three moments in Paris that impacted me the most in terms of considering my identity were the trip to Little Africa, Jake Lamar's lecture, and Ricki Stevenson's short lesson on the Haitian revolution. Little Africa was truly influential to me because it allowed me to get a closer look at my roots, I have never been to Africa so that was the closest I had ever been to witnessing first-hand African culture. It was just amazing to see even how thousands of miles away, African American culture and food is a direct reflection of African culture. Jake Lamar's lecture gave me insight about life in Paris versus life in America. When he said that America is a "Hyper-racialized Society" it made me evaluate how maybe here in America we do put a lot of emphasis on race and ethnicities. Lastly, during our Black Paris Tour and tour of the Alexander Dumas Statue, Ricki Stevenson gave us a short history on Haitian revolution and I realized there was a lot I did not know about my own culture and my mother's home land. That to me was meaningful and it sparked my interest in wanting to research more about Haitian culture as well as Haitian independence.

6. My first moment was watching *Lumieres Noires* by Bob Swaim. I felt like I had discovered a great secret that Paris had been hiding for years. It completely changed what I thought I knew about the civil rights movement and the decolonization of Africa and the Caribbean. It reinforced the fact that a group of people with the right motives and ideals can change the world through sharing knowledge. It made me reflect on how I am to use my education to further others'.

7. My main motivation for taking this study abroad course was exposure to different cultures. Previously, I felt quite naïve, oblivious, and uneducated on the topic of my race and culture, especially when it pertained to historical events. Although my

motivations were not clearly outlined in my final paper, I did
lightly touch on the positive effects of embarking on this journey
in my journal. In addition to desiring maturity, I also wanted to get
in touch with one side of my roots. I heard my great-grandfather
was a Frenchman who moved to Martinique, married a lady there,
and moved to Trinidad. Even before I learned that I had a fetish
for the French romantic language and their culture, I really wanted
my dream of visiting the country to be fulfilled. My professional
plan for the future is to become a pharmacist, and with this
certification, to successfully open my own business.

Witnessing the parallels in intellectual, cultural, and political growth in the
text of my students and the text of the ten study abroad memoirs allowed me
a clearer understanding of the enduring value of reflection. In experiential
education, reflection exercises expose the core of the learning. Service-learning researchers trace the cognitive learning process to reflection prompts in
the form of journals, short assignments, and directed discussions. Including

Fig. 6.8. University of Florida Students, "Café Memoirs." 2011, *l'Autre Bistro*,
22 *bis rue de Ecole*. Author's Collection.

journals for reflection, particularly while written abroad, produces learning opportunities that students can revisit at several stages of their lives and can impact their ability not only to reflect on their experiences, but also to learn how to implement lessons they have learned from those experiences.

MEMOIRS: NARRATIVES OF MOBILITY

Reflective journals can be exponentially enhanced when paired with reflections in other travel memoirs. For example, the student's comment above about having a "rushed spirit" is echoed in Du Bois's writing about his perceptions of Europe's impact on him as he studied at the University of Berlin: "Europe modified profoundly my outlook on life and my thought and feeling toward it, even though I was there but two short years with my contacts limited and my friends few. But something of the possible beauty and elegance of life permeated my soul; I gained a respect for manners. I had been before, above all, in a hurry. . . . Now at times I sat still."[10] Not everyone has the opportunity for physical travel. For those who cannot afford a plane or boat ticket overseas, books are their passports. In the age of all-powerful media, books provide a basis for literacy and vocabulary that frees youth from the confines of their neighborhood and also allows them to expand beyond the images portrayed in social networks, television, movies, music, social media, and other popular culture industries. Though I love the communicative possibilities of Twitter and Facebook, all necessary wisdom cannot be contained within 140 characters or a thumbnail quote. Attention to detail is necessary, this means sustained attention to the relation of ideas, thoughts, and action that only books provide. Few models have achieved the level of concentration and international mobility as Angela Davis and President Barack Obama. Reading their narratives offers a study in what it means to write one's own destiny.

Davis and Obama are clearly two models for the notion of global competence. Both have, quite literally, written their own passports to liberty and power. Keeping in mind the expected personal flaws, they are clear heirs to the legacy of Ida B. Wells and Frederick Douglass.

Angela Yvonne Davis

Angela Davis: An Autobiography (1974). Paris 1963. University of Frankfurt 1965–67.

"Lifetime Conviction by the Court"
Justice work's philosophical, not rhetorical
To absorb the energy of prisoners
Creating families Birmingham to Berlin

Barack Obama

Dreams from My Father (1995, 2004), *Audacity of Hope* (2006). Indonesia 1967; Europe, Kenya 1988; Kenya 2006.

Hyphenated African American, and bi-racial
"Barry" inherits muted radical nature, Afro-Asiatic clashes
Nation's hope; authentically, audaciously, adaptable

Each figure typifies a struggle for personal and intellectual freedom while on a quest to address larger social issues. They approach their work in markedly different ways, one through activism, the other through public service, but they are certainly both measures of how commitment to one's continuing education results in sustainable personal power. Power is a choice.

MODEL: WISDOM IS VIRTUOUS ATTITUDE—
"WATCH YOUR DESTINY"

Dr. Freeman A. Hrabowski, president of University Maryland-Baltimore County, consistently offers a clear message during his public talks: "[W]atch your thoughts, for they become your words; watch your words, for they become your actions; watch your actions, because they become your habits; watch your habits, because they become your character; and watch your character for it becomes your destiny."[11] In presenting his own educational autobiography, Hrabowski focuses on a biography of his mother and credits his success to her creation of a home filled with literature.

My first book, *Black Women in the Ivory Tower, 1850–1954: An Intellectual History* (2007) was an exploration into the historical foundations of empowerment education. I argued that Black women such as Anna Julia Cooper and Mary McLeod Bethune grounded education in four ways: applied learning (community application of theories), standpoint (cultural identity as central to teaching and learning), critical epistemology (critique of ideas as healthy in discussion and debate), and moral existentialism (ethical motives). I concluded by saying, "I pray that this story helps create more equitable and ethical

Fig. 6.9. Dr. Stephanie Y. Evans. 2007, "Give Thanks," *Black Women in the Ivory Tower* Book Signing Party, Gainesville, Florida, Author's Collection.

institutions as time, technology, and circumstance reconfigure the international human landscape."[12] I pray that this collection of stories, including my
own, not only helps create more equitable and ethical institutions, but also
helps guide leaders of institutions to improve our global geographical landscapes and to meet youth's need for guidance.

Folk and popular culture stories told to children often serve as lingering metaphors for how to assist youth on their journey. If revisited, *The Wiz*
reflects many major themes in adolescent literature and mentoring guides.
The book *The Wonderful Wizard of Oz* by L. Frank Baum, the 1939 movie
starring Judy Garland, and Ross's 1978 movie are all reminiscent of the structure found in many cultural folk tales, including African epic hero stories. In
this structure we see a protagonist's family background, battles, victories, and
lessons learned. Challenges or "risk factors" are creatively laid out along the
yellow brick road. Like the characters in *The Wiz*, youth face many troubles
along their life paths. These challenges include difficulties with self-confidence,
fitting in, and group acceptance (Emerald City), deadly environments and
dangerous behaviors (Poisoned Poppies), and obstacles to freedom including
personal, social, and political imprisonment (Evileen's Factory).

In neighborhoods infested with drug dealers, crooked politicians, apathetic adults, or various and sundry characters of ill repute that Charles Green calls "visionless leaders," there are "flying monkeys" around every corner, as henchmen of the evil queen, waiting to take out youth in their own communities, far beyond where the strolling, strutting, spinning, and styled-out citizens of Oz who posed and danced while the city deteriorated. The modern rendition of this is Suzanne Collins' *Hunger Games* trilogy (2008), with leaders and citizens of the capitol oblivious at best, maliciously predatory at worst. But there is always hope. And, like Ms. Copley, there are always a few characters that will be placed at the right time to make a difference.

I am ever the optimist, but I have commonly witnessed that no good deed goes unpunished, so I often "stay in my lane" when it comes to working with others and do not imagine that I have answers for anyone but myself. Like Glenda the Good, my overall suggestion for those seeking advice is to look inside themselves for any answers they seek. Like principles of Nguzo Saba, ancient gauges are plentiful.

However, as this book is about literary mentoring, if I *were* to offer advice to readers, in the spirit of what I believe to be tools for youth empowerment, it would be framed around attitudes loosely based on the seven popular vices and virtues.

Sloth-Diligence
Lust-Chastity
Envy-Kindness
Wrath-Patience
Greed-Charity
Gluttony-Temperance
Pride-Humility

The goal for me is not to work toward "purity" of virtues; we are human, so perfection is impossible. For me, the beauty of wisdom lies in recognizing the tension between virtues and vices and bringing that into equilibrium with self-control and guidance. The goal is to keep in motion but stay in balance. Managing the tension between good and evil in the world helps. This is not an attempt to indoctrinate youth into any one religion because, though these are Christian (specifically Catholic) iterations of morals, these overarching values can be found in every culture, regardless of nation, race, or creed. In philosophy, "virtue ethics," foregrounds character, which classical educator Fanny Jackson Coppin emphasized as essential to pedagogy. Character education is needed in schools, but definitely needed in life-skills training.

Given the need to explore ethics as a tension of vice and virtue, here I interpret how ethics might assist with attitude, behavior, and choices and with competent behaviors (life, school, work, and exchange). Ample autobiographical examples help us contemplate our ways.

Jack Johnson's pride and "unforgivable Blackness" was the cause of his downfall. He loved fast women and fast cars, both of which caused him trouble, and his larger-than-life attitude was "The Greatest" decades before Muhammad Ali. Yet, it was only his pride in self and race that got him to be the world champion. Dorothy Height, like Bethune, was a woman with a spine of steel; she suffered no nonsense and moved through people to get things done. Her resolve meant that her temperament was not always sweet, but her effectiveness meant the solidification of organizations like the National Council of Negro Women, which connected activists and advocates nationwide to advance civil rights causes.

Ruby Dee and Ossie Davis had a rich life filled with fun and purpose. Their story as two strong individuals connected in personal and professional partnership reveals the emotional roller coaster as one pursues a passion of romance (their at-times explosive love for each other) and acting (their work as actor-activists). Mary Church Terrell was famous for her style and radical activism in Washington, D.C., and Europe. She was multilingual, did not shy away from her privileged economic and political position, and was known for her fur coats as much as her antiwar work. Similarly the empire that John H. Johnson built on *Ebony* and *Jet* meant that he wielded considerable economic power, which he did not hesitate to put on grand display. Yet it was the vessels of those magazines that informed Black communities nationwide about domestic terrorist events like the murder of Emmitt Till, where the picture of his mutilated body was shown by Black press in a way not shown by White press, that galvanized a movement.

The entertainment industry is known as a cesspool of lust, and figures like Janet Jackson and Ray Charles can easily be pointed out as exemplars as a model of public sex, drugs, and rock 'n' roll. These and other musicians are not known for their uplift of Puritan ethics. However, the lust in each case is tempered by an admission of insecurity (Jackson) and an unabashed commitment to family (Charles) that complicates the sex-is-pure-evil narrative. Reading these and other texts through the analytical lens of Audre Lorde's power of the erotic could be illuminating for discussions of sexuality in particular and lust for life in general.

Pauli Murray and John Hope Franklin both exemplify the ideal diligence of lifelong learning. Murray's move from law to university professor to priest and Franklin's evolution of academic to public historian show an admirable capacity to push oneself to the limit of learning. Yet each also exemplifies the value of "sloth"; Franklin's love of gardening, especially in his greenhouse full of orchids, enhanced his thought process, and Murray's contemplative retreat into religion and safeguarding of her private life demonstrate the power of repose and opportunity for intellectual growth by being relatively inactive or otherwise occupied outside of formal study.

Work can be an obsession, but you must draw a line of what you will and will not stand for. Barry Gordy's Broadway musical in 2013 reflects his ability to sustain a career of producing Motown talent without limit. His reputation as someone not to cross has endured, but his autobiography title, *To Be Loved*, can also be interpreted simply as a desire to be accepted and move the world through his love of music. Patricia Williams, law professor and author of *Alchemy of Race and Rights,* confronts the injustices she faced within law schools as she pushed for a more progressive interpretation of what constitutes quality legal training. Her narrative interweaves race and gender politics with academic institutions, personifying both agitation for change and commitment to struggle even as she refuses to let the struggle consume her.

Championship tennis requires fortitude, especially by those breaking the color barrier in the era of global desegregation. From Althea Gibson in the 1950s to Arthur Ashe in the 1970s and 80s, penetration of the White-dominated sport, by two athletes from the American South was nothing less than extraordinary. Playing what is often perceived as a White sport at the height of segregationist fervor required diplomatic skills of the highest order. Both players pushed the envelope through maintaining a hard shell of resolve and restraint. However, the resolve to fight for rights on and off the court formed a lasting impression with their peers and the Black communities that they have represented. Ashe's activism is especially notable because of his commitment to multiple causes, including the South African antiapartheid movement and HIV awareness campaigns. His was a tension of kindness and envy (interpreted as radical desire for freedom and license) that was represented in autobiographical prose worthy of nothing short of the word "grace." Ashe's autobiography, *Days of Grace*, is a model of raw emotion, intimate grief, spiritual conviction, and tumultuous earth-shaking life events that makes compelling reading for young and old. Ashe was quintessentially human and his prose a prototype for appreciating the tension of emotional vice and virtue inherent in the human experience.

For many reasons, I hesitate to call myself a role model. I am human and therefore guilty of most vices, and worse, I am nonrepentant in some areas.

For example, I have accepted the fact that I am not a caretaker, and while I feel a sense of social obligation to help when I can, I do not feel obligated to give whatever is asked (or demanded) of me at any given moment by those who feel entitled to my time or energy. Even though I mentor youth, I have no ability or desire to "save" anyone as much as guide them to tools they can use to save themselves. I have been taking care of myself since I moved out of my mother's house at age sixteen, and I am still working on that monumental task, so I have no illusions of my ability to make a difference in other people's lives beyond general support.

Further, in school and exchange, I have yet to move beyond fragments of many tongues and commit to mastering more than one language. Despite my many travels, I am hopelessly monolingual, so this is definitely a "do as I say, not as I do" area for my students. There are ample resources, such as the omniglot website, that provide helpful phrases in multiple languages, but I have not yet been disciplined in fundamental acquisition necessary to truly be globally competent. In work, I am often overwhelmed and take on too many duties that leave me feeling burned out. I have worked too hard for a financial security that may not ever come, and often, I am unhappy with my workload and want to just give up and play the lottery like everybody else. In life, it usually takes me far too long to figure out basic lessons; essentially I am a late bloomer. I am also moody and cry a lot in semidramatic, nearly self-pitying fashion (thank you Mae Jemison for letting me know the crying I do has a name: swup-swup!). Sometimes, I'm just a bit too sensitive for my own good, but sometimes, I'm too hard. Essentially, I continue to work toward greatness but have limitations like everyone else.[13]

However, ethics is not about perfection; it is about finding Grace in imperfection and work toward social justice regardless of our flaws. With that in mind, I offer the following ABCs of power based on my own strivings:

Attitude

Altruism (Heart). *Wishbone.* Love. Feel, like the tin man. Have an attitude of gratitude. Know that you can do anything; however, value humility! Yes, swagger can be powerful, but not without a sincere appreciation for one's limitations. True power lies in equilibrium. Faith is important because, as human beings, we are bound to fail repeatedly and need every moment of opportunity to rebound from missteps and mistakes. This is why humility is a foundational element of happiness. You are imperfect; get over it. By accepting inevitable human failure and committing to aim for perfection anyway, you let yourself off of the hook. Humility will also allow you to give others the benefit of the doubt so that they have an opportunity to do the same. Self-love is inextricably connected to intimate love, social love, and unlimited (spiritual and altruistic) love. Love is the highest virtue.

Behavior

Balance (Brains). *Jawbone.* Meditate. Think, like the scarecrow. Raise your beautiful voice. Beauty is as beauty does. Create something of value, and understand that money is not the equivalent of value. Use your gifts. If you are reading this, you can read, which places you in the most privileged class in the world: the literate class. Material comfort will not bring you joy! Unlike the board game Life™, financial status does not determine whether you win or lose. If every new day you commit to creating your own happiness—if you find and make your own joy—you win the game. Choose work and play according to what brings you joy, and devote yourself to finding a life purpose that exhibits your brilliance and brings you joy. Choose to engage yourself in life-affirming tasks. There is this thing called a "work-life balance," which is usually spoken of in terms of the quality of life. Gluttony, habits of excess and binging, will not fill emotional holes. Life is short and precious. Act accordingly. Bring all of your senses to your life experiences.

Choices

Character (Courage). *Backbone.* Crusade. Be courageous, like the lion. Measure your decisions by timeless definitions of Ma'at (justice); the Ancestors are watching. Fight on your own behalf and for the benefit of others. Don't be politically correct; be spiritually correct. Courage is often a very small act in a very tiny moment. Many courageous acts are quiet and most are anonymous. You almost never control your options, but you always control your choices. No one can make you happy or unhappy. People can enslave your body but not your spirit or your mind unless you give them permission. Choice and will are the source of all freedom. In the movie *Matrix III* when an agent asked Neo, "Why do you keep fighting?" his answer was simple: "Because I choose to." Though oppression is a reality, freedom is a choice.

Most often freedom will require competence and that will take giving up short-term happiness for long-term joy. If you are not free and happy, every *moment* is another chance to reach for that goal. Further, it is only with faith and conviction that those determined to be free, like Harriet Tubman and Solomon Northup, have successfully faced the hundreds of dangers lurking in the journey to gain freedom for others. Therein lays true happiness: working to free one's self and others. Though no one can obligate you to do as they wish (otherwise it is not a choice!), I have found that working with others for common good is one key to happiness. This is especially true of work that benefits children, animals, and others who have more limited control over their circumstances.

Life

Never give up! Stay hungry. My fondest memory is discovering "If" by Rudyard Kipling. I read the poem as valedictorian of Utterback Jr. High in 1983, and the heart and nerve and sinew and hold on when there is nothing left except the *will* to say 'hold on!' resonated loudly with me. The tenacity to keep it moving, through the inevitable failure that comes with being human, is, (at least according to many science fiction movies), humankind's greatest gift to the universe.

My husband's motto is Make It Happen, and he is an amazing role model of how to move beyond mental, physical, and emotional barriers that life throws your way. He has a contagious lust for life, which has shown me fun times in beautiful places. Most important, he has taught me to value home as much as to value adventure. Everywhere else is not always better; the grass is not always greener.

School

Grind before polish! Read, read, read! Oral tradition, music, movies, and other forms of text are critical sites of learning. However, books are the key to power. Frederick Douglass knew it. That is why he hungered for reading lessons. Slaveholders knew it too. That is why antiliteracy laws were passed in the antebellum South. Life is a pop quiz and the more you study, the better positioned you will be to pass the test. Reading is difficult because it takes time, patience, and free headspace. These are not easy to come by in a digital age. Though there is no longer a law against reading, youth have a universe of distractions that can hinder their will to focus. Only those that learn to read the past will fare well in the future. Formal and orderly study is imperative to reach full potential.

Do not ask permission to be excellent! While this book is aimed at mentoring youth, many lessons apply to older audiences, especially graduate students. One of the biggest mistakes I see students in master's or doctoral programs make is waiting for their faculty committee to give them permission to conduct excellent research. Though dissertation or thesis advisors are there to guide you in the process, Fanny Jackson Coppin's *Hints on Teaching* (1913) reminds students that they are to take an active, not a passive part in their own education. There are countless guides to sound research and quality writing. Graduate students need to have the initiative to find and use them. For whatever subject you want to learn, there is a guide, no matter where you are in your academic studies. You have the power to assign yourself extra homework if you really want to improve as a learner.

Work

Do your work! If you don't do your work, your "friends" can't help you; if you do your work, your "enemies" can't harm you. Be nice! Keep your words sweet; you never know when you will have to eat them! It takes sweetness to get sweetness (and, you can catch more flies with sugar than you can with vinegar). "Smile politics" of Gabby Douglas were an important part of her becoming the first African American woman all around champion and gold medal gymnast. A colleague of mine once told me she did not like my "nice-nasty" ways. Though this actually made me giggle (remembering Michel'le's song "Nicety" from the 1980s), the irony lost on this person was that I do not act nice as a passive-aggressive way of being mean. I act nice and professional because that is who I want to be. When people throw tantrums or act unprofessionally, it is often an attempt to divert attention from the fact that they have failed to take care of their own business. That said, I do understand that there is a limit to being well behaved. Jill Nelson had it right about the NBF (look it up). Yes, I too carry a crazy Black woman mask in my back pocket and will pull it out when necessary. And as much as I admire Frederick Douglass, I will go Nat Turner in a situation if need be. But to live life in a constant state of battle doesn't make sense, especially in the work world. Buddha's focus on meditation was revolutionary, and that is why Buddhist monks in popular culture have the most bad-ass reputation as fighters. In countless movies, Chinese, Tibetan, and Japanese monks, nuns, and Ninjas are portrayed as mindful, peace-loving, and spiritual beings, but you wouldn't want to fight one. Nicety. Like Michelle Obama.[14]

When you operate in any professional context, be kind, respectful, and *professional*. There is no need to move through work in anger—even in a hostile environment. You will run into many bullies. Handle with care. If you must fight, fight fair, and fight smart. When you fight with a child, you look childish, and when you fight with a fool, you look foolish. When considering how I have managed to get around destructive people in work settings, I realize I have repeatedly called upon lessons from my adolescent obsession: karate. When facing a fight, I neither turn the other cheek like Martin Luther King Jr., strike back like Malcolm X, nor pick up the gun like Huey P. Newton. I choose Bruce Lee: the art of fighting without fighting. Watch the boat scene and contest scenes in the movie *Enter the Dragon*. They are mindful: when in awful situations, try to maintain your sense of peace and purpose. Many physical fights can be avoided if you use your head. If someone menacing approaches, often all you need to do is give them enough rope . . . Second, as demonstrated with each contest on Han's island, when you are in a larger battle for justice and must engage in combat, each adversary requires careful consideration and a technique suited especially for the situation. Don't try to fight everybody the same way all the damn time. Stick to your goals and principles. Even if you come away bruised, broken, and bloody, it is only when you have lost focus on your own discipline and purpose that you will have actually lost a fight.[15]

Drama in the workplace, like human fallibility, is inevitable. Anticipate it, and don't let it get you off of your game. You will win some, and you will lose some, but either way, keep practicing and be a good sport. As long as you work for yourself (define your own measures of success) and you work for justice (work in a way that expands opportunity for others), you will never be out of work, even if you find yourself out of a job.

Professional athletes know the impact of psychology on winning: when you play the game, play your game your way. Don't let anyone get in your head, and don't try to take care of anyone's business but your own. Practice when no one is looking, and practice as hard as you play in the game when the cameras are rolling.

Exchange

Learn with and from others, but be yourself! Before the Civil War, Black book clubs often were illegal, which is why I believe they remain one of the most powerful spaces for meaningful learning and why school and community book clubs offer untapped potential for meaningful political organization in ways that can improve learning opportunities for all. Take seriously that lifelong learning should involve formal learning spaces. Organizations like Elderhostel (now Road Scholar), which organizes field trips and courses for seniors over sixty years old, is a model learning environment: it is group based and relatively formal, and it involves a voluntary group of people committed to their continued personal growth. Some people enroll in a college degree program only for the paper or credentials; in actuality, formal learning has nothing to do with grades, credentials, or pedigree; learning involves the ongoing quest for wisdom.

Go everywhere. Go where few Black people have gone or where Africans are barely visible or the extreme minority. Explore out-of-the-way nooks and crannies of foreign nations. You will learn about the way that humanity bends and stretches. Go to Africa and other nations where Black people are mainstream or majority. You will learn the ways that Black humanity bends and stretches. When traveling, assume neither sameness nor difference. Both will be true. Your ability to be humble, act graciously, and let people show you who they are (rather than acting like you already know) will largely impact your positive experience. Work collaboratively for environmental, social, and global justice, and your travels will be more fulfilling and fruitful.

In the end, be yourself. It is imperative that you operate as your own axis. While it is great to "do as the Romans do," when in Rome, and it is imperative to observe cultural mores of those in whom homes you visit, if you do not have a clear compass for your direction and actions, you will be swept away into a spiral of actions that may be damaging to you in the long term and from which decisions you may not recover. Be clear about your moral compass, and let your conscience be the fulcrum that keeps you in balance.

Conclusion: "Find Your Future in Your Past": Heritage Is a Cornerstone on the Path to Empowerment

Like many authors, including Oprah in *Finding Oprah's Roots,* and President Obama, in his *Dreams from My Father,* my journey to self-awareness began with a visit to my relatives. When I visited my grandmother Mary Edmonds in Washington, D.C., while in my first year of graduate studies at University of Massachusetts-Amherst, I told her I did not feel smart enough to go through the doctoral process, and I thought I would fail. She smiled and pulled out a letter I had written to her when I was about three years old.

She said to me, "Sugarpuddin', you were born to write. When you moved [to Albuquerque,] you did not *draw me a picture* to send, *you wrote me a letter.* Of course you will finish school. That is what you do, and that is who you are." I distinctly remember writing the letter, even though I had not yet learned

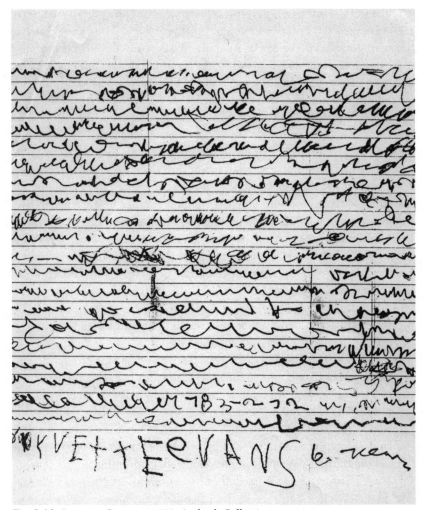

Fig. 6.10. Letter to Gramms, 1972. Author's Collection.

my alphabet or how to write, exactly. I believe we were in a park or backyard, somewhere outside. My mother gave me a piece of paper and a pen, and I scribbled, line by line, a letter, because I had things to tell Gramms about the places I had seen and how much I missed her. When I finished, I had to be helped to spell my name, but when she showed me that letter, it reminded me that I always loved books, reading, and writing.

The work of self-naming is especially important to break down confines of regressive race and gender socialization that prohibit children from realizing their full potential in the world. After all, Makeda was a woman determined to be queen, and she was neither modest about her desires nor embarrassed about her display of power. She was a seeker who traversed national boundaries and scripted her life in her own image.

At Clark Atlanta University, the motto for the Department of History has been Find Your Future in Your Past. These are valuable words for youth and those who seek to teach, mentor, and guide them on their journeys. Wisdom is the best of all treasures, and, surely, the crown jewel of this treasure is knowledge of self, and the key to the kingdom of wealth can be found in the life stories of those ancestors who have not only traveled before but who have left guides for us to follow. As Benin singer Angelique Kidjo sings, "Djin, Djin, Djin, the time is now." Whether traveling, teaching, researching, or writing, a bell sounds daily in my heart as a reminder that my physical life is fleeting, and the children of the world are telling us there is much work still left to do. In his chapter, "I Return to the NAACP," Du Bois writes,

> Above all the American Negro needs to be taught to read and to support a school of art and literature which will preserve his history and culture and add to the great treasure of human accomplishment; rather than let the unique and marvelous life and experience of the black race in America be distorted or even lost to memory as it threatens to be today.[16]

For Du Bois, heritage education and knowledge of cultural identity were the foundation of participation in national and global citizenship.

Black Passports is about freedom, what Afropean Les Nubians call "Liberte" in their *Nu Revolution* track. Through others, like Martin Luther King Jr., Rosa Parks, and the masses of African Americans who rallied to elect President Barack Obama, "I found a way to liberate myself." I wrote the first book for tenure, but I wrote this one for me, and for those who come after me who value both autonomy and connectivity. Professor Valerie Smith wrote, "Black narrative is about narrative authority and autonomy. The example[s] of the slave narrators show us the capacity to create a self lies in language and lies in autonomy."[17] Houston Baker Jr., of Vanderbilt, has argued: "By embodying these experiences and values in expressive form, the writer provides one means through which those who share the same culture can recognize themselves and move toward fruitful self-definition."[18] Life, school, work, and exchange are hard. But with a personal commitment to seeking the guidance of elders and through valuing the treasure of wisdom, struggle on your journey can be managed with relative elegance.

Being Black carries with it many social dangers; however, it is our task as humans to love, interpret, and improve life in our own skin. This balance of quest and acceptance is imperative because, no matter what road youths travel in life, they will still be Black.

For youth looking for an improved quality of life or the "sweet spot" as Sidney Bechet called it, there is much to explore as they prepare for their own journeys, though the road will be strewn with phases of awful attitude, hard lessons of errant behavior, and difficult choices. In her book, *The Womanist Idea*, Layli Maparyan labels a commitment toward positive existence "luxocrasy" as an example of creative resistance. Maparyan shares the touching reality that her commitment to viewing life from a point of light came out of disaster: her daughter committed suicide. Yet, Dr. Maparyan remains one of the most positive, loving, and contagiously peaceful people I know. Life is messy. Empowerment is a journey, and the journey will undoubtedly be rough. Empowerment means different things to different people, but mentoring for empowerment means creating spaces for youth to find and develop their own definitions of joy. Learning the path of others is a step toward the light.

As can be seen in the articulations by mentees (including Saroya Corbet, Frank Moten, myself, and my students), creativity is a central part of mentoring for a good life. Both Katherine Dunham and Dizzy Gillespie led exciting lives based in creativity of music and dance that covered the globe. In the midst of their travels, they impacted the lives of two who are following in their footsteps and in doing so, created a "cycle of voice" that mirrors a creative circle of life. The wisdom provided in memoirs is timeless. It connects the past and the future. In a talk I gave at Texas A&M University in Spring 2013, the title of my comments included tying in the West African concept of Sankofa ("go back and get it") with the fascinating work of Afrofuturism, most notably in Ytasha Womack's new book *Afrofuturism: The World of Black Sci-Fi and Fantasy Culture* (2013). Womack defines the phenomenon as "an intersection of imagination, technology, the future, and liberation," and writes, "Afrofuturism unchains the mind." The book is an important intervention because, as one enthusiast notes, "it gives our young people another way out . . . They need to see people outside of the norm."[19]

I have worked to continue the creative cycle by penning my own autobiography: *Chronicles of the Equator Woman: The Recipe for Justice Soup*, available online and donated to the Worldreader organization, which provides books to remote parts of Africa, Asia, and the Americas. The description of the memoirs conveys my enduring themes of travel (through space and time), mentoring, food, and social justice movements:

> *Equator Woman* is the autobiography of a time-traveling Black woman who saves planet Earth. The author, Axis Heart, shares stories of adventure, soup, and self-defense as her reflections reveal complex identities of females born in the African diaspora. The author begins her life in 10th-century bce Ethiopia, from where readers follow her to several continents during six flavorful lives. This scribe chronicles her viewpoints as an "Equator Woman"—a Black woman of Africa, India, Australia, Brazil, the United States, and beyond—to Kepler-62f, a human-inhabited planet in the Lyra constellation system.
>
> Axis finds herself pitted against powerful forces that perpetuate fear, ignorance, and violence in order to maintain control of society. But ultimately, she vanquishes her treacherous nemesis, Captain G., and joins a group of activists to bring balance to multitudes on the struggling home planet. By challenging readers to "follow your heart" in order to find solutions to human problems, these travel memoirs pose important questions about attitudes, behaviors, and choices we embody. This story of an ancient "sassy" Black girl and her 3,500-year quest offers a tantalizing recipe for organizing social change movements. As publisher of the narrative, Dr. Stephanie Y. Evans serves up a nourishing portion of soup to feed booklovers and advocates for justice far and wide.

Human questions of how to live were pervasive in ancient Africa as they exist in every civilization and should be offered to youth as food for thought. Long before Makeda, Sesheta (Safekh-Aubi) is recognized as the first recorded scribe, and she serves as an important example of the written tradition parallel to the much lauded griot and oral tradition.[20] Further, the ancient Paparus of Ani offers an example of timeless questions of being, knowing, and doing where Anubis-Anapa, guardian of the underworld (guidance) weighed our heart (self-control) against ethics (Maat) to determine our eternal fate. It is important to submit these ancient African traditions not in a grasp for superiority or perfection, but as simple substantiation of African human traditions that warrant attention because their quest(ions) are of value to the world. Our collective future depends on our ability to draw on wisdom from all cultures.

Each unique narrative contributes to our ability to better understand universal themes, and the exploration of creativity allows us to continually step over the existing thresholds of knowledge.

Creative literacy is as important as competence. In the world of information, literacy and management are necessary skill sets. The Association of College and Research Libraries (ACRL) defines information literacy as "the ability to locate, evaluate, and use needed information." I would add that literacy also means that we have an ability to create needed information that may not already exist. "Needed" implies relevance to the larger global community and builds on the idea of adding voices to the human chorus.

Empowerment education, instruction which is applied, cultural, critical, and moral is the path to literacy and freedom. Fortunately there are many tools to guide teachers, mentors, and youth. Autobiography and memoir expand the fields of applied and public history and are especially useful for subject librarians in African American studies and gender studies. Like oral histories, memoirs give us a direct link to preserved voices. Life stories inspire us to "rescue, reconstruct, and restore" humanity. They help us find our place in the

Fig 6.11. Saryoya Corbett. http://www.
dunhamcertification.org/Bio-Saroya.html.

Fig 6.12. Frank Moten. Brigette Hein photographer. http://www.frankmoten.com.

world. Like the jazz tradition of improvisation carried on by Saroya Corbett and Frank Moten, creative mentoring and life stories save and change lives. Dunham, Gillespie, and hundreds of others presented here raised their voices for the collective benefit. Their stories offer wisdom to enliven our hearts, sharpen our minds, and give us courage.

Youth await exposure to this information as a passport to a prosperous and purposeful future, so they can "Go on across the sea" to wherever their heart leads them. May this text bring our lives into balance and strengthen our hearts, nerve, sinew, and *bones* for the joyous work of empowering children and young adults and the next generation of travel writers. So we can all find our way home.

EPILOGUE

Regeneration, A Song for Strong Bones

Grandma LuLu's bones were strong.
Her small frame was sturdied by an iron will.
An iron will for dreams . . . for stories . . . for love.
And an iron will for joy.
It takes strong bones to hold joy in your body
When everything else has been stolen or stripped away.

Family is sometimes those who share your blood.
For LuLu, family was anyone who had strong bones.
Blood ties are thick, but bone ties are mighty.
Yes, blood is the ink of life, but bones are the tablets
on which life is written. And where it is preserved.
Bones are the roots of the tree.
My grandfather's roots.
My grandmother's bones.
Her song is my family

Her favorite singer chanted, "Djin Djin Djin.
Can you hear the clock ticking? It never stops. Now is the time to make your
life worthy.
Djin Djin Djin.

Can you hear the clock ticking? Now is the time to harvest what you sow."
A sister sings harmony; a brother plays horn.

Djin, Djin, Djin . . . the sound of my grandmother's song has been passed
down through ages and over rivers.
Each morning, her words sing me into a new day
Her song is my prayer bell

LuLu surrounded herself with strong-boned women.
They were poets and priests. Physicians and painters.
Market women and lawyers. Leaders and mothers.
Many of these, my other mothers, have crossed over.
But vast libraries of their lives and ideas still exist.
Dissertations. Encyclopedias. Diaries. Accounting ledgers.
Archives of wisdom—for those who knew where to look.
Grandma LuLu kept extensive records . . . with footnotes.
Her textbook is tattooed on my spine.
Her almanac is etched on my femur.
Her dictionary is imprinted on my jawbone
Her song is my birthmark

I have not visited my grandmother's home
for many years. Been gone.
Some places by choice. A wayfarer. Like Makeda.
Some places against my will. A captive. Like Isabell.
Ethiopia, Nubia, Australia, India, Saudi Arabia, Brazil, Haiti.
Georgia, Mississippi, St. Louis. DC, New York, Chicago.
Any direction is one step closer to home.
Her song is my compass

I have not lived in my grandmother's land for many years
But I can tell what time it is.
Her words reverberate in my breastbone
Her stories are hand crafted
and keep better time than a Swiss watch.
Her song is my clock

Bones shout out loud and make hair stand on end.
As centuries pass, blood only whispers.

My grandmother was not interested in being genteel enough to whisper.
She wanted to be heard.
Her hair was thick and her bones were noisy.
Not always respectable, but always respected.
Her song is my respect

LuLu. Grandma said her name twice to make sure folks
remembered. I remember.
I speak her name in the past, present and future tense.
Mercenaries tried to silence her, make her forget
herself—rape and shape her into one thing:
a slave. They failed.
She kept singing.
She kept dancing.
She kept playing and laughing.
Laughing for us. Laughing at them.
In my generation, sons of mercenaries (white and black)
 tried to make me one thing: a whore.
They failed too.
Her song is my freedom

Her song has kept my bones strong for this journey.
Backbone. Wishbone. Jawbone.
And a funny bone too, despite the pains that ail us.
African bones are the fulcrum of this earth.
Her song is my axis.

Grandma LuLu chanted every morning at dawn.
She chants still.
Her prayers are in my bones.
Her words free my feet to walk.
Her memory frees my mind to wander.
Her song is my history.

The myth of the strong Black woman is dead.
The strength of Black women's spirit is necessarily alive.
African women still need strong bones to stand straight
. . . the world is still trying to walk on the backs of our daughters and sons.
Much work still to be done . . .

I am a daughter of Candace
Big bones, dark, quick, heavy, and brazen
I run, I play, I stand tall, and shoot my arrow straight
With bow or ball, bat, or stick, I claim victory
I dance and ride and kick away despair
Her song is my game

I sing Djin Djin Djin.
Her song is my attitude.
Her song is my behavior.
Her song is my choice.
Her song is my Divine wisdom.

—Dr. Stephanie Y. Evans. Dedicated to Association of
Black Women Historians (ABWH) and Association
for the Study of African American Life and History (ASALH), 2012

APPENDIX A

Alphabetical List

Aaron, Hank. *I Had a Hammer: The Hank Aaron Story* (1991). Puerto Rican League 1954; Jamaica 1973; Japan 1974.

Ailey, Alvin. *Revelations* (1995). Dakar 1966; Senegal, London, Barcelona, Paris 1966. Madagascar, Tanzania, Uganda, Kenya, Congo, Ivory Coast, Ghana, Senegal 1967. Germany, Sweden 1968; Russia 1970; Austria 1972; Senegal 1982; Russia 1990; Antigua 1990s.

Ali, Laila. *Reach: Finding Strength, Spirit, and Personal Power.* (2002). Canada, China 2000.

Ali, Muhammad. *The Greatest: My Own Story* (1975). Canada, Germany, England 1966; Switzerland 1971; Canada, Ireland, Japan 1972; Indonesia 1973; Zaire 1974.

Anderson, Marian. *My Lord, What a Morning* (1956, 1984). Europe 1930–1965. Japan, Mexico, Israel 1955.

Angelou, Maya—Marguerite Johnson. *I Know Why the Caged Bird Sings* (1970); *Gather Together in My Name* (1974); *Singin' and Swingin' and Gettin' Merry like Christmas* (1976); *The Heart of a Woman* (1981); *All God's Children Need Traveling Shoes* (1986); *Letter to My Daughter* (2008). Paris, Italy, 22 countries 1954–55; Ghana 1960; Cairo1960; Sweden; Paris, Ghana 1961–64.

Ashe, Arthur. *Days of Grace* (1994). Australia, France, England 1968–79; Sweden 1971; South Africa 1973, 1991.

Atkins, Cholly. *Class Act: The Jazz Life of Choreographer Cholly Atkins* (2003). England 1948.

Bailey, Pearl. *The Raw Pearl* (1969); *Between You and Me* (1989). 1952 London.

Baker, Vernon. *Lasting Valor* (1997). Italy, Germany 1944–47.

Baldwin, James. *Notes of a Native Son* (1955) *The Price of the Ticket* (1985). France 1948–87; Switzerland 1950s; Turkey 1961–67.

Baraka, Amiri. *The Autobiography of Leroi Jones* (1987). Cuba 1959; Tanzania 1974.

Basie, Count. *The Autobiography of Count Basie* (1985). Sweden, Switzerland, Germany, France, Belgium 1954; Europe 1956–62; Japan 1963; Japan, Australia, New Zealand 1971; Canada, St. Thomas, St. Lucia, Caracas, Haiti 1972; Japan 1973; Canada, Europe, Japan 1974–84.

Bassett, Angela, and Vance, Courtney. *Friends: A Love Story* (2009). 1990s.

Bechet, Sidney. *Treat It Gentle: An Autobiography* (1960). London 1919; Paris 1925; Nice 1948, Paris 1955.

Beckwourth, James. *The Life and Adventures of James P. Beckwourth: Mountaineer, Scout and Pioneer, and Chief of the Crow Nation of Indians (1896).* Rocky Mountains 1820s; California 1850s.

Becton, Julius W., Jr. *Autobiography of a Soldier and Public Servant* (2008). Asia, Europe 1944–98.

Belafonte, Harry. *My Song: Memoir* (2011). Senegal 1987; Rwanda 1994; Cuba 1999; South Africa 2001; Kenya 2004; Norway 2007.

Bragg, Janet. *Soaring above Setbacks: The Autobiography of Janet Harmon Bragg, African American Aviator* (1996). London, England, Paris; 1955 Addis Ababa, Ethiopia; 1965 Ethiopia, Dakar Senegal, Nigeria, Cairo; 1972 Ethiopia Mexico, Singapore, Sweden, West Germany, Denmark, Italy 1980s.

Bricktop (Ada Beatrice Queen Victoria Louise Virginia Smith). *Bricktop with Jim Haskins* (1983). 1924–1939 Paris; Mexico City 1945; Paris 1949; Rome 1952.

Brooke, Edward. *Bridging the Divide: My Life* (2006). Italy 1944–45.

Brooks, Gwendolyn. *Report from Part One* (1972), *Report from Part Two* (1996). Ghana 1974; Russia 1982.

Brown, Elaine. *A Taste of Power: A Black Woman's Story* (1992). Beijing, China 1971–74. China, North Korea, Vietnam, Cuba, Algeria to Germany, Italy, Russia, Argentina, Uruguay, Costa Rica, Belize, France 1990–96.

Brown, Henry "Box." *Narrative of the Life of Henry Box Brown* (1849, 1851). England 1850–75.

Brown, William Wells. *Narrative of William W. Brown, a Fugitive Slave* (1847, 1859). Canada 1834; Caribbean 1840; England, France, Scotland 1849–54.

Broyard, Bliss. *One Drop: My Father's Hidden Life—A Story of Race and Family Secrets* (2007). New Orleans 1920.

Bunche, Ralph. *An African American in South Africa: The Travel Notes of Ralphe J. Bunche, 1937–1938* (1992). South Africa, 1937–38.

Bussey, Charles. *Firefight at Yechon: Courage and Racism in the Korean War* (1991). Italy 1942–45; Japan, Korea 1950.

Calloway, Cab. *Of Minnie the Moocher and Me* (1976). London, Manchester, Amsterdam, the Hague, Antwerp, Brussels, Paris 1935; France, Italy, Germany, Britain 1940–50s; Uruguay, South America 1951; South America, Mexico, Cuba, Caribbean 1954.

Campbell, Robert. *A Pilgrimage to My Motherland: An Account of a Journey among the Egbas and Yorubas of Central Africa in 1859–60* (1861).

Carlos, John. *The John Carlos Story: The Ports Moment that Changed the World* (2011). Mexico City 1968.

Carmichael, Stokely. *Ready for Revolution: The Life and Struggles of Stokely Carmichael (Kwame Ture)* with Ekweme Michael Thelwell (2005). Trinidad 1941; New York 1952; Cuba1967; Guinea 1969.

Carson, Ben. *Gifted Hands: The Ben Carson Story* (1990). Australia 1983.

Chamberlain, Wilt. *Just Like Any Other 7-foot Black Millionaire Who Lives Next Door* (1974), *A View from Above* (1991). Europe, Soviet Union 1974.

Charles, Ray. *Brother Ray: Ray Charles' Own Story* (1978, 2004). Europe, South America, Asia, North Africa, Australia, New Zealand 1960s–2003.

Chuck D. *Fight the Power: Rap, Race and Reality* (1998). England, Egypt, Ghana 1992; Europe 1994.

Clark, Poinsette Septima. *Echo in My Soul* (1962), *Ready from Within* (1987). England, Sweden 1964.

Cole, Natalie. *Love Brought Me Back: A Journey of Loss and Gain* (2010). Tokyo 2008.

Commings, Jeff. *Odd Man Out, An Autobiography: True Stories of a Gay Black Swimmer* (2010). Cuba 1991; Australia 2002.

Cooper, Anna Julia. *The Third Step* (1945). London 1900; Paris 1911, 1912, 1913, 1925.

Coppin, Fanny Jackson. *Reminiscences of School Life, and Hints on Teaching* (1913). England 1882; South Africa 1902.

Craft, William and Ellen. *Running a Thousand Miles for Freedom; or The Escape of William and Ellen Craft from Slavery* (1860). Liverpool 1850–68.

Cruz, Celia. *CELIA, My Life: An Autobiography* (2004). Mexico City (from Cuba), Venezuela 1956; Mexico City 1960; Zaire 1974.

Davis, Angela Yvonne. *Angela Davis: An Autobiography* (1974). Paris 1963. University of Frankfurt 1965–67.

Davis, Belva. *Never in My Wildest Dreams: A Black Woman's Life in Journalism* (2010). Cuba 1977; Israel 1980; Jamaica, Guyana 1976; Côte d'Ivoire 1983; South Africa 1994; Cuba, Kenya 1998.

Davis, Miles. *Miles: The Autobiography* (1989). Paris 1949–91; Europe 1960; Japan 1964; Europe 1967; Europe, Japan 1982–83; Japan 1985; Europe, Asia, Australia, New Zealand 1987; Germany, Spain, Japan 1988; Switzerland 1991; Favorites: Paris, Rio, Oslo, Japan, Italy, Poland; No Africa or Mexico.

Davis, Ossie, and Ruby Dee. *This Life Together: With Ossie and Ruby* (1998). Liberia, North Africa (Ossie) 1942–45; Nigeria 1969 (Ossie and Ruby); India 1989.

Davis Jr., Sammy. *Sammy: An Autobiography* (2000). London 1960; London 1964; Paris, London 1964; Canada 1968; Vietnam 1971; Holland, Germany, Sweden, England, France 1972; Australia 1977; Australia 1979; France 1985.

Dean, Harry Foster. *The Pedro Gorino; the adventures of a Negro sea-captain in Africa and on the seven seas in his attempts to found an Ethiopian empire: an autobiographical narrative* (1929). South Africa, Liberia 1876–79.

Delany, Annie and Sara. *Having Our Say: The Delany Sisters' First Hundred Years* (1993). London, Germany, Italy, France, Russia, Lithuania, Estonia, Latvia vacation with mother 1930; Jamaica, Cuba Bessie vacation with dental patient 1932.

Denton, Sandy Pepa. *Let's Talk about PEP: The Salt-n-Pepa Superstar Tells It How It Is* (2008). Born and raised Jamaica 1969. Europe 2006.

Douglas, Gabrielle. *Grace, Gold, and Glory: My Leap of Faith* (2012); *Raising the Bar* (2013). Mexico 2012; Japan, Italy 2011; London 2012.

Douglass, Frederick. *Narrative of the Life of Frederick Douglass, An American Slave: Written by Himself* (1845). England, Scotland, Ireland 1845.

Dryden, Charles W. *A-Train: Memoirs of a Tuskegee Airman* (1997). Morocco, Tunisia, Italy 1943; Korea 1950–52; Germany, London, Greece, Italy, France 1957–62.

Du Bois, W. E. B. *Darkwater* (1920); *Dusk of Dawn: Autobiography of a Race Concept* (1940), *The Autobiography of W. E. B. Du Bois: A Soliloquy on Viewing My Life from the Last Decade of Its First Century* (1968). Berlin

1892–94; Niagara Falls, Canada 1905; London 1900; London 1911; Paris 1919; London, Brussels, Paris 1921; Liberia 1923; Russia 1926; World trip 1936; Haiti, Cuba 1944; Manchester, England 1945; Paris, Moscow 1949; [Passport denied 1951–58]; Soviet Union, Europe 1958–59; China 1959; Accra, Ghana 1961.

Dunham, Katherine. *A Tough of Innocence* (1959), *Island Possessed* (1969). Haiti, Jamaica, Martinique, Trinidad 1936; Mexico, London, Paris 1947–49; South America, Europe, North Africa tour 1950–55; Australia, New Zealand, Japan 1956–58; Europe 1959–60; 1965 Dakar, Senegal; 57 countries in 20 years; 1992 Haiti (hunger strike).

Duster, Michelle. *Ida Abroad* (2010). Mexico, Europe 1983.

Dympna Ugwu-Oju. *What Will My Mother Say?" A Tribal African Girl Comes of Age in America* (1995). Nigeria 1956

Early, Charity. *One Woman's Army: A Black Officer Remembers the WAC* (1989). Bermuda, London, Glaskow, Rouen France 1945; University of Zurich 1951.

Edelman, Marian Wright. *Lanterns: A Memoir of Mentors* (1999). Europe, Paris, Ireland Scotland, Soviet Union 1959.

Elaw, Zilpha. *Memoirs of the Life, Religious Experience, Ministerial Travels and Labours of Mrs. Zilpha Elaw, An American Female of Color: Together with Some Account of the Great Religious Revivals in America* (1846). England 1840.

Ellington, Duke. *Music Is My Mistress* (1974). Holland, France 1932, Europe 1939, 1958–59; Leeds 1958; Turkey, Iraq, Cyprus, Greece, Egypt, Japan 1964; Senegal 1966; Argentina, Chile, Brazil, Mexico 1968; Prague 1969; Latin America, Soviet Union 1971; world tour Europe, Asia, Australia, New Zealand, Southeast Asia 1933–1971.

Estes, Simon. *Simon Estes in His Own Voice* (1999). Germany, Russia, England, Italy, Switzerland, Spain, Portugal, Monoco, Norway, Austria, Sweden 1965–1998; South Africa 1995–96.

Fisher, Antwone. *Finding Fish: A Memoir* (2001). Eleven-year navy tour; Japan 1977.

Forman, James. *The Making of Black Revolutionaries* (1972, 1997). Okinawa 1948; Guinea 1964; Tanzania, Zambia, Congo 1967; Martinique 1969.

Foreman, George. *By George: The Autobiography of George Foreman* (1995, 2000). Mexico City 1968; Kingston Jamaica 1973; Tokyo Japan 1973; Caracas Venezuela 1974; Kinshasa Zaire 1974; England 1990.

Franklin, John Hope. *Mirror to America: The Autobiography of John Hope*

Franklin (2005). Saltsburg 1951, 1958; Cambridge, Australia, Nigeria 1960.

Frazier, Joe. *Smokin' Joe: The Autobiography* (1996). Jamaica, England 1973; Philippines 1975.

Gibbs, Mifflin Wistar. *Shadow and Light: An Autobiography with Reminiscences of the Last and Present Century* (1902). Paris, Israel, Egypt, London, Consul to Madagascar, 1898–1901.

Gibson, Althea. *I Always Wanted to Be Somebody* (1958). Southeast Asia State Department Tour 1955; Australia, France 1956; Wimbledon, Australia 1957; Wimbledon 1958; Rome 1960.

Gillespie, Dizzy (John Birks). *To Be or Not . . . to Bop* (1979). Europe 1948; Europe 1950; 1953; Canada, North Africa, Near East, Asia, Western Europe 1956; London 1965; Nairobi, Kenya 1972; Havana, Cuba 1977.

Gordy, Berry. *To Be Loved: The Music, the Magic, the Memories of Motown* (1994). Korea 1950–53.

Gould, William Benjamin. *Diary of a Contraband: The Civil War Passage of a Black Sailor* (1865, 2002). Holland, Belgium, Spain, Portugal, England 1860s.

Gregory, Dick. *Callus on My Soul: A Memoir* (2003). Australia, Zambia 1970.

Grier, Pam. *Foxy: My Life in Three Acts* (2010).England 1965.

Guillaume, Robert. *Guillaume: A Life* (2002). Okinawa 1945; Vienna 1965; Rome 1973.

Hampton, Lionel. *Hamp: An Autobiography.* with Jim Haskins (1989). France, Denmark, Netherlands, Austria, Spain, Germany, Switzerland, Belgium, Italy, Yugoslavia 1953–83; Japan 1963, 1981, 1983.

Harris, Gail. *A Woman's War: The Professional and Personal Journey of the Navy's First African American Female Intelligence Officer* (2010). Korea 1988; Spain 1989; Middle East 1992–96.

Harrison, Juanita. *My Great, Wide, Beautiful World* ["Explorer"] (1935–36). Europe, Mediterranean, Asia, North Africa, Middle East 1927–1930s.

Height, Dorothy. *Open Wide the Freedom Gates* (2003). Oxford, England 1936; Delhi, India 1952; Liberia, 1955, 1959; Uruguay, 1960; Sierra Leone, Ghana, Nigeria, Guinea, Israel 1966.

Henderson, Jeff. *Cooked: From the Streets to the Stove, from Cocaine to Foie Gras* (2007). Mexico, 1986.

Henson, Josiah. *The Life of Josiah Henson, Formerly a Slave, Now an Inhabitant of Canada, as Narrated by Himself; Truth Stranger Than Fiction. Father Henson's Story of His Own Life; Uncle Tom's Story of His Life: An Autobiography of the Rev. Josiah Henson* (1849, 1858, 1876); Canada 1830.

Henson, Matthew. *Negro Explorer at the North Pole: The Autobiography of Matthew Henson* (1912). North Pole 1909.

Heywood, Harry. *Black Bolshevik: Autobiography of an Afro-American Communist* (1978). Moscow Russia 1926–30.

Holiday, Billie. *Lady Sings the Blues* (1956). Ghostwritten by William Dufty. European Tour 1954; Paris 1958; London, Norway, Sweden, Germany, Italy, France, 1959.

Hughes, Langston. *The Big Sea* (1941), *I Wonder as I Wander* (1956). Mexico 1920–21; Africa, Holland, Paris 1924; Russia 1932–33; Spain 1937.

Hunter-Gault, Charlayne. *New News Out of Africa: Uncovering Africa's Renaissance* (2007). South Africa 1997–2006.

Hurston, Zora Neale. *Dust Tracks on a Road: An Autobiography* (1942). Jamaica, Haiti 1937.

Jackson, Janet. *True You: A Journey to Finding and Loving Yourself.* Paris 2010.

Jackson, Mahalia. *Movin' on Up* (1966). European tours 1948, 1961, 1963–64, 1967–69; Liberia 1970; Europe, Germany 1971.

Jacobs, Harriet. *Incidents in the Life of a Slave Girl* (1852). Published under the pseudonym Linda Brent. England 1845.

James, Etta. *Rage to Survive: The Etta James Story* (1995). Zaire 1974.

James, Rick. *The Confessions of Rick James: Memoirs of a Super Freak* (2007). Europe 1982.

Jamison, Judith. *Dancing Spirit: An Autobiography* (1993). Dakar 1966; Senegal, London, Barcelona, Paris 1966. Madagascar, Tanzania, Uganda, Kenya, Congo, Ivory Coast, Ghana, Senegal 1967. Germany, Sweden 1968; Russia 1970; Austria 1972; Senegal 1982; Russia 1990; Antigua 1990s.

Jefferson, Alexander. *Red Tail Captured, Red Tail Free* (2005). Algeria 1944; Italy, France, Germany 1944.

Jemison, Mae. *Find Where the Wind Blows: Moments from My Life* (2001). Liberia 1983–85; Rio de Janeiro 1989; Space 1992.

Johnson, Jack. *My Life and Battles* (1914, 2009). Australia 1907; Australia, Paris 1908; England, Paris 1911; Canada, Paris, Russia, England, Brazil 1913–14; Cuba 1915.

Johnson, James Weldon. *Along This Way: The Autobiography of James Weldon Johnson* (1933, 1990). Venezuela 1906–08; Nicaragua 1909–13; Haiti 1920; Japan 1929.

Johnson, John H. *Succeeding against the Odds: The Autobiography of a Great American Businessman* (1992). Ghana 1957; Russia, Poland 1959; Ivory Coast 1961; Kenya 1963; Continent feature 1976.

Jones, Quincy. *Q: The Autobiography of Quincy Jones* (2001). Sweden, Paris,

Algiers 1953; Paris, Holland, Belgium, Italy, Yugoslavia, Finland, Austria, Germany, Switzerland, Portugal 1957–59; Turkey 1956; Brazil 195?; Switzerland 1991; France 1998.

Jordan, June. *Some of Us Did Not Die* (2003). Nicaragua 1983; Bahamas 1989.

Kelly, Samuel. *Dr. Sam: Soldier, Educator, Advocate, Friend—An Autobiography* (2010). Japan 1945; South Korea 1951; Japan 1955–56; South Korea 1962.

Kennedy, Florynce. *Color Me Flo: My Hard Life and Good Times* (1976).Canada 1967; Australia, Mexico City, Toronto 1975.

King, B. B. *Blues All Around Me: The Autobiography of B. B. King* (1996). Japan, Australia, Ghana, Nigeria, Chad and Liberia 1971; Russia 1977; Israel 1986, 1996; Europe 1988.

King, Coretta Scott. *My Life with Martin Luther King, Jr.* (1993). Ghana 1957; India 1959; Norway, Paris, Jerusalem, Egypt 1964.

King Jr., Martin Luther. *The Autobiography of Martin Luther King Jr.* (1998). Ghana 1957; India 1959; Norway, Paris, Jerusalem, Egypt 1964.

Kitt, Eartha. *Thursday's Child* (1956), *Alone with Me: A New Autobiography* (1976), *Confessions of a Sex Kitten* (1991). Mexico City 1948; Europe 1948–49; Paris, Istanbul 1950–51; Nigeria 1958; Milan 1968; Swaziland, Southern Africa 1971, 1973; Hong Kong, London 1974.

Lacy, Leslie Alexander. *The Rise and Fall of a Proper Negro: An Autobiography* (1970). Sierra Leone, Liberia, Senegal, Guinea, Ivory Coast, Ghana 1963.

Langston, John Mercer. *From the Virginia Plantation to the National Capitol: Or the First and Only Negro Representative in Congress* (1894). Haiti, Dominican Republic 1877–85.

Latta, Rev. Morgan London. *A History of My Life and Work* (1903). England, Canada 1892–1903.

Lee, Andrea. *Russian Journal* (1981). Russia 1978–79.

Leslie, Lisa. *Don't Let the Lipstick Fool You* (2008). Atlanta 1996; Australia 2000; China 2002; Athens 2004.

Lester, Julius. *Lovesong: Becoming a Jew* (1987, 1995). Vietnam, Cuba 1966.

Lorde, Audre. *Zami: A New Spelling of My Name* (1980). *Sister Outsider* (1984). *Cancer Journals* (1981). Mexico 1954; Russia 1976; Grenada 1978.

Louis, Joe. *My Life: An Autobiography* (1978). England 1944; Canada 1945; Mexico 1946; Mexico, Cuba, Colombia, Chile, Panama, El Salvador 1947; Jamaica, Bahamas, Cuba 1949; Brazil 1950; Japan, China 1951.

Love, Nat. *The Life and Adventures of Nat Love, Better Known in the Cattle Country as "Deadwood Dick," by Himself* (1907). Mexico 1870s.

Lynch, James R. *Reminiscences of an Active Life* (1913). Hawaii, Philippines 1907.

Malcolm X. *Autobiography of Malcolm X* (1965). United Arab Republic, Sudan, Nigeria, Egypt, Mecca, Iran, Syria, Ghana 1959; Germany, Mecca, Saudi Arabia, Sudan, Egypt, Nigeria, Ghana, Liberia, Senegal, Morocco, London, Ethiopia, Kenya, Tanzania, Paris 1964; Canada, London, refused entry to Paris 1965.

Marrant, John. *The Negro Convert: A Poem; Being the Substance of the Experience of Mr. John Marrant, A Negro* (1785). Nova Scotia 1785; England 1790.

Marshall, Paule. *Triangular Road: A Memoir* (2009). Barbados, Grenada 1962; Europe 1965; Lagos, Nigeria 1977.

Mays, Benjamin. *Born to Rebel: An Autobiography* (1987). India, England, Egypt, Jerusalem 1936; China 1937; Egypt 1953.

Mays, Willie. *Say Hey: The Autobiography of Willie Mays* (1988). Japan, Mexico, Venezuela, Latin America 1957-60.

McElroy, Colleen. *A Long Way from St. Louie* (1997). Germany 1940s; Mexico; Fulbright Yugoslavia, Japan Fulbright and Rockefeller 1988;

McKay, Claude. *A Long Way from Home* (1937, 1970); *My Green Hills of Jamaica* (1979). U.S. 1913; London 1919-20; Russia 1922-23; Berlin, Paris 1923; North Africa 1923-33; Paris 1928-29.

Mingus, Charles. *Beneath the Underdog* (1971, 1998). Paris 1964; Europe, Japan, Canada, South America 1964-1977; Mexico, India 1979.

Montague, Magnificent Nathaniel. *Burn, Baby Burn!: The Autobiography of Magnificent Montague* (2003). Holland, Russia, France, Germany, South Africa, Liberia, Nigeria, Senegal, Egypt, Persian Gulf, England 1944.

Morrow, Frederick. *Way Down South Up North* (1973), *Black Man in the White House* (1963), *Forty Years a Guinea Pig* (1980). Ghana 1957.

Morton, Lena. *My First Sixty Years: Passion for Wisdom* (1965). England, France, Scotland, Switzerland, 1956.

Moton, Robert. *Finding a Way Out* (1920). France 1919.

Murray, Pauli. *Pauli Murray: The Autobiography of a Black Activist, Lawyer, Priest, and Poet* (1987). Berkeley (International House). Ghana 1968-73.

Newton, Huey P. *Revolutionary Suicide* (1974). China 1971.

Northup, Solomon. *Twelve Years a Slave: The Autobiography of Solomon Northup* (1853). Canada 1830s, 1857.

Obama, Barack. *Dreams from My Father* (1995, 2004), *Audacity of Hope* (2006). Indonesia 1967; Europe, Kenya 1988; Kenya 2006.

Oliver, Kitty. *Multicolored Memories of a Black Southern Girl* (2001). Canada, Italy 1990s.

O'Ree, Willie. *The Autobiography of Willie O'Ree: Hockey's Black Pioneer* (2000). Born in New Brunswick Canada, NHL 1957.

Owens, Jesse. *Blackthink: My Life as a Black Man and a White Man* (1970), *The Jesse Owens Story* (1970), *I Have Changed* (1972), *Jesse: A Spiritual Autobiography* (1978). Germany 1936; India, Philippines 1955; Australia 1956.

Payne, Daniel. *Recollections of Seventy Years: A Memoir* (1888). Canada, American West 1853; England, France 1864–71; Europe 1881.

Pemberton, Gayle. *The Hottest Water in Chicago* (1998). England 1974.

Pickens, William. *Heir of a Slave* (1911), *Bursting Bonds* (1923). Europe, South America, 1954.

Poitier, Sidney. *This Life (1980), The Measure of a Man: A Spiritual Autobiography* (2000). Cat Island, born in Nassau; Return 1970s.

Powell, Adam. *Adam by Adam: The Autobiography of Adam Clayton Powell, Jr.* (1971). Europe 1930, 1950, 1951; Indonesia 1955; Cuba 1958.

Powell Colin. *My American Journey* (1996). World tour 1958–93; Germany 1959; Vietnam 1962–63; Korea 1974; Vietnam 1968; Germany 1986; Kuwait 1990.

Prince, Nancy Gardner. *A Narrative of the Life and Travels of Mrs. Nancy Prince* (1853). St. Petersburg Russia 1824; Jamaica 1840, 1842.

Pryor, Richard. *Pryor Convictions* (1995). Kenya 1979.

Robin Quivers. *Quivers: A Life (Co-Host of the Howard Stern Show)*. New York: HarperCollins, 1995. Paris n.d.

Rangel, Charles. *And I Haven't Had a Bad Day Since* (2007). Korea 1948–52; South Africa 1994.

Reagon, Bernice Johnson. *We Who Believe in Freedom: Sweet Honey in the Rock . . . Still on the Journey* (1993). Vancouver 1980; Quito, Ecuador, Mexico City; South African Embassy (U. S.); England, Germany, Scotland, Ireland, Moscow, Australia, Cuba 1986–89; France 1991; Australia 1992.

Rice, Condoleezza. *Memoir of My Extraordinary, Ordinary Family and Me (2011); No Higher Honor: A Memoir of the Washington Years* (2011). Iraq, Darfur, North Korea, India, China, Bagdad, Cairo, Georgia, Mumbai 2001–09.

Ringgold, Faith. *We Flew over the Bridge: The Memoirs of Faith Ringgold* (1995). Paris, Rome 1961.

Robeson, Eslanda Goode. *Reminiscences of School Life, and Hints on Teaching*

(1972). London, South Africa, Swaziland, Mozambique, Uganda, Kenya, Egypt, Basutoland (Lesotho) 1936.

Robeson, Paul. *Here I Stand* (1958, 1988). London 1927–39; Soviet Union 1934; Jamaica, Trinidad 1948; Europe, Russia 1949; 1950–58 passport confiscated; [Moscow 1959; Australia, New Zealand, 1960; London, Africa, China, Cuba 1961].

Robinson, Randall. *Defending the Spirit: A Black Life in America* (1998). Tanzania 1970; South Africa 1976, 1997; Sahara 1980; Angola 1989; Jamaica, Haiti 1994; Nigeria, Rwanda 1990s; Dominica, St. Lucia 1996–97; Congo 1997.

Robinson, Sugar Ray. *Sugar Ray* (1969, 1994). Paris, Brussels, Geneva, Frankfurt 1950; Paris, Zurich, London, Antwerpen, Liege, Berlin, Piemonte, London 1951; Spain, London, Vienna, Rhone 1962; Santo Domingo, Quebec, Paris, Rhone, Brussels, Paris 1963; Glasgow, Paris, London, Nice 1964; Mexico 1965.

Ross, Diana. *Secrets of a Sparrow* (1995); Going Back (2002). Europe 1965–70; Solo world tours 1970–2011.

Rowan, Carl T. *The Pitfall and the Proud* (1956), *Breaking Barriers* (1991). India 1954; Cuba 1962; Finland 1963–64.

Rudolph, Wilma. *Wilma* (1977). Australia Olympics 1956; Rome Olympics 1960.

RuPaul, Andre. *Lettin It All Hang Out: An Autobiography* (1995). London 1992, England, Germany, 1993.

Russell, Bill. *Second Wind: Memoirs of an Opinionated Man* (1991). Australia 1956; Liberia, Libya, Ethiopia 1959.

Scarborough, William Sanders. *Autobiography* (nd). England 1901; England, Germany 1911; England, Scotland 1921.

Schuyler, George. *Black and Conservative: The Autobiography of George S. Schuyler* (1966). Liberia 1931; South America, Caribbean 1948–49; West Africa, Dominican Republic 1958.

Shakur, Assata. *Assata: An Autobiography* (1987). Havana, Cuba 1984.

Sheppard, William Henry. *Presbyterian Pioneers in the Congo* (1917). London, Congo 1890–1910.

Simone, Nina. *I Put a Spell on You* (2003). Barbados, Liberia, Switzerland, France 1974–85.

Smith, Amanda. *An Autobiography: The Story of the Lord's Dealings with Mrs. Amanda Smith the Colored Evangelist: Containing an Account of her Life Work of Faith, and Her Travels in America, England, Ireland, Scotland,*

India, and Africa as an Independent Missionary (1893). England, Ireland, Scotland, 1876?(78); India 1879–1881; Liberia, Africa eight years.

Smith, Tommie. *Silent Gesture: The Autobiography of Tommie Smith* (2007). Mexico City 1968.

Steward, Austin. *Twenty-two Years a Slave and Forty Years a Freeman* (1857). Canada 1830s.

Steward, Theophilus Gould. *From 1864–1914: Fifty Years in the Gospel Ministry* (1921) Haiti 1873; Cuba 1898; Philippines 1900; London 1911.

Sullivan, Leon. *Moving Mountains: The Principles and Purposes of Leon Sullivan* (1998). South Africa 1980, 1995; Zimbabwe 1997. France, Germany, Sweden, Finland, Rome 1985–87.

Taylor, Major. *The Fastest Bicycle Rider in the World: The Story of a Colored Boy's Indomitable Courage and Success against Great Odds* (1929). Germany, Belgium, England, Italy, France 1901–03; Australia 1902–04; Europe 1907–09.

Terrell, Mary Church. *A Colored Woman in a White World* (1940). Europe 1884–86; Berlin 1904; Zurich, Switzerland 1919.

Thomas, Claudia Lynn. *God Spare Life: An Autobiography* (2007). St. Thomas 1984–89.

Thompson, Ahmir "Questlove." *Mo' Meta Blues: The World According to Questlove* (2013). Germany 1992-93; London 1994; Berlin, Austria 1995; 1999 Paris, Portugal 2005.

Thompson, Era Bell. *American Daughter* (1945); *Africa the Land of My Father* (1954). Eighteen African countries by 1954; Brazil 1965; Traveled to 124 Countries on 6 continents.

Thurman, Howard. *With Head and Heart: The Autobiography of Howard Thurman* (1981). India 1935; Nigeria 1963.

Toussaint, Rose-Marie. *Never Question the Miracle: A Surgeon's Story* (1998). Haiti 1983.

Turner, Tina. *I, Tina* (1986). Tijuana, Mexico, wedding 1962; Rolling Stones tour 1966; UK and Europe tour 1980; Private Dancer tour Asia, Europe and Australia 1985–86; Munich Break Every Rule tour 1987; Rio World Record crowd 1988; Foreign Affairs 1989; Move to London, Cologne, Germany 1986; Switzerland 1993–94; Wildest Dreams 1996; 24/7 tour 2000.

Tyson, Mike. *Undisputed Truth* (2013). Japan 1988, 1990; Russia 2000; Copenhagen 2001; Cuba, Jamaica 2002

Vaughn, Donald. *Color My World: A Life's Journey* (2012). Germany 1958, Paris 1959.

Verrett, Shirley. *I Never Walked Alone* (2003). Germany 1959; Russia 1963; London 1966; Italy 1969; Paris 1990.

Vincent, Carter O. *The Bern Book: A Record of a Voyage of the Mind* (1956). Bern Switzerland 1950s.

Walker, Alice. *Living by the Word: Selected Writings, 1973–1987* (1988), *Overcoming Speechlessness: A Poet Encounters the Horror in Rwanda, Eastern Congo, Palestine/Israel* (2010). Jamaica, Mexico, Bali 1980s; Greece, England, Ireland, Spain, France, Holland 1990s; China, Bali, Jamaica, Rwanda, Gaza Strip 2009.

Walker, George. *Reminiscences of an American Composer and Pianist* (2009). France, Prague 1947; Paris 1958–59; Italy 1971.

Walker, Rebecca. *Black, White, and Jewish: Autobiography of a Shifting Self* (2001). Jamaica, Mexico, Bali 1980s; Greece, England, Ireland, Spain, France, Holland 1990s.

Wamba, Philippe. Kinship: *A Family's Journey in Africa and America* (1999). Tanzania, Congo 1980.

Ward, Samuel Ringgold. *Autobiography of a Fugitive Negro: His Anti-slavery Labours in the United States, Canada and England* (1853?–55). Canada, Great Britain 1853; Jamaica 1855.

Warwick, Dionne. *My Life as I See It* (2010). Paris 1962; Europe, Asia, Canada 1960s–1980s; Asia, Africa Europe 1987.

Washington, Booker T. *Up from Slavery* (1901). *My Larger Education* (1911). Belgium, Paris, London 1899; Poland, England, Germany 1910.

Washington, Isaiah. *A Man from Another Land* (2011). Namibia, 1996; Sierra Leone, 2006

Waters, Ethel. *His Eye Is on the Sparrow: An Autobiography and to Me It's Wonderful* (1951, 1972). Il de France 1929–30.

Wattleton, Faye. *Life on the Line* (1998). Mexico City 1984; Thailand, Bangladesh, Phillipines, India, Kenya, Jurkina Faso, Ecuador, Bolivia, Sierra Leone, Liberia, Senegal, Zaire, Brazil, Indonesia 1980s.

Wells-Barnett, Ida. *Crusade for Justice: The Autobiography of Ida B. Wells* (1970). By Alfreda Duster. Europe 1893; England 1894.

West, Cornel. *Brother West: Living and Loving Out Loud, a Memoir* (2009). Italy 1990; Addis Ababa Ethiopia 1993; Stockholm Sweden 1993; Germany 2000; Australia 2002, Egypt 2007; South Africa, Chile, Germany, Casablanca, Mexico, Brussels, Istanbul n.d.

White, Walter. *A Man Called White* (1948, 1995). France 1926; Europe 1945.

Wilkins, Roger. *A Man's Life: An Autobiography* (1982). Japan, Korea, China,

Vietnam 1962–63; Algiers, Kinshasa, Dar es Salaam, Nairobi, Addis Ababa, New Delhi, Bangkok 1964; Jamaica 1969; Martinique 1970.

Williams, Patricia. *Open House: Of Family, Friends, Food, Piano Lessons, and the Search for a Room of My Own* (2005). France 1960s, 2004.

Williams, Robert. *Men with Guns* (1960). Canada, Mexico, Cuba, China, Tanzania 1960s.

Williams White, Susie Mae. *Determined in Spite Of . . .* (1998). Germany, England, Israel, France, Switzerland, Italy, India, Thailand, China, Japan 1970.

Willis, Jan. *Dreaming Me: Black, Baptist, and Buddhist* (2008). Tibet 1967; 1970s.

Wilson, Mary. *Dreamgirl and Supreme Faith: My Life as a Supreme* (2000). Europe 1965; England Japan 1975; Europe 1977.

Wright, Richard. *Black Boy* (1940); *The Color Curtin: A Report on the Bandung Conference* (1945). France, Spain, Indonesia 1955.

Young, Andrew. *A Way Out of No Way: The Spiritual Memoirs of Andrew Young* (1994). Colombia 1967; Lesotho, South Africa 1977; Zimbabwe 1979, 1991; Bahamas 1991; South Africa 1994.

APPENDIX B

Passport Geography: Data Set for Viewshare Online Project

SAMPLE LOCATIONS OF TRAVELERS BY REGION/CONTINENT

North America

Marrant, John. Nova Scotia 1785; England 1790.
Beckwourth, James. Rocky Mountains 1820s; California 1850s.
Henson, Josiah. Canada 1830.
Henson, Matthew. North Pole 1909.
O'Ree, Willie. Born in New Brunswick Canada, NHL 1957.

South America and Caribbean

Prince, Nancy Gardner. St. Petersburg Russia 1824; Jamaica 1840, 1842.
Ward, Samuel Ringgold. Canada, Great Britain 1853; Jamaica 1855.
Langston, John Mercer. Haiti, Dominican Republic 1877–85.
Love, Nat. Mexico 1870s.
Bricktop 1924–1939 Paris; Mexico City 1945; Paris 1949; Rome 1952.
Schuyler, George. Liberia 1931; South America, Caribbean 1948–49; West Africa, Dominican Republic 1958.
Hurston, Zora Neale. Jamaica, Haiti 1937.
Calloway, Cab. London, Manchester, Amsterdam, the Hague, Antwerp, Brussels, Paris 1935; France, Italy, Germany, Britain 1940–50s; Uruguay, South

America 1951; South America, Mexico, Cuba, Caribbean 1954.

Pickens, William. Europe, South America, 1954.

Carlos, John. Mexico City 1968.

Smith, Tommie. Mexico City 1968.

Walker, Alice. Jamaica, Mexico, Bali 1980s; Greece, England, Ireland, Spain, France, Holland 1990s; China, Bali, Jamaica, Rwanda, Gaza Strip 2009.

Denton, Sandy Pepa. Born and raised Jamaica 1969. Europe 2006.

Poitier, Sidney. Cat Island, born in Nassau; Return 1970s.

Frazier, Joe. Jamaica, England 1973; Philippines 1975.

Walker, Rebecca. Jamaica, Mexico, Bali 1980s; Greece, England, Ireland, Spain, France, Holland 1990s.

Duster, Michelle. Mexico, Europe 1983.

Jordan, June. Nicaragua 1983; Bahamas 1989.

Toussaint, Rose-Marie. Haiti 1983.

Thomas, Claudia Lynn. St. Thomas 1984–89.

Shakur, Assata. Havana, Cuba 1984.

Turner, Tina. Tijuana, Mexico wedding 1962; Rolling Stones tour 1966; UK and Europe tour 1980; Private Dancer tour Asia, Europe and Australia 1985–86; Munich Break Every Rule tour 1987; Rio World Record crowd 1988; Foreign Affairs 1989; Move to London, Cologne, Germany 1986; Switzerland 1993–94; Wildest Dreams 1996; 24/7 tour 2000.

Europe

Brown, William Wells. Canada 1834; Caribbean 1840; England, France, Scotland 1849–54.

Douglass, Frederick. England, Scotland, Ireland 1845.

Jacobs, Harriet. England 1845.

Elaw, Zilpha. England 1840.

Brown, Henry "Box." England 1850–75.

Craft, William and Ellen. Liverpool 1850–68.

Payne, Daniel. Canada, American West 1853; England, France 1864–71; Europe 1881.

Gould, William Benjamin. Holland, Belgium, Spain, Portugal, England 1860s.

Terrell, Mary Church. Europe 1884–86; Berlin 1904; Zurich, Switzerland 1919.

Latta, Rev. Morgan London. England, Canada 1892–1903.

Wells-Barnett, Ida. Europe 1893; England 1894.

Washington, Booker T. Belgium, Paris, London 1899; Poland England, Germany 1910.

Cooper, Anna Julia. London 1900; Paris 1911, 1912, 1913, 1925.

Scarborough, William Sanders. England, 1901; England, Germany 1911; England, Scotland 1921.

Moton, Robert. France 1919.

Bechet, Sidney. London 1919; Paris 1925; Nice 1948, Paris 1955.

White, Walter. France 1926; Europe 1945.

Waters, Ethel. Il de France 1929–30.

Early, Charity. Bermuda, London, Glaskow, Rouen France 1945; University of Zurich 1951.

Brooke, Edward. Italy 1944–45.

Baker, Vernon. Italy, Germany 1944–47.

Walker, George. France, Prague 1947; Paris 1958–59; Italy 1971.

Atkins, Cholly. England 1948.

Baldwin, James. France 1948–87; Switzerland 1950s; Turkey 1961–67.

Holiday, Billie. European tour 1954; Paris 1958; London, Norway, Sweden, Germany, Italy, France, 1959.

Morton, Lena. England, France, Scotland, Switzerland, 1956.

Vincent, Carter O. Bern Switzerland 1950s.

Ringgold, Faith. Paris, Rome 1961.

Davis, Angela Yvonne. Paris 1963. University of Frankfurt 1965–67.

Williams, Patricia. France 1960s, 2004.

Clark, Poinsette Septima. England, Sweden 1964.

Ross, Diana. Europe 1965–70; Solo world tours 1970–2011.

Grier, Pam. England 1965.

Pemberton, Gayle. England 1974.

James, Rick. Europe 1982.

Oliver, Kitty. Canada, Italy 1990s.

RuPaul, Andre. London 1992, England, Germany, 1993.

Russia

Heywood, Harry. Moscow Russia 1926–30.

Delany, Annie and Sarah. London, Germany, Italy, France, Russia, Lithuania, Estonia, Latvia vacation with mother 1930; Jamaica, Cuba Annie vacation with dental patient 1932.

Lorde, Audre. Mexico 1954; Russia 1976; Grenada 1978.

Verrett, Shirley. Germany 1959; Russia 1963; London 1966; Italy 1969; Paris 1990.

Brown, Elaine. Beijing, China 1971–74. China, North Korea, Vietnam, Cuba,

Algeria to Germany, Italy, Russia, Argentina, Uruguay, Costa Rica, Belize; France 1990–96.

Chamberlain, Wilt. Europe, Soviet Union 1974.

Lee, Andrea. Russia 1978–79.

Edelman, Marion Wright. Europe, Paris, Ireland Scotland, Soviet Union 1959.

Africa

Dean, Harry Foster. South Africa, Liberia 1876–79.

Smith, Amanda. England, Ireland, Scotland, 1876? (78); India 1879–1881; Liberia, Africa eight years.

Gibbs, Mifflin Wistar. Paris, Israel, Egypt, London, Consul to Madagascar, 1898–1901.

Coppin, Fanny Jackson. England 1882; South Africa 1902.

Sheppard, William Henry. London, Congo 1890–1910.

Du Bois, W. E. B. Berlin 1892–94; Niagara Falls, Canada 1905; London 1900; London 1911; Paris 1919; London, Brussels, Paris 1921; Liberia 1923; Russia 1926; world trip 1936; Haiti, Cuba 1944; Manchester, England 1945; Paris, Moscow 1949; [Passport denied 1951–58]; Soviet Union, Europe 1958–59; China 1959; Accra, Ghana 1961.

McKay, Claude. United States 1913; London 1919–20; Russia 1922–23; Berlin, Paris 1923; North Africa 1923–33; Paris 1928–29.

Hughes, Langston. Mexico 1920–21; Africa, Holland, Paris 1924; Russia 1932–33; Spain 1937.

Harrison, Juanita. Europe, Mediterranean, Asia, North Africa, Middle East 1927–1930s.

Montague, Magnificent Nathaniel. Holland, Russia, France, Germany, South Africa, Liberia, Nigeria, Senegal, Egypt, Persian Gulf, England 1944.

Robeson, Paul. London 1927–39; Soviet Union 1934; Jamaica, Trinidad 1948; Europe, Russia 1949; 1950–58 passport confiscated; [Moscow 1959; Australia, New Zealand, 1960; London, Africa, China, Cuba 1961].

Ellington, Duke. Holland, France 1932, Europe 1939, 1958–59; Leeds 1958; Turkey, Iraq, Cyprus, Greece, Egypt, Japan, 1964; Senegal 1966; Argentina, Chile, Brazil, Mexico 1968; Prague 1969; Latin America, Soviet Union 1971; world tour Europe, Asia, Australia, New Zealand, Southeast Asia 1933–71.

Thurman, Howard. India 1935; Nigeria 1963.

Jones, Quincy. Sweden, Paris, Algiers 1953; Paris, Holland, Belgium, Italy, Yugoslavia, Finland, Austria, Germany, Switzerland, Portugal 1957–59;

Turkey 1956; Brazil 195?; Switzerland 1991; France 1998.

Dunham, Katherine. Haiti, Jamaica, Martinique, Trinidad 1936; Mexico, London, Paris 1947–49; South America, Europe, North Africa tour 1950–55; Australia, New Zealand, Japan 1956–58; Europe 1959–60; 1965 Dakar, Senegal; fifty-seven countries in twenty years; 1992 Haiti (hunger strike).

Robeson, Eslanda Goode. London, South Africa, Swaziland, Mozambique, Uganda, Kenya, Egypt, Basutoland (Lesotho), 1936.

Mays, Benjamin. India, England, Egypt, Jerusalem 1936; China 1937; Egypt 1953.

Height, Dorothy. Oxford, England 1936; Delhi, India 1952.

Carmichael, Stokely. Trinidad 1941; New York 1952; Cuba1967; Guinea 1969.

Wilkins, Roger. Japan, Korea, China, Vietnam 1962–63; Algiers, Kinshasa, Dar es Salaam, Nairobi, Addis Ababa, New Delhi, Bangkok 1964; Jamaica 1969; Martinique 1970.

Davis, Ossie, and Ruby Dee. Liberia, North Africa (Ossie) 1942–45; Nigeria 1969 (Ossie and Ruby); India 1989.

Thompson, Era Bell. Eighteen African countries by 1954; Brazil 1965; Traveled to 124 countries on 6 continents.

Jefferson, Alexander. Algeria 1944; Italy, France, Germany 1944.

Jackson, Mahalia. European tours 1948, 61, 63–64, 67–69; Liberia 1970; Europe, Germany 1971.

Gillespie, Dizzy (John Birks). Europe 1948; Europe 1950; 1953 Canada; North Africa, Near East, Asia, Western Europe 1956; London 1965; Nairobi, Kenya 1972; Havana, Cuba 1977.

Forman, James. Okinawa 1948; Guinea 1964; Tanzania, Zambia, Congo 1967; Martinique 1969.

Kitt, Eartha. Mexico City 1948; Europe 1948–49; Paris, Istanbul 1950–51; Nigeria 1958; Milan 1968; Swaziland, Southern Africa 1971, 73; Hong Kong, London 1974.

Bailey, Pearl. London 1952.

Robinson, Sugar Ray. Paris, Brussels, Geneva, Frankfurt 1950; Paris, Zurich, London, Antwerpen, Liege, Berlin, Piemonte, London 1951; Spain, London, Vienna, Rhone 1962; Santo Domingo, Quebec, Paris, Rhone, Brussels, Paris 1963; Glasgow, Paris, London, Nice 1964; Mexico 1965.

Angelou, Maya—Marguerite Johnson. Paris, Italy, twenty-two countries 1954–55; Ghana 1960; Cairo1960; Sweden; Paris, Ghana 1961–64.

Bragg, Janet. London, England, Paris 1955; Addis Ababa, Ethiopia 1965; Ethiopia, Dakar Senegal, Nigeria, Cairo 1972; Ethiopia Mexico, Singapore, Sweden, West Germany, Denmark, Italy 1980s.

Cruz, Celia. Mexico City (from Cuba), Venezuela 1956; Mexico City 1960; Zaire 1974.

Russell, Bill. Australia 1956; Liberia, Libya, Ethiopia 1959.

King Jr., Martin Luther. Ghana 1957; India 1959; Norway, Paris, Jerusalem, Egypt 1964.

King, Coretta Scott. Ghana 1957; India 1959; Norway, Paris, Jerusalem, Egypt 1964.

Morrow, Frederick. Ghana 1957.

Johnson, John H. Ghana 1957; Russia, Poland 1959; Ivory Coast 1961; Kenya 1963; continent feature 1976.

Malcolm X. United Arab Republic, Sudan, Nigeria, Egypt, Mecca, Iran, Syria, Ghana 1959; Germany, Mecca, Saudi Arabia, Sudan, Egypt, Nigeria, Ghana, Liberia, Senegal, Morocco, London, Ethiopia, Kenya, Tanzania, Paris 1964; Canada, London, refused entry to Paris 1965.

Franklin, John Hope. Saltsburg 1951, 1958; Cambridge, Australia, Nigeria 1960.

Baraka, Amiri. Cuba 1959; Tanzania 1974.

Williams, Robert. Canada, Mexico, Cuba, China, Tanzania 1960s.

Charles, Ray. Europe, South America, Asia, North Africa, Australia, New Zealand 1960s–2003.

Marshall, Paule. Barbados, Grenada 1962; Europe 1965; Lagos, Nigeria 1977.

Lacy, Leslie Alexander. Sierra Leone, Liberia, Senegal, Guinea, Ivory Coast, Ghana 1963.

Estes, Simon. Germany, Russia, England, Italy, Switzerland, Spain, Portugal, Monoco, Norway, Austria, Sweden 1965–1998; South Africa 1995–96.

Lester, Julius. Vietnam, Cuba 1966.

Young, Andrew. Colombia 1967; Lesotho, South Africa 1977; Zimbabwe 1979, 1991; Bahamas 1991; South Africa 1994.

Ali, Muhammad. Canada, Germany, England 1966; Switzerland 1971; Canada, Ireland, Japan 1972; Indonesia 1973; Zaire 1974.

Jamison, Judith. Dakar 1966; Senegal, London, Barcelona, Paris 1966. Madagascar, Tanzania, Uganda, Kenya, Congo, Ivory Coast, Ghana, Senegal 1967. Germany, Sweden 1968; Russia 1970; Austria 1972; Senegal 1982; Russia 1990; Antigua 1990s.

Murray, Pauli. Ghana 1968–73.

Foreman, George. Mexico City 1968; Kingston Jamaica 1973; Tokyo Japan 1973; Caracas Venezuela 1974; Kinshasa Zaire 1974; England 1990.

Gregory, Dick. Australia, Zambia 1970.

Robinson, Randall. Tanzania 1970; South Africa 1976, 1997; Sahara 1980;

Angola 1989; Jamaica, Haiti 1994; Nigeria, Rwanda 1990s; Dominica, St. Lucia 1996–97; Congo 1997.

Williams, White Susie Mae. Germany, England, Israel, France, Switzerland, Italy, India, Thailand, China, Japan 1970.

King, B. B. Japan, Australia, Ghana, Nigeria, Chad, Liberia 1971; Russia 1977; Israel 1986, 1996; Europe 1988.

Simone, Nina. Barbados, Liberia, Switzerland, France 1974–85.

James, Etta. Zaire 1974.

Brooks, Gwendolyn. Ghana 1974; Russia 1982.

Davis, Belva. Cuba 1977; Israel 1980; Jamaica, Guyana 1976; Côte d'Ivoire 1983; South Africa 1994; Cuba, Kenya 1998.

Pryor, Richard. Kenya 1979.

Wamba, Philippe. Tanzania, Congo 1980.

Sullivan, Leon. South Africa 1980, 1995; Zimbabwe 1997. France, Germany, Sweden, Finland, Rome 1985–87.

Belafonte, Harry. Senegal 1987; Rwanda 1994; Cuba 1999; South Africa 2001; Kenya 2004; Norway 2007.

Obama, Barack. Indonesia 1967; Europe, Kenya 1988; Kenya 2006.

Harris, Gail. Korea 1988; Spain 1989; Middle East 1992–96.

Wattleton, Faye. Mexico City 1984; Thailand, Bngladesh, Phillipines, India, Kenya, Jurkina Faso, Ecuador, Bolivia, Sierra Leone, Liberia, Senegal, Zaire, Brazil, Indonesia 1980s.

West, Cornel. Italy 1990; Addis Ababa Ethiopia 1993; Stockholm Sweden 1993; Germany 2000; Australia 2002, Egypt 2007; South Africa, Chile, Germany, Casablanca, Mexico, Brussels, Istanbul.

Chuck D. England, Egypt, Ghana 1992; Europe 1994.

Hunter-Gault, Charlene. South Africa 1997–2006.

Rice, Condoleeza. Iraq, Darfur, North Korea, India, China, Bagdad, Cairo, Georgia, Mumbai 2001–09.

Asia

Steward, Theophilus Gould. Haiti 1873; Cuba 1898; Philippines 1900; London 1911.

Johnson, James Weldon. Venezuela 1906–08; Nicaragua 1909–13; Haiti 1920; Japan 1929.

Lynch, James R. Hawaii, Philippines 1907.

Anderson, Marian. Europe 1930–1965; Japan, Mexico, Israel 1955.

Powell, Adam. Europe 1930, 1950, 1951; Indonesia 1955; Cuba 1958.

Owens, Jesse. Germany 1936; India, Philippines 1955; Australia 1956.

McElroy, Colleen. Germany 1940s; Mexico; Fulbright Yugoslavia, Japan Fulbright and Rockefeller 1988.

Bussey, Charles. Italy 1942–45; Japan, Korea 1950.

Dryden, Charles W. Morocco, Tunisia, Italy 1943; Korea 1950–52; Germany, London, Greece, Italy, France 1957–62.

Louis, Joe. England 1944; Canada 1945; Mexico 1946; Mexico, Cuba, Colombia, Chile, Panama, El Salvador 1947; Jamaica, Bahamas, Cuba 1949; Brazil 1950; Japan, China 1951.

Becton, Julius W. Jr. Asia, Europe 1944–98.

Guillaume, Robert. Okinawa 1945; Vienna 1965; Rome 1973.

Kelly, Samuel. Japan 1945; South Korea 1951; Japan 1955–56; South Korea 1962.

Rangel, Charles. Korea 1948–52; South Africa 1994.

Gordy, Berry. Korea 1950–53.

Hampton, Lionel. France, Denmark, Netherlands, Austria, Spain, Germany, Switzerland, Belgium, Italy, Yugoslavia 1953–83; Japan 1963, 1981, 1983.

Aaron, Hank. Puerto Rican League 1954; Jamaica 1973; Japan 1974; Korea 1970s.

Rowan, Carl T. India 1954; Cuba 1962; Finland 1963–64.

Basie, Count. Sweden, Switzerland, Germany, France, Belgium 1954; Europe 1956–62; Japan 1963; Japan, Australia, New Zealand 1971; Canada, St. Thomas, St. Lucia, Caracas, Haiti 1972; Japan 1973; Canada, Europe, Japan 1974–84.

Wright, Richard. France, Spain, Indonesia 1955.

Mays, Willie. Japan, Mexico, Venezuela, Latin America 1957–60.

Powell Colin. World tour 1958–93; Germany 1959; Vietnam 1962–63; Korea 1974; Vietnam 1968; Germany 1986; Kuwait 1990.

Davis Jr., Sammy. London 1960; Paris, London 1964; Canada 1968; Vietnam 1971; Holland, Germany, Sweden, England, France 1972; Australia 1977; Australia 1979; France 1985.

Warwick, Dionne. Paris 1962; Europe, Asia, Canada 1960s–1980s; Asia, Africa Europe 1987.

Mingus, Charles. Paris 1964; Europe, Japan, Canada, South America 1964–1977; Mexico, India 1979.

Wilson, Mary. Europe 1965; England, Japan 1975; Europe 1977.

Willis, Jan. Tibet 1967, 1970s.

Fisher, Antwon. Eleven-year navy tour; Japan 1977.

Bassett, Angela, and Vance, Courtney. 1990s.

Australia

Ashe, Arthur. Australia, France, England 1968–79; Sweden 1971; South Africa 1973, 1991.

Johnson, Jack. Australia 1907; Australia, Paris 1908; England, Paris 1911; Canada, Paris, Russia, England, Brazil 1913–14; Cuba 1915.

Carson, Ben. Australia 1983.

Rudolph, Wilma. Australia Olympics 1956; Rome Olympics 1960.

Taylor, Major. Germany, Belgium, England, Italy, France 1901–03; Australia 1902–04; Europe 1907–09.

Commings, Jeff. Cuba 1991; Australia 2002.

Davis, Miles. Paris 1949–91; Europe 1960; Japan 1964; Europe 1967; Europe, Japan 1982–83; Japan 1985; Europe, Asia, Australia, New Zealand 1987; Germany, Spain, Japan 1988; Switzerland 1991.

Gibson, Althea. Southeast Asia State Department tour 1955; Australia, France 1956; Wimbledon, Australia 1957; Wimbledon 1958; Rome, Italy 1960.

Kennedy, Florynce. Canada 1967. Australia, Mexico City, Toronto 1975.

Space

Jemison, Mae. Liberia 1983–85; Space 1992.

APPENDIX C

Passport Vocabulary:
A Thirteen-Hundred Word Guide for Youth Empowerment

Wells, *Crusade for Justice*, (1970)

1. abetted
2. accosted
3. acquiesced
4. agitation
5. ameliorating
6. apprentice
7. assaulted
8. atrocities
9. auspices
10. bar association
11. barbarity
12. bedlam
13. boycott
14. carpetbag
15. character
16. chattel slavery
17. cessation
18. compunction
19. condemnation
20. condone
21. confinement
22. congregated
23. conscience
24. consolidated
25. conspiracy
26. contempt / contemptuously
27. courteous
28. cowardly
29. crystallize
30. debauch
31. deliberations
32. denounce
33. denominations
34. descendants
35. dictation
36. discrediting
37. disinclination
38. dispatch
39. disposition
40. efficiency
41. eloquent
42. encroachment
43. epidemic
44. epithets
45. erstwhile
46. evidently
47. exponents
48. Fifteenth Amendment
49. figuratively
50. gang plank
51. goose quill
52. gouged
53. gratifying
54. grievances
55. grogshop
56. humanity
57. humiliation
58. impotency
59. incited
60. indicative
61. innocence
62. locomotion
63. lyceum
64. lynching
65. manhood
66. microscopic
67. misrepresen- tation
68. munificent
69. muster
70. northern capitalists
71. novelty
72. oblivion
73. oblong
74. palliation
75. partitioned
76. passerby
77. pedestrian
78. penitentiary
79. pigeonhole
80. posterity
81. presiding
82. press
83. propaganda
84. proprietor
85. pulpit
86. quarantine
87. remonstrance
88. repudiation
89. reputation
90. resolutions
91. retaliation
92. rigidly
93. self-restraint
94. self-sustaining
95. sensational
96. sentiment
97. specious
98. spinal meningitis
99. spindles
100. stenographer
101. streetcar
102. subsequent
103. successor
104. suffrage
105. suspicious
106. sympathizers
107. temperance
108. testimonials
109. traduce
110. ubiquitous
111. ultimatum
112. unanimity
113. ungentlemanly
114. unimpassioned
115. utterances
116. vengeance
117. vigorous
118. vocation
119. voracious
120. yellow fever

Douglass, *The Narrative of* . . . , (1845)

1. abolitionists
2. accurate
3. advisedly
4. aft
5. annihilate
6. anxiety
7. apprentices
8. ascertaining
9. barbarity
10. betwixt
11. blasphemy
12. breeder
13. bushel
14. callous
15. complexion
16. compliance
17. comprehension
18. conjecture
19. consequence
20. considerable
21. console
22. conspicuous
23. consummate
24. contempt
25. contradiction
26. cowardice
27. cunning
28. dehumanizing
29. depravity
30. desolate
31. devour
32. dialogue
33. discontented
34. discord
35. disposition
36. dread
37. duration
38. emancipation
39. endurance
40. estate
41. evidence
42. exultingly
43. famished
44. fiendish
45. forte
46. flesh-mongers
47. gallant
48. glimmering
49. gratification
50. humane
51. human rights
52. hypocrites
53. ignorant
54. immutable
55. impudence
56. incoherent
57. incompatible
58. ineffable
59. inevitable
60. inferred
61. infernal
62. intelligence
63. inevitable
64. invariably
65. lacerated
66. obdurate
67. ordained
68. possession
69. profligate
70. manifestation
71. maxim
72. misdemeanor
73. non-compliance
74. parentage
75. partiality
76. pernicious
77. perpetrating
78. perplexed
79. philosophy
80. pious
81. pirates
82. plantation
83. presumptuous
84. profane
85. profitable
86. providence
87. privation
88. rapture/rapturous
89. reputation
90. resistance
91. restless
92. resurrection
93. reverence
94. sanction
95. scow
96. self-confidence
97. semblance
98. soul-killing
99. starboard
100. stratagems
101. stupor
102. subsist
103. tedious
104. tenfold
105. testimonial
106. tranquil
107. treacherous
108. turbid
109. unbroken
110. unmanageable
111. utterance
112. valuation
113. vindication
114. wretched
115. yonder

Cooper, *The Third Step*, (1945)

1. accommodate
2. accumulate
3. affidavit
4. ambassador
5. ambition
6. anticlimax
7. apprehensive
8. astonishing
9. atheist
10. audacious
11. auspices
12. balustrade
13. bailiff
14. bolster
15. brazen
16. carafe
17. commissioner
18. competent
19. compensation
20. concession
21. concocted
22. conscious/ consciousness
23. contrary
24. conviction
25. courageous
26. crimson
27. delegate
28. designated
29. determination
30. devastating
31. distinguished
32. doctorate
33. doctrine
34. dossier
35. dread
36. efficient
37. emblazon
38. emphatic
39. endorse
40. esclavage
41. exhaustive
42. expedient
43. foolhardy
44. goblet
45. gracious
46. grueling
47. intellectual
48. inevitable
49. landscaping
50. laudable
51. nurture
52. manipulate
53. marvel
54. matriculate
55. misgiving
56. monument
57. ostensible
58. partisan
59. preconceive
60. preoccupied
61. preponderance
62. pronouncement
63. promulgate
64. prostrate
65. quadrangle
66. refurbish
67. reign
68. rejoinder
69. reorganization
70. scrapping
71. solemn
72. specification
73. stimulating/ stimulus
74. soutenance
75. supplementary
76. thesis
77. transcript
78. transpire
79. upheaval
80. vociferation

Du Bois, *Darkwater*, (1920)

1. aberration
2. arbitrate
3. abundant
4. abutting
5. accusations
6. aggrandizement
7. antagonism
8. apprentice
9. assimilation
10. assumption
11. austere
12. Bantu
13. barbarism
14. barter
15. birthright
16. blasphemous
17. braggadocio
18. brawny
19. cataclysm
20. catastrophe
21. chasten
22. clapboards
23. clamor
24. clannish
25. composite
26. conception
27. confiscated
28. conflagration
29. conjure
30. conquest
31. consciousness
32. contradicted
33. cozenage
34. console
35. criterion
36. credo
37. culminating
38. daunted
39. debauched
40. demeanor
41. discourse
42. disillusion
43. divert
44. eagerness
45. emerging
46. emprise
47. endeavor
48. entrenched
49. epitomize
50. epoch
51. extemporaneous
52. garner
53. glib
54. graft
55. guise
56. ideological
57. illuminate
58. imperialism
59. impracticable
60. impudent
61. indictment
62. indolent
63. inordinate
64. indignation
65. intangible
66. interloper
67. intolerance
68. intrigue
69. lotus
70. manacled
71. mannerism
72. manifest / manifestation
73. manikin
74. manufactured
75. masquerade
76. microcosm
77. mongrel
78. mulatto
79. mundane
80. pestilence
81. pittance
82. plausible
83. postulate
84. peonage
85. prestige
86. propaganda
87. prophecy
88. provincial
89. Pullman car
90. punitive
91. redolent
92. regime
93. reverberate
94. sectarian
95. seething
96. short shift
97. shrewd
98. sociology
99. sojourn
100. solemnity
101. socialist
102. soul
103. spinster
104. suffrage
105. superlative
106. supplication
107. swagger
108. talisman
109. transmute
110. unanimity
111. Veil / veiled
112. vengeance
113. veritable
114. vicariously
115. wanton
116. warp
117. wassail
118. whirlwind
119. weltering
120. willy-nilly

Dunham, *Island Possessed*, (1969)

1. advent
2. accessible
3. accustomed
4. acquaintancs
5. anecdotal
6. anonymous
7. anthropology
8. anxiety
9. approximatin
10. atrocious
11. authoritative
12. basins
13. bohemian
14. bourgeoisie
15. brocade
16. capitulate
17. carnival
18. ceremonial
19. chagrin
20. chamois
21. circumspection
22. cloister
23. consummation
24. conversion
25. crepe
26. creole
27. deliberate
28. deracinated
29. discrimination
30. discern
31. drowse
32. ebb
33. elite
34. eligible
35. ellipse
36. embroidery
37. emissaries
38. emulate
39. endear
40. engenders
41. ensemble
42. equivalent
43. escort
44. exhibition
45. exuberance
46. flamboyant
47. gazebo
48. geographically
49. histrionic
50. hygienic
51. immaculate
52. indigenous
53. indignation
54. ingrown
55. insinuation
56. interrogator
57. inverse
58. kaleidoscopic
59. maneuver
60. manipulate
61. metamorphosis
62. mime
63. myopic
64. mysterious
65. mulatto
66. niggling
67. nuance
68. organdy
69. ornate
70. patriarch
71. paunchy
72. persona non grata
73. phenomenon/
    phenomenal
74. personable
75. pique
76. poinsettia
77. precarious
78. precautionary
79. prestige
80. presume
81. proprietor
82. quaquaversal
83. recommendation
84. revelry
85. ritual
86. scrutiny
87. simultaneous
88. solemn
89. spatter
90. sensuous
91. sporadic
92. staccato rhythm
93. stimulus
94. telepathy
95. unitiated
96. unpredictability
97. veranda
98. voyeur
99. vulgar
100. waver

Gillespie, *To Be or Not to . . . Bop!*, (1979)

1. abscond
2. adversity
3. African derivation
4. Afro-Cuban
5. ambush / battle /
   cutting contest
6. animal husbandry
7. avant-garde
8. Bahá'i
9. bario
10. bebop
11. capitalize
12. chauffeur
13. chromaticsim
14. commercialism
15. commensurate
16. communists
17. Conga drum
18. conjugate
19. conventional
20. cultivate
21. descendency
22. deprivation
23. detrimental
24. disc jockey
25. diluted
26. effrontery
27. embedded
28. embellish
29. embouchure
30. entrenched
31. esoteric
32. ferment
33. finesse
34. fundamentals
35. gangster
36. goatee
37. gig
38. groove
39. gumbo
40. gyrations
41. hardheaded
42. harmony
43. humanitarian
44. improvisation
45. impromptu
46. incorruptible
47. inquisitive
48. inversion
49. innovation
50. jazz
51. jitterbug
52. jive
53. jurisdiction
54. machinations
55. melody
56. methodically
57. mischievous
58. modern / modernist
59. music theory
60. mutiny
61. nationalism
62. nepotism
63. notorious
64. orchestration
65. paradiddle
66. phonic
67. Pig Latin
68. polyrhythmic
69. prevail
70. progression
71. pummel
72. ratamacue
73. rejuvenation
74. rhythm
75. resurrection
76. revolutionary
77. ruptured
78. Samba
79. sanctified
80. self-discipline
81. septet
82. serenity
83. spawn
84. stimulating
85. stylistically
86. swinging
87. symptom
88. syncopation
89. syndrome
90. synthetic
91. technique
92. tone
93. uninitiated
94. unpredictable
95. vogue

Willis, *Dreaming Me*, (2008)

1. ablution
2. amends
3. analogy
4. annihilation
5. awestruck
6. auspicious
7. beckon
8. blissful
9. bristle
10. brooding
11. burlap
12. caste
13. circumambulate
14. compassion
15. compliance
16. confluence
17. crestfallen
18. cringing
19. debilitating
20. dejected
21. detention
22. doctrine
23. eerie
24. electrical
25. enlightenment
26. ephemeral
27. etiquette
28. ethereal
29. existential
30. gaunt
31. geneological
32. glaring
33. glib
34. gilded
35. grassy knoll
36. historical trauma
37. hordes
38. idyll
39. impermanence
40. inadequacy
41. inconsolable
42. indignities
43. inkling
44. inlaid
45. inordinate
46. insurmountable
47. intensive
48. interminable
49. invective
50. jibe
51. jostle
52. lama
53. liturgical
54. luminous
55. mantras
56. mausoleum
57. meditation
58. menacing
59. monastery / monastic
60. monk
61. palpable
62. penance
63. pilgrim
64. poignant
65. prankster
66. prattle
67. predawn
68. prideful
69. rarified
70. raucous
71. reliquary
72. regimen
73. reiterate
74. repugnant
75. retribution
76. rote memorization
77. rickshaw
78. ruddy
79. sari
80. saffron
81. scrumptious
82. self-absorption
83. self-worth
84. shame
85. sitar
86. soot
87. sophisticated
88. squat
89. spree
90. suppression
91. switchbacks
92. tantric
93. tarmac
94. tirade
95. transit
96. unscrupulous
97. untethered
98. unworthiness
99. verdant
100. vulnerability

El-Shabazz, *Autobiography of . . .* , (1965)

1. ablution
2. animosity
3. aplomb
4. applied
5. appraise
6. arose
7. associate
8. assumption
9. astonishment
10. astounded
11. atmosphere
12. batch
13. bound
14. cavern
15. chanting
16. circumambulation /
    circumambulated
17. communal
18. compartment
19. complexion
20. consecration
21. cordial
22. culturally
23. curiosity
24. demanded
25. derives
26. disbelief
27. discomforted
28. disembarkation
29. disposal
30. domineering
31. economics
32. effect
33. embracing
34. eminent
35. essence
36. exclaimed
37. experienced
38. financing
39. frustrate
40. graciousness
41. hesitantly
42. honor
43. hospitality
44. humane
45. humility
46. impulse
47. inconvenienced
48. indicating
49. industrialization
50. inevitably
51. instrument
52. intending
53. interceded
54. intricate
55. invited
56. jammed
57. jestering
58. judged
59. manufacture
60. modern
61. mosque
62. notwithstanding
63. peasant
64. personages
65. pernicious
66. Pilgrimage
67. plight
68. political science
69. posture
70. praise
71. proclaim
72. protesting
73. psychological
    castration
74. reassurance
75. refuge
76. represented
77. restless
78. ridiculous
79. shuffling
80. sensed
81. signified
82. spectacle
83. spellbound
84. spiritual
85. stun
86. strain
87. stricken
88. surprise
89. suburb
90. surplus
91. subsidized
92. tremendous
93. trampled
94. unfolds
95. utter
96. unison
97. vacant
98. valuable
99. versatile
100. vocabulary

Davis, *An Autobiography*, (1974)

1. aberration	31. gaudy	61. remnants
2. abominable	32. grubby	62. resort
3. advisability	33. disorientation	63. satire
4. assassination	34. incomprehensible	64. sequence
5. baguette	35. indiscriminate	65. seize
6. bedraggled	36. inquisitive	66. severance
7. bibliography	37. immaculate	67. squander
8. cobblestone	38. incongruous	68. spectacular
9. Communists	39. infuriating	69. socialist
10. compelling	40. inadvertent	70. staggering
11. consolation	41. ironically	71. stipend
12. consciousness-raising	42. liberation	72. stimulating
13. contradiction	43. logical	73. stratum
14. conviction	44. metamorphoses	74. struggle
15. correspondence	45. mobilization	75. subside
16. decadent	46. monopolies	76. survival
17. deserted	47. muster	77. symbolism
18. demonstrations	48. objective	78. teeming
19. doctoral dissertation	49. parasitic	79. terrain
20. dilapidated	50. pathological	80. tranquility
21. dismember	51. phenomenological	81. transformation
22. contemporary	52. philosophy	82. tremendous
23. emerge	53. predecessors	83. trinket
24. emigrate	54. preparatory	84. unapproachable
25. emphasis	55. racists	85. unilaterally
26. enchanted	56. ravaging	86. unsystematic
27. episodes	57. recuperate	87. variation
28. extremist	58. recurring	88. vehement
29. fascists	59. reenactment	89. vicarious
30. fingerprinted	60. rekindle	90. voracious

Obama, *Dreams from My Father*, (1995)

1. acculturation
2. affirmative action
3. Afrocentrism
4. aggrievement
5. ancient
6. antebellum
7. authentic
8. awkward
9. bamboo
10. baobab tree
11. bigots
12. binge
13. birthright
14. bolstering
15. bureaucrats
16. Burning Spear
17. calibrate
18. capitalist imperialism
19. caricature
20. caste system
21. colonialism
22. community organizer
23. conscripted
24. consolation
25. consigned
26. demons
27. dignity
28. disaffection
29. diversion
30. elongated
31. embassy
32. empowerment
33. enticement
34. Eurocentrism
35. Extracurricular
36. female circumcision
37. green tea ice cream
38. optimistic
39. Garveyite
40. genteel
41. grotesquely
42. grudges
43. hierarchies
44. homilies
45. humiliation
46. hypocrisy
47. inaugurated
48. Indian reservation
49. indulgent
50. indignities
51. indiscriminant
52. inexhaustible
53. ingratiating
54. irretrievably
55. Japanese internment
56. jive
57. Luo
58. Madman
59. Meandered
60. melancholy
61. menacing
62. mesmerized
63. miscegenation
64. moralism
65. mosque
66. multiracial
67. muttering
68. nationalist
69. needlepoint
70. nihilism
71. nonalignment
72. nuance
73. omission
74. paramilitary
75. pastoral
76. patriarchy
77. patronage
78. pavilion
79. persistent
80. phosphorescent
81. power
82. progressive
83. prototype
84. provincialism
85. proximity
86. purge
87. quiet desperation
88. Reader's Digest
89. reconciliation
90. respectable
91. revoked
92. revolt
93. savages
94. savannah
95. servitude
96. social construct
97. solicitude
98. sophistication
99. stucco
100. scrawny
101. smugness
102. soukous beat
103. Swahili
104. Temperance
105. toast
106. tilapia
107. transcendentalist
108. translation
109. tribe
110. unvarnished

Jemison, *Find Where the Wind Goes*, (2001)

1. accelerating
2. African dance
3. altitude
4. anathema
5. ancestors
6. analytic geometry
7. Archozoic
8. alacrity
9. architectural
10. astronaut
11. atmospheric
12. Azoic
13. bazaar
14. Black Power
15. Bid Whist
16. cadaver
17. calculations
18. cardio funk
19. chemical engineering
20. Cenozoic
21. centrifuge
22. computer
23. community health
24. consciousness
25. constellations
26. cosmology
27. currents
28. decipher
29. Doppler effect
30. diligence
31. dinosaurs
32. discharges
33. dissection
34. disheveled
35. enchanted
36. emphatically
37. epicenter
38. epoxy
39. formaldehyde
40. galaxy
41. geology
42. gravity
43. gross anatomy
44. hard head
45. heart murmur
46. hemoglobin
47. hematology
48. horizon
49. hydrogen
50. hypothesize
51. imagination
52. incision
53. indignant
54. ingratiating
55. interdepartmental major
56. Katherine Dunham technique
57. laissez-faire
58. latch-key children
59. launch
60. luminous
61. manifest
62. material science
63. Mesozoic
64. metaphorical
65. meteorology
66. Milky Way
67. modern dance
68. modus operandi
69. nappy hair
70. natural hair
71. nautical miles
72. 'nuff said
73. orbit
74. oxygen tank
75. perturbed
76. Paleozoic
77. pharaoh
78. phenomenon
79. physics
80. physical sciences
81. "pimp" walk
82. planetology
83. precocious
84. puberty
85. qualms
86. quasicelebritydom
87. radio communication signals
88. refugee
89. reminisce
90. research-experimentation-hypothesis
91. roughhoused
92. sci-fi
93. self-induced
94. shuttle
95. sickle cell anemia
96. sit-ins and walkouts
97. skid
98. skirmish
99. space laboratory
100. stars
101. stoop
102. student hostel
103. swup-swup
104. talisman
105. telescope
106. temperature
107. thought insertion
108. thyroid
109. timelessness
110. torrential rains
111. universe
112. vesicular stage
113. volatile
114. waft
115. weightlessness

Henderson, *Cooked*, (2007)

1. accumulating
2. administrative
3. aesthetic
4. anxious
5. appetizer
6. associate degree
7. bandwagon
8. bang (streets vs. kitchen)
9. black-on-black crime
10. blanche
11. blueprint
12. braise
13. broiler
14. burgundy
15. canapés
16. carte blanche
17. cayenne
18. chef de cuisine
19. chef tournot
20. clogs
21. cognizance
22. compassion
23. comfort zone
24. confectionary
25. conspiracy
26. Corning Ware Pyrex
27. chrome
28. creme de la creme
29. cuisine
30. culinary arts
31. delegate
32. dope
33. dregs
34. drizzle
35. drudgery
36. evidentiary
37. executive chef
38. experimenting
39. foie gras
40. furlough
41. gang banging, gangsterism
42. garnish
43. GED (General Education Development)
44. Good Samaritan
45. goatee
46. gorgonzola
47. griddle
48. Hobart mixer
49. honing skills
50. hustler
51. hydraulics
52. immaculate
53. impeccable
54. intensive care
55. increment
56. infraction
57. influential
58. institutionalized
59. invigorated
60. kleptomaniac
61. knead
62. kosher
63. legitimately
64. lowrider
65. lurking
66. maneuver
67. manhandling
68. mentality
69. meticulous
70. mimic
71. miscalculation
72. mise en place
73. newbie
74. obligatory
75. observe
76. OG (original gangsta)
77. palate
78. pastry chef
79. penitentiary
80. PhD
81. phyllo dough
82. precise
83. prep cook
84. professionalism
85. progressive
86. reconnaissance mission
87. Ramadan fast
88. roux
89. redemption
90. reimaging
91. responsibility
92. resurrect
93. sabbatical
94. sauté
95. scallop
96. sear
97. self-talk
98. sensation
99. shock (cooking)
100. solitary confinement
101. sous-chef
102. snitch
103. strudel
104. suave
105. sushi
106. Stroganoff
107. sweating (cooking)
108. subconscious
109. surplus
110. technique
111. tweak
112. toque
113. think tank
114. venturing
115. weeds (cooking)

APPENDIX D

Nenoku Poetry

Aaron, Hank. *I Had a Hammer: The Hank Aaron Story* (1991). Puerto Rican League 1954; Jamaica 1973; Japan 1974.

"Keep Hammering Away"
Number 715 brought hate mail
No *arigato*: So you stir the pot
Batting against national Confederate deliveries

Anderson, Marian. *My Lord, What a Morning* (1956,1984). Europe 1930–1965. Japan, Mexico, Israel 1955.

"Oh! Graceful Daughter of the Revolution"
Whispering Shubert in Sunday's best
Einsteinian genius. *Madame.* Wings on the wind
Greeting 75,000 with practiced spirit

Angelou, Maya—Marguerite Johnson. *I Know Why the Caged Bird Sings* (1970); *Gather Together in My Name* (1974); *Singin' and Swingin' and Gettin' Merry Like Christmas* (1976); *The Heart of a Woman* (1981); *All God's Children Need Traveling Shoes* (1986); *Letter to My Daughter* (2008). Paris, Italy, Croatia, twenty-two countries 1954–55; Ghana 1960; Cairo1960; Sweden; Paris, Ghana 1961–64.

"Phenomenal Speakerboxx"
Poet strutting, emotional remembrances rising
Canadian voyeur, European chorus girl, Ghanaian queen
Weaving a world-wide speakerly rug

Ali, Muhammad. *The Greatest: My Own Story* (1975). Canada, Germany, England 1966; Switzerland 1971; Canada, Ireland, Japan 1972; Indonesia 1973; Zaire 1974.

"Allah's Greatest Poet"
Humble vanity, worthy, most high
Springtime ringmaster, dancing will, Zaire skill. Rebounding.
Going to thank the Lord

Ashe, Arthur. *Days of Grace* (1994). Australia, France, England 1968–79; Sweden 1971; South Africa 1973, 1991.

"Respectable Rebel"
Revolutionary racquet in tighty whities,
Fighting "intellectual violence": Richmond, HIV, Johannesburg Afrikaans
Heart-broken child turned fuzzy-ball activist

Atkins, Cholly. *Class Act: The Jazz Life of Choreographer Cholly Atkins* (2003). England 1948.

"Panache Paradigm"
Choreographing "theatrical etiquette" art forms
Swing had no class without Cholly's polish
Shellacking (un)even dreary Dover stages

Bailey, Pearl. *The Raw Pearl* (1969); *Between You and Me* (1989). London 1952; Middle East, Russia, Senegal 1980s.

"Hello! Pearl"
Touching feet drumming Zimbabwe hustle
Studied theology, country biscuits, show biz. *Lawdy!*
Warming presidential hearts, Russian bears

Baker, Vernon. *Lasting Valor* (1997). Italy, Germany 1944–47.

"Double-Crossing Distinguished Service"
52 years climbing mountainous terrain
Cheyenne hunter, engineering Gothic Line, Aghinolfi victories
First in honor, scurrilously ignored

Baldwin, James. *Notes of a Native Son* (1955) *The Price of the Ticket* (1985). France 1948–87; Switzerland 1950s; Turkey 1961–67.

"Escrivain de Les Misérables"
Preacher's son holding church soirees
Turkish coffee and cigarettes, St. Germain cafés
Gorgeous observer transmutes ugly world

Baraka, Amiri. *Home: The Autobiography of Leroi Jones* (1987).Cuba 1959; Tanzania 1974.

"A Luta Continua para LeRoi Jones"
Evolutionary scientist, 25-hour train ride
Revisiting life rhymes from Cuban take-home speeches
New-ark *Norteamericano Libre* Black destination

Basie, Count. *The Autobiography of Count Basie* (1985). Sweden, Switzerland, Germany, France, Belgium 1954; Europe 1956–62; Japan 1963; Japan, Australia, New Zealand 1971; Canada, St. Thomas, St. Lucia, Caracas, Haiti 1972; Japan 1973; Canada, Europe, Japan 1974–84.

Question: Which is more intoxicating?
Stockholm vodka and tartar or Parisian secrets
Neither: Both make you stomp

Belafonte, Harry. *My Song: Memoir* (2011). Senegal 1987; Rwanda 1994; Cuba 1999; South Africa 2001; Kenya 2004; Norway 2007.

"Chant Day-O"
Suave sway, convening righteous indignation.
Baying Abukur breeze. UNICEF chant activist spirits.
Ackee-and-saltfish for all. Rights godfather.

Bragg, Janet. *Soaring above Setbacks: The Autobiography of Janet Harmon Bragg, African American Aviator* (1996). London, England, Paris 1955; Addis Ababa, Ethiopia 1965; Ethiopia, Dakar Senegal, Nigeria, Cairo 1972; Ethiopia Mexico, Singapore, Sweden, West Germany, Denmark, Italy 1980s.

"Black Wings over Lake Tana"
Flight captain sheparding Salassie-I's youth
Healing Atlanta hands: Tuskegee bodies, engines
Piloting Empress, Addis Ababa bird

Bricktop *Bricktop with Jim Haskins* (1983). (Ada Beatrice Queen Victoria Louise Virginia Smith). 1924–1939 Paris; Mexico City 1945; Paris 1949; Rome 1952.

"Confessions of a Redheaded Recluse"
West Virginian empress, vaudevillian to Roman saint
Hostess of highest royalty and lowliest poets
Joint jumpin'—saloon Charleston devotees

Brown, Henry "Box." *Narrative of the Life of Henry Box Brown* (1849, 1851). England, Wales 1850–75.

"Heaven save me from kind masters"
To ease slavery's friendly yolk
Please donate funds: 21 Cornhill Street, Boston
My wife's box to Wales

Brown, William Wells. *Narrative of William W. Brown, A Fugitive Slave* (1847, 1859). Canada 1834; Caribbean 1840; England, France, Scotland 1849–54.

"The Wonderment of Freedom's Crystal Palace"
Adieu to war-hungry American shores.
World's steamship, addressing *La Presse*. Peace Delegate.
Gaining utmost respect of lions.

Carmichael, Stokely. *Ready for Revolution: The Life and Struggles of Stokely Carmichael (Kwame Ture)* with Ekweme Michael Thelwell (2005). Trinidad 1941; New York 1952; Cuba 1967; Guinea 1969.

"Toure *Boum aye*: Stay Ready, Jack!"
Gracious embodiment, Power-full revolutionary prophecy
Organizing your triangular bloodlines: PtSpainTrinidad, LowdnesCo, ConakryGuinea
World stirring, uniting Mother Africa

Carson, Ben. *Gifted Hands: The Ben Carson Story* (1990). Australia 1983.

Detroit rage, blinded by fatherlessness
Bennie, go inside down under, find your
Prayer needle—heal bonded babies

Charles, Ray. *Brother Ray: Ray Charles' Own Story* (1978, 2004). Europe, South America, Asia, North Africa, Australia, New Zealand, Japan 1960s–2003.

"RC's St. Augustine ~~Blues~~ Swing"
Seven years picturing Panhandle country
Ruined early by boogie-woogie jukebox and bicycles
Jazzing red music All Over

Cole, Natalie. *Love Brought Me Back: A Journey of Loss and Gain* (2010). Tokyo 2008.

"World Class Hermanita"
Singing *Unforgettably*, swinging, Tokyo reprise
Organs failing: liver indignant; kidney following stubbornly
Sweetie, embracing four sisters' union

Cooper, Anna Julia. *The Third Step* (1945). London 1900; Paris 1911, 1912, 1913, 1925.

"One Whole Woman"
From *esclavage* to Sorbonne doctorate
Southern Black woman's *studere*, measuring men
Conjoined identities, physio-conative separation impossible

Coppin, Fanny Jackson. *Reminiscences of School Life, and Hints on Teaching* (1913). England 1882; South Africa 1902.

Advocating excellence; pedagogies of freedom.
Educating restless natives is always a tricky venture
Realizing limitations of proscriptive training

Craft, William and Ellen. *Running a Thousand Miles for Freedom; or The Escape of William and Ellen Craft from Slavery* (1860). Liverpool, 1850–68.

"Genteel Performance . . . Tender Mercies of the Wicked"
Redbone daughter, auction-block son: self-possessed.
Dred(ful) Yankee tyrannies: Macon masquerade, engendering gentlemen
Liberty (un)bound: leaping for Liverpool

Cruz, Celia. *CELIA, My Life: An Autobiography* (2004). Mexico City (from Cuba), Venezuela 1956; Mexico City 1960; Zaire 1974.

"Pedro's love, La Negra, Queen of Salsa"
After coffee, July 15, 1960
Trenta años exile, rumbling *Guantanamera* . . . imprisoned freedom
Surviving life: celebrating dancing *Azúcar*!

Davis, Angela Yvonne. *Angela Davis: An Autobiography* (1974). Paris 1963. University of Frankfurt 1965–67.

"Lifetime Conviction by the Court"
Justice work's philosophical, not rhetorical

To absorb the energy of prisoners
Families from Birmingham to Berlin

Davis, Belva. *Never in My Wildest Dreams: A Black Woman's Life in Journalism* (2010). Cuba 1977; Israel 1980; Jamaica, Guyana 1976; Côte d'Ivoire 1983; South Africa 1994; Cuba, Kenya 1998.

"Bringing Black Stories to the Light"
From Castro's charm to Kenyan blasts
Confronting double-barreled racist backlash with your pen-sword
Scooping hidden realities; corresponding overachievement

Davis Jr., Sammy. *Sammy: An Autobiography* (2000). London 1960; London 1964; Paris, London 1964; Canada 1968; Vietnam 1971; Holland, Germany, Sweden, England, France 1972; Australia 1977; Australia 1979; France 1985.

"Glass half full"
OG socialite, Vegas high life
Bon vivant cat with the swinginest pack
Entertainer hugging royalty and non-convention

Denton, Sandy Pepa. *Let's Talk about PEP: The Salt-n-Pepa Superstar Tells It How It Is* (2008). Born and raised Jamaica 1969. Europe 2006.

Expressive hiphop thrillseeker. Chasing worthyness.
Not simply surviving; Spittin' definitively instructional treatise
Joyride: the Autobon of life

Douglass, Frederick. *Narrative of the Life of Frederick Douglass, An American Slave: Written by Himself* (1845). England, Scotland, Ireland 1845.

"Independent Ambassador"
Wit sharper than Covey's whip
Third-eye North Star clarity of purpose
Tough as Haiti's limestone foundation

Du Bois, W. E. B. *Darkwater* (1920); *Dusk of Dawn* (1940), *Soliloquy: Autobiography* (1968). Berlin 1892–94; Niagara Falls, Canada 1905; London 1900; London 1911; Paris 1919; London, Brussels, Paris 1921; Liberia 1923; Russia 1926; world trip 1936; Haiti, Cuba 1944; Manchester, England 1945; Paris, Moscow 1949; [Passport denied 1951–58]; Soviet Union, Europe 1958–59; China 1959; Accra, Ghana 1961.

"No Apologies"
Disciplined professor. Hopes. Races Pan-Africa
Humbly attached. Agitating against Atalanta's greed
Vindicating human . . . *Souls* . . . suffering indignities

Dunham, Katherine. *A Tough of Innocence* (1959), *Island Possessed* (1969). Haiti, Jamaica, Martinique, Trinidad 1936; Mexico, London, Paris 1947–49; South America, Europe, North Africa tour 1950–55; Australia, New Zealand, Japan 1956–58; Europe 1959–60; 1965 Dakar, Senegal; fifty-seven countries in twenty years; 1992 Haiti (hunger strike).

"Bravo Company"
Chi-town feet pounding Port-au-Prince clay
Geographically sensuous, Creole initiate
Excavating primitive technique, visionary possession

Edelman, Marian Wright. *Lanterns: A Memoir of Mentors* (1999). Europe, Paris, Ireland Scotland, Soviet Union 1959.

"No Child Left Constrained"
Advocate for youth's legal rights
Lamppost, passing forward newfound freedoms of 1959
Spelman's paradigm of mobile inspiration

Fisher, Antwone. *Finding Fish: A Memoir* (2001). Eleven-year navy tour; Japan 1977.

"Sailing Away to Find Home"
Rape of Black boys? Hush.
Who's ever heard of such a thing?
Screenwriting happiness: unlikely *arigato* sunsets.

Gillespie, Dizzy (John Birks). *To Be or Not . . . to Bop* (1979). Europe 1948; Europe 1950; 1953 Canada; North Africa, Near East, Asia, Western Europe 1956; London 1965; Nairobi, Kenya 1972; Havana, Cuba 1977.

Cheeks for weeks; slick mischief-maker
Diplomatic charmer, chanting South Carolina peanut melodies
Faithfully trumpeting Afro-mestizo vibrato jive

Gordy, Berry. *To Be Loved: The Music, the Magic, the Memories of Motown* (1994). Korea 1951–53. Rome 1975.

"Farnsworth Cadence"
Lyrics of the Hitsville Maestro
Blockbuster groovemaster, knockout bandleader. Parading through Koreatown
Heading towards West Grand Boulevard

Grier, Pam. *Foxy: My Life in Three Acts* (2010). England 1965.

"An Appetite for Balanced Living"
Swindon fish-n-chips cures childhood stuttering
Baaad mama: (actor, rebel, rape/cancer survivor)
Fiercely nourishes desire and respect

Harris, Gail. *A Woman's War: The Professional and Personal Journey of the Navy's First African American Female Intelligence Officer* (2010). Korea 1988; Spain 1989; Middle East 1992–96.

"Adakian Logic. Two Things to Do about Any Problem: Something or Nothing"
Cairo women, laughing . . . professional warriors
Irish hospitality, Japanese driving, Korean Christmas shopping
SONAR, cyber warfare on barriers

Henderson, Jeff. *Cooked: From the Streets to the Stove, from Cocaine to Foie Gras* (2007). Mexico, 1986.

"Twelve Steps Away from Ten Years of Hard Time"
56-grams of sugar tastes sweeter
Than 56-grams of coke at Mexican boarder
And, though expensive, costs less

Henson, Josiah. *The Life of Josiah Henson, Formerly a Slave, Now an Inhabitant of Canada, as Narrated by Himself; Truth Stranger Than Fiction. Father Henson's Story of His Own Life; Uncle Tom's Story of His Life: An Autobiography of the Rev. Josiah Henson* (1849, 1858, 1876). Canada 1830.

"Maryland Dusk, Ontario Dawn"
Servile Negroes, too, want freedom
Preaching a British-American Institute into Canadian existence
London labour, loyal lumbering legend

Holiday, Billie. *Lady Sings the Blues* (1956). European Tour 1954; Paris 1958; London, Norway, Sweden, Germany, Italy, France, 1959.

"Unfinished Business"
Steel magnolias are sometimes sad
But steel gardenias are anything but pitiful
Besides, Eleanora didn't write blues

Hughes, Langston. *The Big Sea* (1941), *I Wonder as I Wander* (1956). Mexico 1920–21; Africa, Holland, Paris 1924; Russia 1932–33; Spain 1937.

"The Other Mexican Revolution"
Unabashedly loving Black people's funk
Writing books—poetic hook, line and sinker
Painting Africa's diasporan multi-shaded blues

Hunter-Gault, Charlayne. *New News Out of Africa: Uncovering Africa's Renaissance* (2007). South Africa 1997–2006.

"Round Trip . . . Robbin Island Township:Twenty Years of Eyes and Ears"
Reporting resurrection, critical Indigenous ink

Harvesting Soweto words. Johannasburg journal-isms. Conferring.
Athens correspondent, amplifying democratic demands

Hurston, Zora Neale. *Dust Tracks on a Road: An Autobiography* (1942).
Jamaica, Haiti 1937.

"The most interesting thing that I saw was the horizon"
Infamous child in Chinaberry tree
Eatonville's will, founded jook joint anthropology, story-telling
Zombies, "My People, My People"

Jacobs, Harriet. *Incidents in the Life of a Slave Girl* (1852). England 1845.

"Reminiscences of Troubled Seas"
Rooming house for Whig desires
Beyond reach, seven-year loophole: a Carolina Adalaide
Graceful. Strictly escaping women's bondage

Jamison, Judith. *Dancing Spirit: An Autobiography* (1993). Dakar 1966; Senegal, London, Barcelona, Paris 1966. Madagascar, Tanzania, Uganda, Kenya, Congo, Ivory Coast, Ghana, Senegal 1967. Germanu, Sweden 1968; Russia 1970; Austria 1972; Senegal 1982; Russia 1990; Antigua 1990s.

"Born to Cry the Spirit"
Long-winged angle, never-ending riverboat legs
Revelatory protégé; rural-rooted Moscow blues. Blood movement
Dakar nomad, rotating inside out

Jemison, Mae. Liberia 1983–85; Space 1992. *Find Where the Wind Goes: Moments from My Life* (2001).

NASA afros and African science
Sporting Chi-town smile. Migrant dancer-doctor commands
questions
*Endeavor*ing: finding the real thing

Johnson, Jack. *My Life and Battles* (1914, 2009); *Jack Johnson Is a Dandy* (1927, 1969). Australia 1907; Australia, Paris 1908; England, Paris 1911; Canada, Paris, Russia, England, Brazil 1913–14; Cuba 1915.

"Black Matador in Powder Blue Trunks"
Seeker of Beasts. Women. Liberty.
Mes Combats driving blades through White hope
Noble artist, Chivalrous. Driven mad

Johnson, John H. *Succeeding against the Odds: The Autobiography of a Great American Businessman* (1992). Ghana 1957; Russia, Poland 1959; Ivory Coast 1961; Kenya 1963; Continent feature 1976.

"High Stakes Dreams"
Mastering the politics of business
Ebony Jetting: South African Ivory Coast, tops-n-tails
Publishing Ghanaian and Kenyan Independence

Jordan, June. *Soldier: A Poet's Childhood* (2000). *Some of Us Did Not Die* (2003). Jamaica 1974; Nicaragua 1983; Bahamas 1989.

"Daughter of a Little Bull Dances the Immigrant Calypso on the Pages"
Among Brooklyn's West Indian nations
Granville Ivanhoe scolds his daughter's common penchants
Her mother's Clonmel grit enduring

Kennedy, Florynce. *Color Me Flo: My Hard Life and Good Times* (1976). Canada 1967. Australia, Mexico City, Toronto 1975.

"Order of Discovery"
KC feminist organizer wields her
Pink cowboy hat, fist and middle finger
Testifying against foolishness even NOW

King, B. B. *Blues All around Me: The Autobiography of B. B. King* (1996). Japan, Australia, Ghana, Nigeria, Chad and Liberia 1971; Russia 1977; Israel 1986, 1996; Brazil 1986; Europe 1988.

Beating Moscow, Jerusalem, SaoPaolo hearts
B. B. loves women but Lucille comes first
Indianola blues will never die

Kitt, Eartha. *Thursday's Child* (1956), *Alone with Me: A New Autobiography* (1976), *Confessions of a Sex Kitten* (1991). Mexico City 1948; Europe 1948–49; Paris, Istanbul 1950–51; Nigeria 1958; Milan 1968; Swaziland, Southern Africa 1971, 73; Hong Kong, London 1974.

> "Eaaaartha, Misssstressss of Ssssound"
> Sex appeal: Dean, Dunham, Dover
> Far to go: *Rue de Pantehon* Ennnngenou.
> Mother Kitt, Eartha Mae, puuuurrrrr.

Malcolm X. *Autobiography of Malcolm X* (1965). United Arab Republic, Sudan, Nigeria, Egypt, Mecca, Iran, Syria, Ghana 1959; Germany, Mecca, Saudi Arabia, Sudan, Egypt, Nigeria, Ghana, Liberia, Senegal, Morocco, London, Ethiopia, Kenya, Tanzania, Paris 1964; Canada, London, refused entry to Paris 1965.

> "The Witness Rests His Case"
> Wisdom seeker prosecuting false realities
> Smiling with conviction, indicting *all* spiritual liars
> Interrogates even his own definitions

Marshall, Paule. *Triangular Road: A Memoir* (2009). Barbados, Grenada 1962; Europe 1965; Lagos, Nigeria 1977.

> "Bed-Stuy Brownstone's Bookworm, or The Rainmaker's Protégé"
> Paul-e. E for editor. Eden-dweller
> Traversing tobacco rivers, Bajan seas, *Omawale* oceans
> Ever faithful to the story

McElroy, Colleen. *A Long Way from St. Louie* (1997). Germany 1940s; Mexico; Fulbright Yugoslavia, Japan 1988.

> "The Road between Butterflies and Dragons"
> Comforting self-defining movement. Recollecting survivalists.

Chasing Baker's forbidden Victrola voice. Nonlinear meanderings . . .
Goree, Auschwitz, Hiroshima. Invisible Aboriginals.

McKay, Claude. *A Long Way from Home* (1937, 1970); *My Green Hills of Jamaica* (1979). U.S. 1913; London 1919–20; Russia 1922–23; Berlin, Paris, North Africa 1923–33; Paris 1928–29.

"No Place like Home"
Belonging neither here nor there
Wandering poet, artist of *persona non grata*
Perennial outsider, but fighting back

Montague, Magnificent Nathaniel. *Burn, Baby Burn!: The Autobiography of Magnificent Montague* (2003). Holland, Russia, France, Germany, South Africa, Liberia, Nigeria, Senegal, Egypt, Persian Gulf, England 1944.

"Record Player Promises"
Music merchant, hustlin' historical grooves
Riotous museum, burning Black Atlantic souls
Feeling heartbeats through drum speakers

Murray, Pauli. *Pauli Murray: The Autobiography of a Black Activist, Lawyer, Priest, and Poet* (1987). Ghana 1968–73.

"Nomadic Spirit"
Raising consciousness of perennially rejected
A priest's army of demons eventually vanquished
Durham daughter ordaining lasting peace

Newton, Huey P. *Revolutionary Suicide* (1973). China 1971

Student of Merritt, UC PhD
Murdered: Black man's fist-clutched gun. Incomplete revolution.
Monroe anti-reactionary of People's Republic

Obama, Barack. *Dreams from My Father* (1995, 2004), *Audacity of Hope* (2006). Indonesia 1967; Europe, Kenya 1988; Kenya 2006.

Hyphenated African American, and bi-racial
"Barry" inherits muted radical nature, Afro-Asiatic clashes
Nation's hope; authentically, audaciously, adaptable

Poitier, Sidney. *This Life (1980)*, *The Measure of a Man: A Spiritual Autobiography* (2000). Cat Island, born in Nassau; Return 1970s.

"Acting Black: From Black Ash and Blacklist to *Blackboard* and
Black-tie"
Lifestyle? Moving-on. Temperament? Volatile charm
Hurricane principles, non-negotiable as your skin color
Traveling clear-blue stage's far galaxies

Rangel, Charles. *And I Haven't Had a Bad Day Since: From the Streets of Harlem to the Halls of Congress* (2007). Korea 1950–52; South Africa 1994.

"Pleasant Reminiscences of Mastering the Deck of Cards Called
American Politics"
Thirty-six Ways-and-Means surviving Kuni-ri ditches
Le GARCON, pushing Watergate, anti-apartheid and Aristide
Litigating smile, mortician's poker face

Rice, Condoleezza. *No Higher Honor: A Memoir of the Washington Years* (2011). Iraq, Darfur, North Korea, India, China, Baghdad, Cairo, Georgia, Mumbai 2001–09.

Black boots, culture, conservative confidence
Marching X continents . . . revising current perceptions for posterity
Surrogate weapons of mass deconstruction

Robeson, Eslanda Goode. *African Journey* (1972). London, South Africa, Swaziland, Mozambique, Uganda, Kenya, Egypt, Basutoland (Lesotho), 1936.

"Latitudinal Sketches of African Horizons"
Digging soil with non-hierarchical tools
Diaries logging African humanity; vivid portraits
Research focus on Pauli's people

Ross, Diana. *Secrets of a Sparrow* (1995); *Going Back* (2002). Europe 1965–70;
Solo world tours 1970–2011.

> "Domestic Diva, World Boss"
> 400,000 in Central Park rain
> Situated somewhere between all heart and untouchable
> Tomboy, Lady, Josephine, Maasai warrior

Ringgold, Faith. *We Flew over the Bridge: The Memoirs of Faith Ringgold* (1995).
Paris, Rome 1961.

> "Harlemite Women Seen Riding Magic Quilt over Manhattan Bridge"
> Desocializing Parisian Paint, Patchwork, Performance
> Super real daughtermother: flying but not high
> Loss gain. Fighting artist's invisibility

RuPaul, Andre. *Lettin It All Hang Out: An Autobiography* (1995). London 1992,
England, Germany, 1993.

> "You Betta (Work)"
> California Black boy in heels
> Cannes Queen, having one thing to say
> Soulful blonde bombshell fashioning self-love

Schuyler, George. *Black and Conservative: The Autobiography of George S.
Schuyler* (1966). Liberia 1931; South America, Caribbean 1948–49; West
Africa, Dominican Republic 1958.

> Before FOX News irritated mainstream
> African American gadfly contraryan, opposite even himself
> Refused even black righteous indignation

Shakur, Assata. *Assata: An Autobiography* (1987). Havana, Cuba 1984.

> "Cuba Libre?"
> Robbery, kidnapping, murder? No fingerprints!

Escaping U.S. prison of lies: "Political refugee"
Hands up! for 40 years.

Sheppard, William Henry. *Presbyterian Pioneers in the Congo* (1917). London,
Congo 1890–1910.

"Christian Conqueror"
Heir to Presbyterian missionary martyrdom
Enlightening with Virginian benevolence, Hampton manhood
"Civilizing savages," whitening Luebo blackness

Simone, Nina. *I Put a Spell on You* (2003). Barbados, Liberia, Switzerland
1974–78; Cannes, Israel 1978; Paris 1979–85.

"This Is the World You Have Made"
Father's pride, unsettled Liberian bride
C'est la vie; Goddamn wisdom; ghostly memories
Raising hell, piano fanning flames

Smith, Tommie. *Silent Gesture: The Autobiography of Tommie Smith* (2007).
Mexico City 1968.

"On the Banks of Resurrection River"
Tommie on top; muted gold.
John, unequivocally Black; unquietly bronze. Shoeless platforms.
200 meters distancing East-West coast protest

Terrell, Mary Church. *A Colored Woman in a White World* (1940). Europe
1884–86; Berlin 1904; Zurich, Switzerland 1919.

"Indignant Style"
Upper–class Memphis Fraulein—International clubwoman
Socialite picketing segregated eateries in your fur
Railing angrily, carrying on, unbounded

Thompson, Era Bell. *American Daughter (1945); Africa the Land of My Father* (1954). Eighteen African countries by 1954; Brazil 1965; traveled to 124 countries on 6 continents.

"A Prodigal Daughter's Temporary Return"
Investigating diversities: colonized Continental self-love
Mining Dr. Malan's dark-hearted apartheid, exposing color bars
Typing eighteen-thousand complicated Black tomorrows

Toussaint, Rose-Marie. *Never Question the Miracle: A Surgeon's Story* (1998). Haiti 1983.

Haitian *oungan* foretelling your future
Seven-year old visions: aberrant Holy transplant surgeon
Possibilities of the improbable 6%

Turner, Tina. *I, Tina* (1986). Tijuana, Mexico 1962; Rolling Stones tour 1966; UK and Europe tour 1980; Private Dancer tour Asia, Europe and Australia 1985–86; Munich Break Every Rule tour 1987; Rio 1988; Foreign Affairs 1989; London, Cologne, Germany 1986; Switzerland 1993–94; Wildest Dreams tour 1996; 24/7 tour 2000.

"Queen of Rhythm, Disciple of Soul"
Acid rising, remixing spiritual emergence
Foolish escapes, enchanting those ready to hear
Proud legs, Rough-rocking London thunderdomes

Vincent, Carter O. *The Bern Book: A Record of a Voyage of the Mind* (1956). Bern Switzerland 1950s.

"The Mindful Exile"
Black nonlinear mind running . . . slowly
Swiss Alps's flora questioning a writers' motivation
While the author darkens himself

Wells-Barnett, Ida. *Crusade for Justice: The Autobiography of Ida B. Wells* (1970). Europe 1893; Liverpool, Manchester, Bristol, London England 1894.

"Vigilant Liberty. Run tell that!"
World's Fair, America's radical elocutionist
Parading *Red Record* to Queen and Parliament
Organizing protest campaigns; liberty's *Defender*

Willis, Jan. *Dreaming Me: Black, Baptist, and Buddhist* (2008). Tibet 1967;
1970s.

"Luminous Lions"
Putting down guns at Cornell
Non-violence: not a dream, but a journey
Mother's rainbow on Buddha's robe

NOTES

PROLOGUE

1. Budge, *Queen of Sheba*, 16, 25; Clapp, *Sheba*, 139; Lassner, *Demonizing the Queen of Sheba*, 12, 174; von Sivers *et al., Patterns of World History*, 459; Williams and Finch, "Great Queens of Ethiopia," 16–17; Flemming and Pryde, *Distinguished Negroes Abroad*, 307–10.
2. Hausman, Gerald. *The Kebra Nagast: The Lost Bible of Rastafarian Wisdom and Faith from Ethiopia and Jamaica*, introduction by Ziggy Marley (New York: St. Martin's, 1997), 57.
3. Based on numerous ancient testaments, particularly the forty-two Proclamations of Innocence in the Egyptian *Book of Coming Forth by Day*, ten Commandments and thirty Proverbs of Wisdom in the Bible, virtue is the basis of wisdom. Makeda concerned herself with virtue in both individual growth and social justice. Accordingly, Jesus himself is recorded as saying, "The Queen of the South shall be the final judge of us all" (Matthew 12:38–42; Luke 11:31; First Kings 10:1–5; Second Chronicles 9:1–12. Qu'ran: 27 sura). However, in this text, I use ethics as a pervasive set of social values rather than assuming moral instruction as the sole purview of religion.
4. Stevens, *Smart and Sassy: The Strengths of Inner-City Black Girls* (New York: Oxford University Press, 2002) 93, 189.
5. For those interested in Ancient African civilization, access the organization ASCAC (Association for the Study of Classical African Civilizations) http://www.ascac.sqsp.com/ and Dr. Greg Carr, head of Howard

University's Department of African American Studies http://www.coas. howard.edu/afroamerican/faculty_carr.html are great places to start as Dr. Carr actually studies hieroglyphics and is immersed in community education centers around the nations.

6. South African site, http://www.southafrica.info/about/history/saa-rtjie-270209.htm.

7. Alston. "Race-Crossings at the Crossroads of African American Travel in the Caribbean." PhD diss., 2004.

8. For syllabi, visit "Teaching" page, http://www.professorevans.net/Teaching.html (accessed April 10, 2013).

CHAPTER 1. INTRODUCTION

1. Gomez, "Nina Turner's Future Bright Due to Gutsy Stand on Issue 6," *The Plain Dealer Online*.

2. Eyler and Giles, "Where Is the Learning in Service Learning?"

3. "About Us," Big Brothers Big Sisters, accessed June 28, 2012, http://www. bbbs.org/site/c.9iILI3NGKhK6F/b.5962351/k.42EB/We_are_here_to_ start_something.htm.

4. Ladner's work is essential reading as a forerunner model for those interested in Black adolescent gender studies. Other groundbreaking work includes Diane Caroll (*Sugar in the Raw: Voices of Young Black Girls in America*), and Darrell Dawsey (*Living to Tell about It: Young Black Men in America Speak Their Piece*).

5. Green, *Manufacturing Powerlessness*, 167.

6. See "Introduction" in *African Americans and Community Engagement in Higher Education*, ed. Stephanie Y. Evans, Colette Taylor, Michelle Dunlap, and DeMond Miller for outline of Septima Clark's contribution toward understanding community voice, collaborative learning, and the centrality of race in "town-gown" relations; "Mentoring 'At-Risk' Youth Syllabus" online at www.professorevans.net.

7. Krenn, *Black Diplomacy*, 163.

8. David Levering Lewis, Talk at Brooklyn Public Library, February 13, 2013. Carter V. Good "Functional History of Education" (Editorial), *The Journal of Educational Research* 33, no. 2 (October 1939): 136–38. Pero Dagbovie, *African American History Reconsidered*. Champaign-Urbana: University of Illinois, 2010.

9. As in the *African American Lives* reference volume, truncated citation style is used to preserve space. Full references are listed in the bibliography.

10. Stevens, *Smart and Sassy,* 189.

11. Heather Williams, *Self-Taught: African American Education in Slavery and Freedom* (Chapel Hill: University of North Carolina Press, 2005), 207. See also Janet Duitsman Cornelius, *When I Can Read My Title Clear: Literacy, Slavery, and Religion in the Antebellum South* (Columbia: University of South Carolina Press, 1991).

12. See especially Mari Evans, *Black Women Writers, 1950–1980: A Critical Evaluation* (New York: Anchor, 1984); Angelyn Mitchell, ed., *Within the Circle: An Anthology of African American Literary Criticism from the Harlem Renaissance to the Present* (Durham: Duke University Press, 1994).

13. There are roughly 100 authors—James Haskins being of great significance to children's literature and author of 130 of the books on Thompson's list—accessed September 18, 2011, http://www.pauahtun.org/aakidlit.html.

14. Anderson, *My Lord, What a Morning,* xv.

15. See Augustus Wood, Clark Atlanta University, forthcoming thesis.

16. King, *Blues All around Me,* 2.

17. Du Bois, *Soliloquy,* 12.

18. I characterize Dr. Du Bois as a "conductor" in three ways: in writing about his life, he transferred massive amount of vibrancy and energy (physics); in his school life he conducted research and formed research collectives with the skill, direction and smoothness of a symphony maestro (music); and in his work for social justice, he was a social engineer, directing organizations like the National Association for the Advancement of Colored People (NAACP), to bend the arc of sociology in favor of liberation and freedom like directing a train on an alternate track (engineering).

19. This work also enhances Black male narratives, as found in Henry Louis Gates' *Thirteen Ways of Looking at a Black Man.*

20. Lassner, *Demonizing the Queen of Sheba,* 51.

21. In the early stages of research at the University of Florida, I taught a course called "U.S. Women of Color," which became an important predecessor to the "Black Autobiography" class I taught at Clark Atlanta University. The "Women of Color" curriculum centered on autobiographies: *Paper Daughter* (M. Elaine Mar), *When I Was Puerto Rican* (Esmeralda Santiago), *In My Place* (Charlayne Hunter-Gault) and *I Am Woman: A Native Perspective on Sociology and Feminism* (Lee Maracle). At other times, I assigned *No Disrespect* (Sista Souljah), and considered using *Strong*

Medicine Speaks: A Native American Elder Has Her Say (Hearth). These initial explorations into the memoirs began with Native, Asian, Latina, and Black women.

22. Blassingame, "Black Autobiography as History and Literature," 2–9.

23. Olaudah Equiano, *Interesting Narrative of the Life of Olaudah Equiano* (1789).

24. *From Behind the Veil: A Story of Afro-American Narrative.*

25. *African American Autobiography*, 30.

26. Houston Baker Jr. also provides an argument for Black literature as historical evidence, regardless of lack of absolute accuracy, "Meaning and its expression are one; hence, in the Black word resides the culturally specific meaning that grows out of the physical circumstances where language begins. As a vehicle of a rational agent's thought, the language of the Black author (as embodied in a literary text) can be taken as historical evidence."Baker, "On the Criticism of Black American Literature," 128.

27. Braxton, *Black Women Writing Autobiography*, 9–13.

28. Perkins, *Autobiography as Activism*, xvi, xvii, 149–50.

29. See also Shawn Alexander, *An Army of Lions: the Civil Rights Struggle before the NAACP* (Philadelphia: University of Pennsylvania Press, 2011).

30. Wells, *Crusade for Justice*, 415.

31. "Oprah Talks to Maya Angelou," http://www.oprah.com/omagazine/ Oprah-Interviews-Maya-Angelou; Academy of Achievement, Profile of Kareem Abdul Jabar, http://www.achievement.org/autodoc/page/ abd0int–5.

32. In *Smart and Sassy*, Stevens defines self-efficacy as "the ability to exercise *mastery* and competence in one's social environment to achieve desirable social goals" (italics added). Stevens, *Smart and Sassy*, 93, 189.

33. World Savvy, http://worldsavvy.org/blog/evaluating-global-competency/.

34. Colleen McElroy, *A Long Way from St. Louis*, 40–41.

35. Omniglot see http://www.omniglot.com/ (accessed April 9, 2013).

36. Greg Carr, "The Impact and Implications of the Maafa: Africana Studies, the HB[M]CU and Acts of Remembering." Clark Atlanta University, Lecture. November 2,2012.

37. "NIA Statement of Purpose, Youth Summits," accessed July 15, 2012. http://www.professorevans.net/Service.html.

38. Gwen Kirk and Margo Okazawa-Rey, *Women's Lives: Multicultural Perspectives* (New York: McGraw Hill, 2006).

CHAPTER 2. LIFE

1. Tucker and Herman, "Using Culturally Sensitive Theories . . . ," 767.
2. "I Am Not a Role Model, *Newsweek*, Accessed June 29, 2012, http://www.thedailybeast.com/newsweek/1993/06/27/i-m-not-a-role-model.html; "I Am Not a Role Model," YouTube, accessed June 29, 2012, http://www.youtube.com/watch?v=nMzdAZ3TjCA; "Niggas in Paris," YouTube, accessed June 29, 2012, http://www.youtube.com/watch?v=x1eMlgN39O8.
3. See "Five Ways Talib Quali Can Be a Better Ally to Women in Hip Hop" http://www.crunkfeministcollective.com/2013/04/05/five-ways-talib-kweli-can-become-a-better-ally-to-women-in-hip-hop/ and "Five Ways CrunkFeminist.com Could Actually Be a Reliable Source of INformaiton http://talibkweli.tumblr.com/post/47248623360/5-ways-crunkfeminist-com-could-actually-be-a#_=_ accessed, April 8, 2013.
4. Higginbotham, "Politics of Respectability," in *Righteous Discontent.*
5. "The Chef Jeff Project," Food Network, accessed June 30, 2012, http://www.foodnetwork.com/the-chef-jeff-project/index.html.
6. Washington, *A Man from Another Land*, 73.
7. OK, really, I just love Richard Pryor. I know long quotes are taboo. Get over it.
8. Pryor, *Pryor Convictions*, 173–74.
9. Robeson, *Here I Stand*, 25.
10. Ibid., 109.
11. "Assata Shakur," African American Registry, accessed March 5, 2012, http://www.aaregistry.org/historic_events/view/revolutionary-text-assata-shakur.
12. Assata, *Assata*, 240.
13. Personal correspondence, November 30, 2011 (Moten) and December 20, 2011 (Corbett); Frank Moten, "Growing Up in New Jersey," accessed December 1, 2011, http://frankmoten.com/growing_up_in_new_jersey_might_n.html; Steven Weisz, "A New Generation of Dance Innovators with Fresh Juice and The Requisite Movers," Dance Bloggers, September 26, 2011, accessed December 1, 2011, http://www.dancebloggers.com/2011/09/a-new-generation-of-dance-innovators-with-fresh-juice-and-the-requisite-movers/.
14. See http://frankmoten.com/ for full details. Accessed November 30, 2011.
15. Reichert House Youth Academy, accessed June 30, 2012, https://www.gainesvillepd.org/index.php/community-programs/reichert-house.

16. Reichert House Curriculum Handout, January 2010.

17. For multiple resources to discuss Black masculinity, see the 2007 course syllabus in "Black Gender." The reading list reveals limitless possible texts for exploring Black manhood http://www.professorevans.net/Teaching. html.

18. Child Welfare League of America, accessed June 7, 2002, http://www.cwla. org/voice/0909girls.htm.

19. Movie trailer, accessed February 26, 2012, http://www.youtube.com/ watch?v=2DkwSqNDJbM; Beifuss review, accessed February 26, 2012, http://www.gomemphis.com/news/2009/jun/30/beifuss-wiz-scarecrow-role-last-straw-jackson-movi/; World Trade Center video, accessed February 26, 2012, http://www.youtube.com/watch?v=XuFrQXpmw3U.

20. Jones, Q, 229.

21. Ross, *Secrets of a Sparrow*, 198.

22. Ibid., 233.

23. Ibid., 278.

24. V. P. Franklin, *Living Our Stories, Telling Our Truths*, 20.

25. A cluster of reading in postcolonial feminism that would reveal theoretical contrasts of identity and location would be to match *Black Body* with Jacqui Alexander and Changra Mohanty's edited *Feminist Genealogies, Colonial Legacies, and Democratic Futures*, Uma Narayan's *Dislocating Cultures: Identities, Traditions, and Third World Feminism*, Chris Weedon's *Feminism, Theory, and the Politics of Difference*, and Jennifer DeVere Brody's *Impossible Purities: Blackness, Femininity, and Victorian Culture*. Since these authors reference each other, discussions of convergent and divergent viewpoints would be especially rich. Mohanram's analysis very necessarily depends on deconstructing White, male, heterosexual, Western paradigms. However, at some point it is necessary to move beyond deconstruction, thus using Mohanram's work in tandem with other theorists like Brody, Mohanty, and Narayan would decentralize the focus of European male theory.

CHAPTER 3. SCHOOL

1. Larose and Tarabulsy, "Academically At-Risk Students," 443–44.

2. Ibid.

3. The course syllabus is available online at http://www.professorevans.net/ Teaching.html.

4. Stephanie Y. Evans, Book Review, Joyce West Stevens, *Smart and Sassy: The Strengths of Inner-City Black Girls* in *Sex Roles: A Journal of Research* 47, nos. 3–4 (August 2002): 199–200.

5. Those wishing to add to this curriculum can certainly take advantage of the three-volume memoir of Dr. Edmond W. Gordon, a long-standing faculty member at Columbia University Teachers College, *Pedagogical Imagination, Volume I: Using the Master's Tools to Change the Subject of the Debate* (Third World Press, 2012). There are also excellent programs such as David Wall Rice's work on Black manhood at Morehouse College in Atlanta, Niambi Jaha-Echols's *Project Butterfly* in Chicago and Ohio, Ralph Steele's book *Mentoring and the Rites of Passage for Youth*, and Aiesha Turman's *Black Girl Project* in New York. "Identity Orchestration Lab," Rice, accessed June 19, 2012, http://iorl.tumblr.com/; "Project Butterfly," accessed June 19, 2012, http://campbutterfly.org/about/cb-national/; "The Black Girl Project," Turman, accessed June 19, 2012, http://blackgirlproject.org/.

6. "Language Arts Requirement," Georgia Department of Education, accessed June 30, 2012, https://www.georgiastandards.org/standards/Georgia%20Performance%20Standards/Multicultural%20Literature%20Reading%20Across%20the%20Curriculum.pdf.

7. McMillen, "The Impact of Academic Vocabulary Instruction," 30–32. These and other stories can be supplemented by online resources: Black Past, www.blackpast.org and African American Registry, www.aaregistry.org.

8. Clark, *Echo in My Soul*, 153–66; Evans, "Introduction," in *African Americans and Community Engagement in Higher Education*.

9. Hayat Mohamed, "Kemba Walker UConn Star Reads First Book," *The Root*, April 20, 2011, http://www.theroot.com/buzz/kemba-walker-uconn-star-reads-first-book.

10. McMillen, "The Impact of Academic Vocabulary Instruction," 42.

11. Ibid., 104–23.

12. I was initially inclined to limit the list to exactly one thousand words, but I was inspired by Nikki Giovanni's 100 Best African American Poems * But I Cheated, in which she exceeds the initial number of the "top 100."

13. Thanks to Ayana Flewellen and Alisa Valentine who helped construct the Malcolm X word list.

14. NCHS History Standards, accessed June 22, 2012, http://www.nchs.ucla.edu/Standards/historical-thinking-standards-1/1.-chronological-thinking.

15. University of California–Los Angeles, accessed June 22, 2012, http://nchs. ucla.edu/Standards/us-history-content-standards/us-era-9-1.

16. Georgia Department of Education, accessed June 30, 2012, https://www. georgiastandards.org/standards/Georgia%20Performance%20Standards/ World%20Geography%208-27-2007.pdf.

17. Carter, *The Bern Book,* 208.

18. Ibid., 279.

19. "Exploring Poetry and Poets," Georgia Department of Education, http:// gadoe.georgiastandards.org/DMGetDocument.aspx/9th%20Grade%20 Exploring%20Poets%20and%20Poetry.pdf?p=39EF345AE192D900F620 BFDE9C014CE65F48E7E4CC6532400C474024B483C9ADB45AB5C070 9A6D57&Type=D.

20. Angelou, "Senegal," in *Letter to My Daughter,* 89.

21. Hughes, *The Big Sea,* 335.

22. Rampersad, "Introduction," *Anthology of African American Poetry* (add publ info 2006), xxiv.

23. Mottoes of Clark Atlanta University.

24. Black Passports, Viewshare http://viewshare.org/views/drevans/swag-diplomacy-web-resource/. Google Maps™ or StatPlanet can also create outstanding geographic lesson plan guides.

25. The Viewshare tool builds on another online mentoring tool I created to enhance past mentoring classes: the NIA Statement of Purpose project. The project guided students to create a Haiku, spoken word poem, and standard college or graduate school application essay. They filmed their own poetic statements and uploaded them onto YouTube, which both served the students by helping them find their voice and served hundreds of viewers who viewed the videos. Biren, *Guided Autobiography*, a useful tool with elders, could work as a structural model and be reconfigured with a youth audience in mind.

26. Available online at: www.ProfessorEvans.net; Professor Haskins is the author of The Cotton Club (the book on which the movie was based) and almost 200 books, mainly books for youth. For published collection of Diaries of a Prolific Professor : Undergraduate Research from the James Haskins Manuscript Collection, visit http://ufdc.ufl.edu/AA00007589/.

CHAPTER 4. WORK

1. Georgia Steppers League information, accessed March 11, 2013 http:// georgiasteppersleague.pbworks.com/w/page/3599319/About%20Us.

2. National Association for Urban Debate Leagues. http://www.urbandebate. org/index.shtml accessed April 8, 2013.

3. MyPlan, accessed June 29, 2012, www.myplan.com.

4. Rice, *No Greater Honor,* 734.

5. Powell, *My American Journey,* 564.

6. Ibid., 566–67.

7. Ibid., 613.

8. Davis, *Never in My Wildest Dreams,* 217, 221.

9. Sullivan, *Moving Mountains,* 205–08.

10. Anderson, *My Lord, What a Morning,* 191.

11. Ibid., 38.

12. Ibid., 40.

13. Ibid., 45.

14. Ibid., 189.

15. Ross, *Secrets of the Sparrow,* 83, 117.

16. Jemison, "Wind Currents: What I Intended to Be," in *Find Where the Wind Goes,* vii.

17. James Baldwin, "The Creative Process," in *The Price of the Ticket, Collected Nonfiction, 1948–1985* (1962; repr., New York: St. Martin's, 1985).

18. Stephanie Y. Evans, *Black Women in the Ivory Tower, 1850–1954: An Intellectual History.* (Gainesville: University Press of Florida, 2007), 87.

19. Paul D. Leedy and Jeanne Ellis Ormrod, *Practical Research: Planning and Design,* 8th edition (New Jersey: Pearson, 2005).

20. Evans, *Black Women in the Ivory Tower,* 8–9.

21. Ibid.

22. See Heather Williams, *Self-Taught: African American Education in Slavery and Freedom* (Chapel Hill: UNC Press, 2007).

23. *The Root,* July 21, 2010.

24. Stephen Hawking, a well-known British theoretical physicist and cosmologist at the University of Cambridge, has argued that humans must quickly work to inhabit other planets because we have ruined earth. This planet, he argues, is no longer sustainable. In a rebuttal to Dr. Hawking, I employed an argument based on interrogating the underlying injustices of our practices, particularly those of research (art, science, and policy) that has contributed to our preventable demise. See Hawking, "The Beginning of Time," http://www.hawking.org.uk/lectures/bot.html; BBC, http://news.bbc.co.uk/2/hi/science/nature/6594821.stm; New York Times online, http://www.nytimes.com/aponline/us/AP-Hawking-Flight.html?_r=1&oref=slogin; Washington Post online http://www.

washingtonpost.com/wp-dyn/content/article/2007/04/26/AR2007
042602709.html?hpid=artslot.

25. Player, "Over the Tumult," 4–8.

26. Ibid., in Evans, *Black Women in the Ivory Tower*, 209.

CHAPTER 5. EXCHANGE

1. Lewis Gordon, *Existencia Africana*, 37–40.

2. Nat Love, *The Life and Adventures of Nat Love, Better Known in the Cattle Country as "Deadwood Dick" by Himself; a True History of Slavery Days, Life on the Great Cattle Ranges and on the Plains of the "Wild and Woolly" West, Based on Facts, and Personal Experiences of the Author* (1907), 37.

3. See "Trail of Tears," U.S. Park Service, http://www.nps.gov/trte/index.htm and "Buffalo Soldiers," http://www.nps.gov/goga/planyourvisit/upload/sb-buffalo-2008.pdf.

4. "Luminoir Noir," Bob Swaim, http://www.bobswaim.com/home_bs/index.htm.

5. *Harvard Gazette* online, accessed June 30, 2012, http://www.news.harvard.edu/gazette/2002/10.17/02-wamba.html.

6. Letter excerpt in "Mecca" chapter, *The Autobiography of Malcolm X*, 339–42.

7. For details, visit www.bobswaim.com (accessed June 30, 2012).

8. National CARES Mentoring Movement http://www.caresmentoring.org/. Black Girls Rock http://www.blackgirlsrockinc.com/ (accessed April 9, 2013).

9. Williams, "Conceived in Transit, Delivered in Passage"; Steadman, "Travel Writing and Resistance"; Thomas, "Traveling Eyes."

10. See Steven W. Shirley's 2006 dissertation "The Gender Gap in Post-secondary Study Abroad: Understanding and Marketing to Male Students."

11. For a summary of Black women's study abroad, see Stephanie Evans, "African American Women Scholars and International Research: Dr. Anna Julia Cooper's Legacy of Study Abroad," *Frontiers: The Interdisciplinary Journal of Study Abroad* 18 (Fall 2009): 77–100. Also see Flemmie Kittrell Papers, Moreland Spingarn Research Center, Howard University.

12. Cooper, "The Third Step," in *The Voice of Anna Julia Cooper*, 327.

13. Patricia Schechter, *Ida B. Wells-Barnett and American Reform, 1880–1930* (Chapel Hill: University of North Carolina Press, 2001), 16. For additional examinations of social location, see Gwen Kirk and Margo Okazawa-Rey,

Women's Lives: Multicultural Perspectives (New York: McGraw Hill, 2006).

14. Dunham, *Island Possessed*, 109.

15. Ibid., 105–16.

16. Ibid., 109.

17. Osumare writes "Summarily, Dunham created performance ethnographies on the world's greatest stages, privileged the voices of her informants in her publications, created visions of cross-cultural communication, and engaged in self-examination within the fieldwork process that far exceeded any of her contemporaries." Halifu Osumare, "Katherine Dunham, a Pioneer of Postmodern Anthropology" in *Kaiso: Writings by and about Katherine Dunham*, ed. VeVe Clark and Sara Johnson, 612.

18. Kaiso, 430–35.

19. Davis, 134–36.

20. Ibid.

21. Ibid., 145.

22. Willis, *Dreaming Me: Black, Baptist and Buddhist*, 95, 102, 130–37.

23. Ibid., 139.

24. Ibid., 144.

25. Stevens, *Smart and Sassy*, 28–29.

26. Terrell, *Colored Woman in a White World*, 68.

27. Morton, *My First Sixty Years*, 16–30.

28. Ibid., 128–43.

29. Ibid., 56.

30. Marian Wright Edelman, *Lanterns: A Memoir of Mentors*, 36.

31. Ibid., 38.

32. In addition to her 1892 social critique, *Voice from the South by a Black Woman of the South* and the 1925 dissertation, Cooper translated *Le Pelerinage de Charlemagne* (1925). She worked on the epic poem about the ninth-century ruler Charlemagne, converting the text from Old French to Middle French as a proposed doctoral thesis. She finished the piece at the same time as completing her dissertation, not for Sorbonne credit but rather for her own scholarly ambition. See Evans, *Black Women in the Ivory Tower* and May, *Anna Julia Cooper, Visionary Black Feminist*. Cooper was not alone among African Americans in the benefit she received from the international post–World War I education boom: in 1925, the year she graduated from the Sorbonne, Mercer Cook (Amherst College), John Matheus (Columbia University), and Jessie Fauset (Cornell University; University of Pennsylvania) were all studying and writing in France.

33. Cooper, "The Third Step," 327–29.

34. Ibid.

35. Emery, "The Zombie in/as the Text," 327–36.

36. Ibid., 328.

37. Ibid.

38. Ibid.

39. Hurston, *Dust Tracks on a Road,* 175–76.

40. Ibid., 192.

41. Colleen McElroy, *A Long Way from St. Louis,* 40–41.

42. Ibid., 42.

43. Ibid., 45.

44. Ibid., 224, 240.

45. Gayle Pemberton, *The Hottest Water in Chicago,* 134.

46. Ibid., 142.

47. AZ HB 2281, accessed June 30, 2012, http://www.azleg.gov/legtext/49leg/2r/bills/hb2281s.pdf.

48. Wells, *Crusade for Justice,* 21–22.

49. Chronicle blogger commenting on Northwestern Conference.

50. Gordon, "Like play, writing affords a moment's recognition of agency," *Existencia Africana,* 166.

51. Evans, "*Black Body* Book Review," 171–73.

52. Mohanram, *Black Body,* xv, 91, 123.

CHAPTER 6. CONCLUSION

1. In Rampersad, *African American Poetry,* 29.

2. The Du Bois Legacy Project was completed with the support of Clark Atlanta University president Carlton E. Brown. For details visit http://cauduboislegacy.net/.

3. Du Bois, "Of the Wings of Atalanta," in *Souls of Black Folk,* pp. 88–89; and *Soliloquy,* 423.

4. Anna Julia Cooper, "Higher Education of Women," in *Voice from the South,* 82, in Evans, *Black Women in the Ivory Tower,* 143–44.

5. LIGMO, accessed June 30, 2012, http://www.ligmo.com/.

6. Evans, *Atlas of Race,* 254–56.

7. See http://www.youtube.com/watch?v=JkIiauRlcpo; Virtual Montmartre, http://www.montmartre-virt.paris-sorbonne.fr/; Sylvana Ah-laye, graduate student project (Anna Julia Cooper), http://www.montmartre-virt.

paris-sorbonne.fr/Anna%20Julia%20Cooper/AnnaCooper_fichiers/
frame.htm.

8. YouTube video, http://www.youtube.com/watch?v=L_VbcWTBcdE;
Online syllabus, http://www.professorevans.net/uploads/2011AA
ParisClassEvans.pdfhttp://www.professorevans.net/uploads/2011AA
ParisClassEvans.pdf.

9. Anonymous student surveys answered questions about how the class
impacted their identity, in particular three moments that mattered. April
18, 2011, response in author's possession, used by permission.

10. Du Bois, *Dusk of Dawn*, 45.

11. Keynote Speech, Sunday, June 23, 2012. SAEOPP/McNair Conference.
Atlanta, Georgia.

12. Evans, *BWIT,* 216.

13. Omniglot website for useful phrases http://www.omniglot.com/language/
phrases/langs.htm#lang. accessed March 8, 2013.

14. Though there was much turmoil surrounding me in my seven years as a
junior faculty member, I only earned tenure because I wrote, taught, and
served the institution in a way recognizable to objective colleagues in
national and international arenas. When my book was on sale in Japan or
was positively reviewed in *Jahrbuch fur Universitatsgeschichte* (Yearbook
of University History), a German journal at a university in Berlin, it indicated to me that my work was valuable without a need for nepotism or a
"hook up" that young professionals can too often rely upon to get ahead.
See Review essay, including *Black Women in the Ivory Tower.* Accessed July
15, 2012. http://www.professorevans.net/uploads/EvansSJahrbuchfurUni-
versitatsgeschichte.pdf.

15. See *Enter the Dragon,* "What's your *schtyle*?," accessed June 21, 2012,
http://www.youtube.com/watch?v=o_Ycw0d_Uow.

16. Du Bois, *Autobiography*, pp. 336–38.

17. Valerie Smith, "Self-Discovery and Authority in Afro-American Narrative" in *Women, Autobiography, Theory: A Reader,* ed. Sidonie Smith and
Julia Watson (Madison: University of Wisconsin Press, 1998), 64.

18. Houston Baker Jr., "On the Criticism of Black American Literature" in
African American Literary Theory: A Reader, ed. Winston Napier (add
publication info), 113.

19. Womack, Ytasha. *Afrofuturism: The World of Black Sci-Fi and Fantasy Culture.* (Chicago: Lawrence Hill Books, 2013), 9, 15.

20. See Egypt online http://ancientegyptonline.co.uk/seshat.html (accessed
April 10, 2013).

21. Thompson, Ahmir "Questlove"; Greenman, Ben. *Mo' Meta Blues: The World According to Questlove* (Grand Central Publishing. Kindle Edition, 2013), 282. For Jazz Age Motmartre virtual research collaboration visit http://llc.oxfordjournals.org/content/early/2005/07/22/llc.fqi032.extract.

BIBLIOGRAPHY

Alston, Vermonja Romona. "Race-Crossings at the Crossroads of African American Travel in the Caribbean." PhD diss., University of Arizona, 2004.

Anderson, Benedict. *Imagined Communities. Reflections on the Origin and Spread of Nationalism.* London: Verso, 2006.

Andrews, William. *African American Autobiography: A Collection of Critical Essays.* New Jersey: Prentice Hall, 1993.

Angelou, Maya. *Letter to My Daughter.* New York: Random House, 2008.

Baca Zinn, Maxine, and Bonnie Thorton Dill, eds. "Difference and Domination." In *Women of Color in U.S. Society*, Philadelphia: Temple University Press, 1994. *Introduction to Women of Color in U.S. Society.* http://www.temple.edu/tempress/chapters/657_ch1.pdf.

Baker, Houston, Jr. "On the Criticism of Black American Literature." In *African American Literary Theory: A Reader*, ed. Winston Napier. New York: New York University, 2000.

Birren, J., and K. Cochran. *Telling the Stories of Life through Guided Autobiography Groups.* Baltimore: Johns Hopkins University Press, 2001.

Blassingame, John. "Black Autobiography as History and Literature." *The Black Scholar: Journal of Black Studies and Research* 5, no. 4 (December 1973–January 1974): 2–9.

Braxton, Joanne. *Black Women Writing Autobiography: A Tradition within a Tradition.* Philadelphia: Temple University Press, 1989.

Canada, Geoffrey. *Reaching Up for Manhood: Transforming the Lives of Boys in America.* Boston: Beacon, 1998.

Carroll, Karanja Keita. "The State of Graduate Studies in Africana/Black Studies: An Interview with Stephanie Evans." *Journal of Pan-African Studies* 2, no. 10 (2009): 6–11.

Chan, Zenobia. "Cooking Soup to Writing Papers: A Journey through Gender, Society, and Self." *International Journal of Women's Studies* 4, no. 1 (2002): 93–106. http://www.bridgew.edu/soas/jiws/fall02/cooking_soup.pdf.

Clapp, Nicholas. *Sheba: Through the Desert in Search of the Legendary Queen.* New York: Mariner, 2001.

Cooper, Anna Julia. "The Third Step" (1945). In *The Voice of Anna Julia Cooper,* ed. Charles Lemert and Esme Bhan. Maryland: Rowman and Littlefield, 1998.

Costa, Margaret D., Stephanie Y. Evans, and Evelyn Haralson. "A Cultural Framework for the Study of Sport History and Brazil." *VI Congresso Brasileiro De Historia Do Esporte, Lazer E Educacao Fisica.* 39–45. Rio De Janeiro, Brazil: Gama Filho University Press. 1998.

Coulibaly, Modibo. "The Characteristics of the African Epic Hero as a Reflection of the Kemetic Tradition." PhD diss., Temple University, 1997.

Damon, William. "What Is Positive Youth Development?" *Annals of the American Academy of Political and Social Science* 591, no. 1 (January 2004): 13–24.

Dortch, Thomas. *The Miracles of Mentoring: How to Encourage and Lead Future Generations.* New York: Broadway Books, 2009.

Dunlap, Michelle. *Reaching Out to Children and Families: Students Model Effective Community Service.* Maryland: Rowan and Littlefield, 2000.

Eby, John. "Why Service Learning Is Bad." Messiah University. National Service-Learning Clearing House. 1998. http://www.messiah.edu/external_programs/agape/servicelearning/articles/wrongsvc.pdf.

Emery, Amy Fass. "The Zombie in/as the Text: Zora Neale Hurston's *Tell My Horse.*" *African American Review* 39, no. 3 (Fall 2005): 327–36.

Evans, Stephanie Y. "African American Women and International Research: Dr. Anna Julia Cooper's Legacy of Study Abroad." *Frontiers: The Interdisciplinary Journal of Study Abroad* 18 (2009): 77–100.

———. *Black Women in the Ivory Tower, 1850–1954: An Intellectual History.* Gainesville: University Press of Florida, 2007.

———. "Gender and Research in the African Academy: 'Moving against the Grain' in the Global Ivory Tower." *Black Women, Gender, and Families* 2, no. 2 (2008): 31–52.

———. "Introduction." In *African Americans and Community Engagement in*

Higher Education, edited by Stephanie Y. Evans, Colette Taylor, Michelle Dunlap, and DeMond Miller. New York: State University Press of New York, 2010.

———. "'I Was One of the First to See Daylight': Black Women at Predominantly White Colleges and Universities in Florida since 1959." *Florida Historical Quarterly* 85, no. 1 (2006): 42–63.

———. "Major Service: Combining Students' Academic Disciplines with Community Service-Learning in an Introductory Women's Studies Course." *Feminist Teacher* 17, no. 1 (2006): 1–14.

———. "Mary McLeod Bethune's Research Agenda: Thought Translated to Work." *African American Research Perspectives* 12, no. 1 (2008): 22–39.

———. Review of *Black Body: Women, Colonialism, and Space,* by Radhika Mohanram. Journal of International Women's Studies 6, no. 2 (2005): 171–73.

———. "The State and Future of the PhD in Black Studies: Assessing the Role of the Comprehensive Examination." *Griot: Southern Conference on African American Studies* 25, no. 1 (Spring 2006): 1–16.

———. "'This Right to Grow': African American Women's Intellectual Legacy." *International Journal of the Humanities* 3, no. 7 (2006): 163–74.

———. "Women of Color in American Higher Education." *Thought and Action* 23 (Fall 2007): 131–38.

Evers, Frederick, James C. Rush, and Iris Berdrow. *The Bases of Competence: Skills for Lifelong Learning and Employability.* San Francisco: Jossey-Bass Higher and Adult Education Series, 1998.

Flemming, Beatrice Jackson, and Marion Jackson Pryde. *Distinguished Negroes Abroad.* Washington, D.C.; Associated Publishers, 1946. Reprint 1988.

Franklin, V. P. *Living Our Stories, Telling Our Truths: Autobiography and the Making of the African American Intellectual Tradition.* New York: Scribner, 1995.

Gardner, Howard. *Frames of Mind: The Theory of Multiple Intelligences.* New York: Basic Books, 1983.

Gates, Jr., Henry Louis. *Finding Oprah's Roots: Finding Your Own.* New York: Crown, 2007.

———. *Thirteen Ways of Looking at a Black Man.* New York: Crown, 1997.

Giovanni, Nikki. *The Best 100 African American Poems, * But I Cheated.* Illinois: Sourcebooks, 2010.

Goldman-Price, Irene, and Melissa McFarland Pennell. *American Literary Mentoring.* Gainesville: University Press of Florida, 1999.

Gomez, Henry. "Nina Turner's Future Bright Due to Gutsy Stand on Issue 6." *The Plain Dealer Online*, November 22, 2009. http://blog.cleveland.com/metro/2009/11/nina_turners_future_bright_due.html.

Gordon, Lewis. *Existentia Africana: Understanding Africana Existential Thought*. New York: Routledge, 2000.

Green, Charles. *Manufacturing Powerlessness in the Black Diaspora: Inner-city Youth and the New Global Frontier*. Walnut Creek, CA: AltaMira, 2001.

Hausman, Gerald, ed. *Kebra Nagast: The Lost Bible of Rastafarian Wisdom and Faith from Ethiopia and Jamaica*. New York: St. Martin's, (1997).

Higginbotham, Evelyn. *Righteous Discontent: The Women's Movement in the Black Baptist Church, 1880–1920*. Cambridge, MA: Harvard University Press, 1993.

Inscoe, John. *Writing the South through the Self: Explorations in Southern Autobiography*. Athens: University of Georgia Press, 2011.

Joyce, Joyce. *Black Studies as Human Studies: Critical Essays and Interviews*. New York: SUNY Press, 2004.

Kirk, Gwen, and Margo Okazawa-Rey. "Social Location Theory." In *Women's Lives, Multicultural Perspectives*. New York: McGraw-Hill, 2000.

Krenn, Michael. *Black Diplomacy: African Americans and the State Department, 1945–1969*. New York: M. E. Sharpe, 1999.

Ladner, Joyce. *Tomorrow's Tomorrow: The Black Woman*. Lincoln: University of Nebraska Press, 1971.

Larose, Simon, and George Tarabulsy. "Academically At-Risk Students." In *Handbook of Youth Mentoring*, edited by David L. DuBois and Michael Karcher, 443–44. Thousand Oaks, CA: Sage: 2005.

Lassner, Jacob. *Demonizing the Queen of Sheba: Boundaries of Gender and Culture in Post-Biblical Judaism and Medieval Islam*. Chicago: University of Chicago, 1993.

Lee, Elaine. *Go Girl!: The Black Woman's Book of Travel and Adventure*. Portland: Eight Mountain, 1997.

Mahaffy, Kimberly. "Gender, Race, Class, and the Transition to Adulthood: A Critical Review of the Literature." In vol. 9 of *Sociological Studies of Children and Youth*, edited by Katherine Brown Rosier and A. Kinney. UK: JAI/Elsevier Science, 2003.

Maparyan, Layli. *The Womanist Idea*. New York: Routledge, 2012.

May, Vivian. *Anna Julia Cooper, Visionary Black Feminist: A Critical Introduction*. New York: Routledge, 2007.

McKay, Nellie. "The Narrative Self: Race, Politics, and Culture in Black American Women's Autobiography," (1995). In *Women, Autobiography, Theory:*

A Read, edited by Sidonie Smith and Julia Watson. Madison: University of Wisconsin Press, 1998.

McMillen, Margaret. "The Impact of Academic Vocabulary Instruction on Reading Performance of Sophomore Students on the Florida Comprehensive Assessment Test from 2008 and 2009." PhD diss., University of Central Florida, 2009.

Norment, Nathaniel. *The African American Studies Reader.* 2nd Ed. Durham: Carolina Academic, 2007.

Perkins, Margo. *Autobiography as Activism: Three Black Women of the Sixties.* Jackson: University of Mississippi Press, 2000.

Rainer, Tristine. In Center Autobiographic Studies, http://www.storyhelp.com/autotypes.html.

Sanchez, Sonia. *Morning Haiku.* Boston: Beacon, 2010.

Schechter, Patricia. *Ida B. Wells-Barnett and American Reform, 1880–1930.* Chapel Hill: University of North Carolina Press, 2001.

Shirley, Steven W. "The Gender Gap in Post-secondary Study Abroad: Understanding and Marketing to Male Students." Dissertation, University of North Dakota, 2006.

Shockley, Evie. *Renegade Poetics: Black Aesthetics and Formal Innovation in African American Poetry.* City: University of Iowa Press, 2011.

Smith, Sidone, and Julia Watson. "Tool-Kit: Twenty-Four Strategies for Reading Life Narratives." In *A Guide for Interpreting Life Narratives: Reading Autobiography.* City: Publisher, 2001.

Smith, Valerie. *Self-Discovery and Authority in Afro-American Narrative.* Cambridge: Harvard University Press, 1981.

Steadman, Jennifer Bernhardt. "Travel Writing and Resistance: A Feminist Reading of Travel Narratives by African American and Euro-American Women, 1820–1860." PhD diss., Emory University, 2000.

Steele, Ralph. *Mentoring and the Rites of Passage for Youth.* Baton Rouge, LA: Ralvon, 1998.

Stepto, Robert. *From Behind the Veil: A Study of Afro-American Narrative.* Champaign-Urbana: University of Illinois Press, 1991.

Stevens, Joyce West. *Smart and Sassy: The Strengths of Inner-City Black Girls.* New York: Oxford University Press, 2002.

Thomas, Karin Michele. "Traveling Eyes: African American Travelers Create a World, 1789–1930." PhD diss., Yale University, 2001.

Tijerina Revilla, Anita. "Inmensa Fe en la Victoria: Social Justice through Education." *Frontiers: A Journal of Women's Studies* 24, nos. 2–3 (2003): 282–301.

Tucker, Carolyn, and K. Herman. "Using Culturally Sensitive Theories and Research to Meet the Academic Needs of Low-Income African American Children." *American Psychologist* 10 (2002): 762–773.

Ueshiba, Morihei. *The Art of Peace*. Boston: Shambala Press, 2007.

Umoja, Akinyele. *We Will Shoot Back: Armed Resistance in the Mississippi Freedom Movement*. New York: New York University Press, 2013.

von Sivers, Peter, Charles Desnoyers, and George Snow. *Patterns of World History* (Combined Volume), 459. New York: Oxford University Press, 2012.

Williams, Cheryl. "'Conceived in Transit, Delivered in Passage': Travel and Identity in Nineteenth-Century African-American Women's Narratives." PhD diss., University of Pennsylvania, 1999.

Williams, Larry, and Charles Finch. "Great Queens of Ethiopia." In *Black Women in Antiquity*, edited by Ivan Van Sertima. New Brunswick: Transaction, 1984.

Williams, Roland. *African American Autobiography and the Quest for Freedom*. West Port: Greenwood, 2000.

Womack, Ytasha. *Afrofuturism: The World of Black Sci-Fi and Fantasy Culture*. Chicago: Lawrence Hill Books, 2013.

INDEX